CHEROKEE CIVIL WARRIOR

Principal Chief John Ross circa 1850. Image courtesy of the Library of Congress Prints and Photographs Division, DAG No. 1413.

CHEROKEE
CIVIL WARRIOR

Chief John Ross and the
Struggle for Tribal Sovereignty

W. DALE WEEKS

UNIVERSITY OF OKLAHOMA PRESS : NORMAN

This book is published with the generous assistance of the Wallace C. Thompson Endowment Fund, University of Oklahoma Foundation.

Library of Congress Cataloging-in-Publication Data

Names: Weeks, W. Dale, 1964–, author.
Title: Cherokee civil warrior : Chief John Ross and the struggle for tribal sovereignty / W. Dale Weeks.
Description: Norman : University of Oklahoma Press, [2023] | Includes bibliographical references and index. | Summary: "How the Cherokee Nation, led by Principal Chief John Ross, navigated the duplicity of the federal government during much of the nineteenth century, seeking to use constitutional law to retain tribal autonomy and land ownership"—Provided by publisher.
Identifiers: LCCN 2022016221 | ISBN 978-0-8061-9157-7 (hardcover)
ISBN 978-0-8061-9491-2 (paper)
Subjects: LCSH: Ross, John, 1790–1866. | Cherokee Indians—Government relations—19th century. | Cherokee Indians—Land tenure—19th century. | Cherokee Indians—Legal status, laws, etc.—19th century. | Cherokee Nation—History—19th century.
Classification: LCC E99.C5 W44 2023 | DDC 975.00497557—dc23
LC record available at https://lccn.loc.gov/2022016221

The paper in this book meets the guidelines for permanence and durability of the Committee on Production Guidelines for Book Longevity of the Council on Library Resources, Inc. ∞

Copyright © 2023 by the University of Oklahoma Press, Norman, Publishing Division of the University. Paperback published 2024. Manufactured in the U.S.A.

All rights reserved. No part of this publication may be reproduced, stored in a retrieval system, or transmitted, in any form or by any means, electronic, mechanical, photocopying, recording, or otherwise—except as permitted under Section 107 or 108 of the United States Copyright Act—without the prior written permission of the University of Oklahoma Press. To request permission to reproduce selections from this book, write to Permissions, University of Oklahoma Press, 2800 Venture Drive, Norman OK 73069, or email rights.oupress@ou.edu.

For Merri Jo, who expresses her belief in me

CONTENTS

List of Maps / ix

Preface / xi

Introduction / 1

1. Removal and the Struggle for Sovereignty / 29
2. Secession and the Preservation of a Nation / 50
3. Autonomy and the Confederate Alliance / 73
4. Abraham Lincoln and the Indian Expedition / 98
5. The Fort Smith Council and the Dismantling of U.S. Indian Policy / 129

Conclusion / 158

Notes / 179

Bibliography / 205

Index / 221

MAPS

Indian Territory, 1861 / 92

The Plains, 1866 / 154

Oklahoma and Indian Territory, 1890 / 167

PREFACE

I admired my maternal grandfather. During the 1930s, he was a farmer in Cherokee County, Texas, and, at the outbreak of the war in Europe, moved his young wife and infant daughter to the Texas coast to go to work in an oil refinery as part of Roosevelt's "Lend-Lease" program. For the next four decades, he worked at the Humble Oil refinery and raised a family in the quiet community of Baytown. What I admired most about him, however, was that he was Choctaw. During the heyday of the citizens-band radio craze, he was known on the air as "Chief" and carried that moniker in reflective letters on the back glass of his camper shell for most of my childhood. I, however, was never allowed to call him "Chief." To me, he was Peepaw.

What intrigued me most about Peepaw was the knowledge that if he was Choctaw, I was Choctaw. But no one ever seemed to talk about it, especially him. There were no exciting stories about growing up in a Choctaw family, no tales about Choctaw culture and traditions, and no mention of Choctaw ancestors. For a young boy, this was puzzling. My mother, who also would have been Choctaw, only knew the names of her grandfather, Eli, and his father, Oliver. Other than that, she had no knowledge of her indigenous ancestry. If only I could find information on Eli and Oliver, I would know the truth about my own heritage. Sometime after Peepaw's funeral in 1982, I walked into the Choctaw Cultural Center in Bryan County, Oklahoma, ready to solve the mystery. I searched the rolls for hours, looking for Eli or Oliver. I enlisted help from staff members. Yet we found nothing.

While conducting research for this book three decades later at the Oklahoma History Center in Oklahoma City, I struck up a conversation one morning with Brian Bashore, the librarian. I told him of my desire to return someday to further investigate the mystery behind my own family heritage. He casually asked me to write down the names for which I had been searching, and while I began my research, he went to work. I had not been at my computer more than ten minutes when he walked up and handed me a photocopy. I was shocked and excited to read the name Eli Davis on a page of the Dawes Rolls dated 1906. Listed as Eli's father was Oliver Davis. Why could I not find this on my own? Was the technology just that much better in 2019? Then I saw it. At the top of the page were the words "Creek Nation Rolls." Peepaw was not Choctaw. He was Creek. Eli's mother, a woman named Rose Grayson, was Creek Indian. Oliver was not. We had had the wrong information all along.

What the family did know about Eli came from my Aunt Linda, Peepaw's daughter-in-law, who lives in Laurel, Mississippi. Family tradition holds that when Eli was about twelve years old, Oliver married a woman named Mary Ellen McKeachem in Lamar County, Texas. Mary Ellen immediately announced to her new husband that she would never live in the same house as a "half-breed." So, at the age of twelve, Eli moved out. My search of the 1910 census found Eli Davis, a white man, living in Prescott, Arkansas, with the Niemeyers, an immigrant family from Germany. Eli's father was listed as having been born in Texas, his mother in Indian Territory. Yet, for the remainder of his life, Eli was a white man. He rarely spoke of his Creek heritage, and his family could only surmise the details. Eli married Mary Edna, one of the Niemeyer daughters, and they had a son. I called him Peepaw. Eli died when Peepaw was only eighteen, and somewhere between 1910 and the invention of the CB radio, Peepaw became known as Choctaw.

The dismantling of indigenous culture and identity in the United States has been a forced and, sadly, too often a voluntary process. If not compelled to give up their indigeneity and assimilate, many Native Americans, especially those of mixed ancestry, like Eli, chose to become white and avoid much of the racism directed at indigenous people. As a young student, I learned that the people of the United States threw themselves into the great "melting pot" in order to transform a diverse society into one coherent nation. I learned later that what that really meant is that white people threw other races into the pot in an effort to eliminate diversity of culture, thought, and identity. In recent years, however, we have learned to embrace difference and to celebrate diversity. However, for many indigenous people, like Eli, it was too late.

For over a century, the story of Eli Davis, the Muscogee (Creek) citizen, was hidden by the racism within his own familial circle. His family did not know the truth about their own identity because Eli felt the need to hide from his. Too often, the stories of Native North America have been rendered invisible by a dominant culture that believed racial invisibility was akin to progress. Acculturation and assimilation were supposed to move the nation forward because indigenous societies somehow stood in the way of that progress. The popular claim that racism will disappear only when we no longer see race in our culture keeps us tied too closely to the old melting pot. Instead, it is time for us to see race in everything we do, to embrace it, to celebrate its presence among us, and to not ignore it—only then can a little boy sit at his grandfather's knee and celebrate a shared heritage rather than negate it.

The same can be said about Native American history. The United States was at its most diverse before the arrival of European intruders who quickly went to work transforming the continent into a European colony. The tenets of this settler-colonialist agenda sought to reshape the continent into an extension of Western "civilization." This meant the indigenous people of North American either had to avoid this new society or join it and become "civilized." Eventually, the European population became so large that the Native peoples had nowhere else to migrate. The only option was to assimilate. As Native nations, like the Cherokees, adapted, they surrendered much of their culture and identity to the waters of the melting pot. What emerged were indigenous societies relegated to mere support roles of U.S. history. Moreover, the histories and identities of these indigenous societies disappeared over time as "civilization" taught us to forget them, much as it taught Eli to forget his. Soon, historians began to reintroduce diversity into our scholarship by including the Native American perspective in our narratives. The Cherokee Nation provides a bounty of those sources. However, simply including indigenous sources adds a new dimension to our story, but it does not fundamentally change it, and it certainly does not undo centuries of acculturation.

In 2015, historian Brian DeLay suggested we change that by placing Native Americans at the center of our narratives of U.S. history, rather than on the margins. Centering indigenous voices helps to reverse the effects of the melting pot and reintroduces the stories of our indigenous past. Eli claimed to be white, but his mother did not, nor did her mother, nor her mother. As a little boy, I did not get to hear the stories of those indigenous ancestors from my grandfather because Eli refused to tell them. However, if we as historians follow Professor DeLay's advice, as I have done here, perhaps the little boys and girls of the Cherokee Nation and other tribes can one day hear those stories from the voices of their own ancestors and can help rebuild the diversity that existed on our continent prior to the melting pot.

So many deserve my gratitude for this project. I am indebted to my reviewers for their timely and valuable feedback, and to copyeditor Helen Robertson for her expert eye. Any errors in this book are most certainly my fault, not theirs. I would be remiss if I did not thank Linda Chameron and David Thorpe for hosting us in their basement for a summer of research. They have become sweet friends. Thank you to Heather, Veronica, Karla, and Scott, and the rest of the team at Stephen F. Austin Middle School for supporting me while I completed my degree. Without a doubt, you are the hardest working group of people I have ever met. Special thanks go to Walter Kamphoefner, Al Broussard, Lorien Foote, Kate Unterman, Alston Thoms, Tom Wagy, Mike Perri, and Doris Davis for molding me into an historian and writer. Your fingerprints are all over this work.

Finally, the Lord has placed three people in my life who make all of the work worthwhile. Lealah Plummer insists that we are related. Her willingness to claim me as family makes me smile. Perhaps more than any other, she has taught me that racial identity is foundational to who we are as a people; therefore, we must understand it. Finally, I am blessed to be loved by two of the most brilliant, independent, and capable people I will ever know. Katie Allgood is the model of love and grace. She has put up with me her entire life yet, somehow, hangs around. I include her name here because of how important she is to me. However, she is destined to make her own name in this world. Watch for her. I am beyond proud of the woman she has become. And then, Merritt Royal Weeks—Merri Jo—has more faith in me than anyone I have ever known. She speaks life into me and encourages me daily. Her skills as a writer and editor are second to none. I am a better person because of her. I shudder to think where I would be without her. Thank you, Merri Jo, for your love for me and your passion for my work. We both rely on it.

INTRODUCTION

The late spring day was growing steadily warmer as the young warrior hid among the brush overlooking the winding river below. Pleasant Bluff, his hiding place, was carefully chosen for its commanding view of the river. The dilapidated house nearby reminded him how important this place was to his people in the years after their arrival from their ancestral homes in the East. He was glad when the leader of the ambush, a warrior from the tribe across the river, looked on his hiding spot with approval. The young warrior and his men waited almost seven days until word finally came that the enemy was approaching. His heart pounded as he watched a boat round a distant bend and slowly ply its way upstream toward them. The young warrior waited patiently while the vessel slowed to navigate the sharp bend in the river below his hiding place. When the boat reached a spot directly in front of him, he jumped to his feet and shouted, setting the attack in motion.[1]

The first cannon fired a warning shot over the steamboat's bow to encourage the crew to surrender. When that did not come, a second shot struck the stack, sending the men on deck scurrying. A perfectly aimed third shot destroyed the pilot house only moments before a final blast took out the boiler, sending a cloud of steam spewing into the air. By this time, the crew had abandoned the boat, which had run aground along the opposite bank of the river. Quickly a group of Indians boarded the vessel and towed it to the south bank where they unloaded what they could of its cargo. Carrying over $120,000 worth of supplies for the Federal post upriver, the boat, the *J. R. Williams*, had left Fort Smith, Arkansas, bound for Fort Gibson in the Cherokee Nation.[2] The Indians, fighting as allies of the Confederate States during the American Civil War, quickly unloaded about 150 barrels of flour and eight tons of bacon, packing it onto their horses and scurrying away with the bounty to feed their starving families.[3] Other Indians confiscated the abundance of tinware on board, lashing it to their horses, and clanking away with their spoils. The young warrior, a Creek named George Washington Grayson, served with a band of pro-Confederate Indians led by a

Cherokee named Stand Watie. Watie and Grayson remained with the boat, hoping to salvage the remainder of the cargo when their allies returned. However, approaching Union troops drove them away. Before they departed, they set the wreck ablaze, releasing it to drift downstream for nearly a mile as it burned.[4]

Tales of Confederate victory and Union defeat at Pleasant Bluff fill the pages of the historiography of the Civil War in Indian Territory. The attack, which took place on June 15, 1864, near present Tamaha, Oklahoma, has been celebrated by historians. Clarissa W. Confer calls it "a story of daring in the annals of Indian Territory warfare."[5] LeRoy H. Fischer asserts that the victory "cheered the despondent Confederates."[6] Mary Jane Warde argues that the capture "came at a particularly inopportune time for the Union occupation of Fort Gibson."[7] Wilfred Knight would agree. He claims the capture crushed Federal plans for an invasion of northern Texas through southern Indian Territory.[8]

Although historians view the attack as an important victory for Confederate forces, at least one white Confederate officer at the time questioned its success. Major Rhesa Walker Read, regimental surgeon for the 29th Texas Cavalry, claimed that the supplies could have fed the entire Confederate department for two months "if Watie's Indians would have staid [sic] with their commander."[9] This was not the first time Read ranted about Watie's forces and their apparent lack of commitment to the Confederate cause. Following the defeat at the First Battle of Cabin Creek in July 1863, in present Mayes County, Oklahoma, Read bemoaned the fact that Watie had been unable to hold the line against a much larger Federal advance across the creek. Watie was forced to defend the road with his small force without the help of two regiments of Texans who were unable to join them due to high water. Regardless, Read told his wife that "our Indians stampeded again."[10] Five months later, he celebrated the segregation of Confederate troops in Indian Territory in a vituperative letter to his wife. He wrote, "I hope I don't see another Indian this side of H__l!"[11]

Read's displeasure with the pro-Confederate Indians was more commonplace than historians have imagined. In November 1863, seven months before the attack on the *J. R. Williams,* Brigadier General William Steele, who commanded Confederate forces in Indian Territory, denounced plans to raise a brigade of Indians by accusing Watie of leading an imaginary force that always seemed to be scattered around the country, rendering itself useless as an organized body. He even claimed the Indians always managed to take more than their share of provisions whenever the opportunity presented itself.[12] Yet many Confederate leaders openly praised Watie for his gallantry, promoting him to brigadier general a month prior to the capture of the Federal steamboat. This contradiction raises some important questions. Why would Confederate leaders shower so much praise on Watie if his force seemed so uncommitted to the Southern cause? And why were many white Confederates on the ground in Indian Territory unconvinced that Watie and his men deserved any praise? Finally, if Watie was so pro-Confederate, why did he and his men so frequently disappoint white leadership in Indian Territory? Were they as apathetic about the cause as white Confederates assumed? These questions rise from a sense of dissonance that often fills large portions of the historiography of the Civil War in Indian Territory and are unanswerable if historians continue to interpret the events only through a North-versus-South lens.

This book views the Civil War from the Cherokee capital at Tahlequah in Indian Territory. However, it is not a book about the Civil War. I merely use the war as a prop expanding our understanding of the Cherokee Nation and its attempt to defend the integrity of the U.S. Constitution from the very men sworn by oath to protect it. By allowing the Cherokees to tell their own story, we learn that many of the events that took place in Indian Territory between 1861 and 1865 had little to do with the Civil War per se. As a result, this becomes a story of Indian policy, failed foreign relations, and the white man's conquest of the North American West. It becomes an epic tale of how the Cherokee Nation and its leader John Ross withstood the onslaught of white America in an attempt to protect tribal autonomy during the nineteenth century.[13]

Our memory of the Civil War in Indian Territory has been constrained by the North-South binary, forcing all the events into the same familiar storyline of the Civil War. Perhaps the most glaring example is the story of the venerable Creek headman, Opothle Yahola, who had no desire to participate in the white man's war. He chose instead to remain loyal to the tribe's treaties with the United States. Moreover, when he petitioned President Abraham Lincoln for relief, the president encouraged him to remain neutral in a fight that was not his.[14] Within months of the war's outbreak, as many as 8,000 Indians from the various tribes of Indian Territory gathered at the headman's farm seeking to join him in that neutrality. Even though the Creek national government had signed a treaty of alliance with the Confederate States, Opothle Yahola and his followers wanted nothing to do with the war. Confederate and Creek leaders felt threatened by such a large gathering of Indians who did not share the same political opinions as the Creek national government. They quickly assumed that if Opothle Yahola was against the Confederate alliance, he must be pro-Union. In a series of three attacks in November and December 1861, Confederate forces—both white and Indian—chased Opothle Yahola and his followers from Indian Territory, killing many and leaving the remainder to fight starvation, frostbite, and death in refugee camps in southern Kansas. These attacks are commonly referred to as the first "battles" of the Civil War in Indian Territory.

The idea that Opothle Yahola and his followers were pro-Union emerged from the perspective of many Confederates who, in the turbulent political climate of the day, were unwilling to accept the idea that Indians could really be neutral. If an Indian was not pro-Confederate, did he have to be pro-Union? Apparently, most Confederates thought so. It seems that many historians do as well.[15] Our use of the label "Union" is of particular interest here in that it is a construct of white society. When viewed from the Native perspective, the discourse was of loyalty to the treaties, not to the Union. Obviously, the North-South binary has heavily influenced, if not hindered, our memory and interpretation here. If we continue to force our narratives to follow the constraints of that binary, every Indian is forced to take one side or the other. Unless we seek to match the discourse in our narratives with that of the Indian perspective, we can never fully comprehend the stories they wish to tell us.

The problem is not that historians have failed to include Indian perspectives. In fact, we have sought increasingly to include Native voices and, in doing so, have made great strides in removing much of the savagery and barbarism that once dominated the historical impression of American Indians. In the 1930s, Angie Debo refuted the claim of Frederick Jackson Turner that the conquest of the American frontier had been a tale of westward expansion and settlement. Debo claims that, instead, the frontier had been obliterated on the back of the exploitation of American Indians.[16] Debo's willingness to include the perspectives of Native participants inspired subsequent historians to do the same. By the early twenty-first century, historians such as Clarissa W. Confer and Mary Jane Warde had rewritten the narratives of the Civil War in Indian Territory by building their works primarily on the voices and perspectives of Indian participants. This book delves yet deeper into the perspective of the Cherokee Nation by allowing Cherokee voices to tell their own unfamiliar story.

To continue using Cherokee voices to tell the story of the Civil War era in Indian Territory is problematic because those voices actually have been trying to describe a different narrative, one not so compatible with the North-South conflict. This book does not view the Civil War from the perspective of the Indians in the same way previous historians have. Instead, it places the Cherokee Nation at center stage in its own narrative, using the Civil War as a backdrop rather than a plotline. In this way, an entirely new account emerges. Although much of the following narrative is set between 1861 and 1865, it does not tell the story of the Civil War in Indian Territory. Rather, it tells the story of the Cherokee Nation and its efforts to survive the Civil War era. Even though Cherokee voices may be crying out from the wartime battlefields, they are not all telling the same story as their Confederate or Union allies.

At the heart of these Cherokee voices is the one belonging to John Ross. Ross, the son of a Scottish father and a mixed-blood Indian mother, served the Cherokee Nation in a public capacity for nearly fifty years, even though he was but one-eighth Cherokee by blood. He served as clerk of the Cherokee National Council for two decades before being elected principal chief under the tribe's new constitution in 1828. Moreover, he was reelected every four years until his death in 1866. Ross is perhaps best known for his interaction with President Andrew Jackson during the forced removal of the Cherokee Nation along the "Trail of Tears" in the 1830s. However, his most important contribution to the tribe's legacy did not occur until the Civil War. Unfortunately, our proclivity to force the round peg of Ross's perspective into the square hole of our Civil War narratives has hidden the bulk of that contribution. This book extricates Ross and the Cherokee Nation from the restrictions of that square hole and places the tribe more securely into the round hole of its own narrative.

During his lengthy service, Ross communicated extensively with tribal leaders and officials of the U.S. government. His collection of letters and public addresses offers important insight into the perspective of the Cherokee national leadership as it led the tribe through the gauntlet of nineteenth-century U.S. Indian policy and directly into the Civil War. While the Cherokee Nation enjoyed consistent leadership for much of the nineteenth century, the U.S. government continually changed the way it defined and administered its Indian policy. Beginning in 1824 when Secretary of War John C. Calhoun established an Indian office within the Department of War to oversee trade with Native nations, U.S. Indian affairs were guided primarily by the army.

In 1830, however, Congress inserted itself into the discussion of Indian affairs by giving the president the authority to exchange land in the newly acquired region west of the Mississippi River for their ancestral homelands in the eastern United States. The president was to employ the existing treaty-making process to accomplish this objective. Conducted under the guise of foreign relations, these Senate-ratified treaties did more than just satisfy an immediate need. They helped create two important legacies that came to define this treaty-making process. First, treaties elevated Indian tribes—even tiny ones—to nation status, granting them a certain level of autonomy and independence. Second, they placed constitutional restrictions and limitations on how the United States could deal with these nations. An existing treaty could be honorably replaced only with a new one. This process gave the Indians a heightened sense of control over their own fortunes and came under heavy criticism from some in the federal government over the years because of the Indians' unwillingness to alter their treaties every time the federal government's changing needs required them to do so.

In 1832, Congress informally approved Calhoun's Indian office by granting the president the authority to appoint a commissioner to head the nation's Indian affairs and work beneath the auspices of the secretary of war. This new commissioner was simply directed to carry out the Indian policies of the president.[17] The president's sole control over Indian affairs, and the enforcement of presidential decisions by the U.S. military, became the modus operandi of U.S. Indian policy during the remainder of the nineteenth century.

However, the enforcement of Indian policy was not always an easy matter. Each president had his own idea of how the nation should interact with indigenous people. For the most part, Indian policy was not written into nineteenth century legal codes, leaving each administration to devise its own policy as it saw fit. The problems with this system are obvious. Promises made to Indians by one president did not obligate future presidents to deliver on them; future presidents usually had their own opinions and plans for the nation's Indians. When Andrew Jackson carried out his policy of forced removal in the 1830s, he promised to protect the Indians in their new homes as an inducement for their submission. However, later presidents were left to fulfill a promise they did not make and perhaps did not support. In the wake of this ever-shifting policy, the Indian tribes could only hope that each successive president would fulfill the promises of the ones before him.

The failure of the U.S. government to codify its Indian policy in the mid-nineteenth century, coupled with a revolving door on the White House, frustrated U.S.-Indian relations. Between 1828 and 1866, the United States had eleven different presidents, and only one of them, the anti-Indian Andrew Jackson, served for two full terms. Moreover, five of the remaining ten held office for less than four years. Over the twenty-nine years following Jackson's departure in 1837, Ross encountered a new president every 2.9 years on average, a new secretary (Department of War or Department of the Interior) every 2 years, and a new

Indian commissioner every 2.6 years. Ross's desire to interact directly with the executive leadership in Washington met with crippling inconsistency as U.S. Indian policy was in a constant state of change.

The ever-changing federal government stood in stark contrast to the consistent and stable leadership of the Cherokee Nation. Not only did Ross serve thirty-eight consecutive years as the constitutionally elected principal chief, but he led his nation with a consistent ideology almost unmatched in Washington. Ross's faith in the processes of U.S. constitutional law remained steadfast, even during the parade of presidents, many of whom approached Indian matters with questionable ethics. During Ross's lengthy tenure as chief, only two presidents won reelection for a second term. The first, Andrew Jackson, who served from 1829 to 1837, led the most consistent Indian policy in the first half of the nineteenth century. He was able to initiate and implement his policy of forced removal without interference or disruption. The second was Abraham Lincoln, who won reelection in 1864 only to be assassinated six months later. Historians can only surmise how a consistent second Lincoln administration would have addressed the nation's Indian affairs in the postwar years. Lincoln reportedly told one Indian advocate in 1864, "You may rest assured that as soon as the present matter of this war is settled the Indian shall have my first care and I will not rest until Justice is done to their . . . satisfaction."[18] If Lincoln was serious, American Indians had reason to lament his assassination as one of the most significant events in the history of nineteenth-century U.S.-Indian relations.

Although the Cherokees signed numerous treaties with various British colonies prior to the American Revolution, formal interaction between the tribe and the United States began in 1785 with the signing of the Treaty of Hopewell, Georgia, in which the Cherokees placed themselves under the protection of the new nation. As an inducement for signing, the United States offered the Cherokees the right to send "a deputy of its own choosing" to Congress to intercede on behalf of the tribe whenever it felt its rights had been violated. This article was included so that "the Indians may have full confidence in the justice of the United States respecting their rights."[19] This incentive became a linchpin of nineteenth-century Cherokee political ideology as the Cherokee Nation sent nearly two dozen delegations to Washington between 1816 and 1866 alone.[20]

When Tennessee citizens encroached on Cherokee lands in 1788, the United States realized that the central government under the Articles of Confederation lacked the authority to enforce the protection clause of the Treaty of Hopewell. Congress could address Indian trade, but the central government did not possess the power to intercede in matters pertaining to the individual states. In short, no governmental entity had the authority to compel a state to honor federal Indian policy. Following ratification of the U.S. Constitution in 1789, the United States sought a new treaty with the Cherokees to update the one signed under the Articles of Confederation. The new treaty, signed in Holston, Tennessee, in 1791, amended the Hopewell treaty but did not replace it. Moreover, the new constitutional government now had the power to provide the protection promised to the Indians in their previous treaties.

The most important aspect of the Treaty of Holston, however, was that it declared the sovereignty of the U.S. government by adding a line to the protection clause of the former treaty. The new stipulation forbade the Cherokees from signing treaties of any kind with any other governmental entity, including any state government or any individual other than the United States. Moreover, in an effort to eliminate future conflict between the Cherokees and white settlers, the treaty sought to transform the Cherokees into sedentary subsistence farmers by promising to provide them with the necessary tools and training. The hope was that the tribe would embrace a more sedentary lifestyle, abandoning the hunt and restricting themselves to a circumscribed territory, thereby limiting the frequency of Indian-white interaction.[21]

While peace was the goal of the Hopewell treaty, the Treaty of Holston had a different purpose: the acculturation of the Cherokee Nation. Acculturation sought to change many of the habits of indigenous society while allowing that society to retain much of its "Indianness," as long as it did not interfere with an advancing white settler population. Many Americans believed that as long as the proper tools and support were provided, the process of acculturation would teach the Indians to behave like "civilized" white people.[22]

To teach the Cherokees the intricacies of subsistence farming, the U.S. government turned to Colonel Return Jonathan Meigs Sr. His experience with Indians in Ohio, where he had settled and helped establish a territorial government, helped prepare him for his position among the Cherokees. His interest in Cherokee success endeared him to tribal leadership, many of whom often sought his counsel on matters of national importance. He regularly encouraged the tribe to embrace the tenets of "civilization" in order to perpetuate the nation's existence among the rapidly encroaching white horde.[23]

Under Meigs's supervision, the Cherokees readily adopted European-style agriculture, which accelerated the acculturation process in two significant ways. First, the adoption of an agrarian lifestyle allowed for the further development of African chattel slavery within the Cherokee Nation. As a result, the traditional redistributive economic model evolved into a capitalist free-for-all for many Cherokees.[24] Slaveholders took advantage of the tribe's communal landholdings by improving larger tracts of land for personal gain. Cherokee land could be used at will as long as it was occupied by its user and did not interfere with uses other Cherokees made of it. Needless to say, slavery grew steadily among the Cherokee people as readily available land encouraged larger plantations.[25]

Second, intermarriage between Cherokees and white settlers created conflict between traditional Cherokee social norms and the social values espoused by European societies.[26] As interracial marriages produced a growing population of mixed-blood Cherokees, many mixed-bloods adopted much of the dress and culture of their white ancestors. By the early nineteenth century, many Cherokees had also become Christian and learned to read and write English, driving a wedge between the traditional full-blood Cherokees and the semiacculturated mixed-bloods of the tribe. It is important to note that the mixed-blood portion of the tribe constituted a small segment of Cherokee society, as only 17 percent of the near 17,000 or so living in the Cherokee Nation prior to removal had white ancestors. Moreover, less than 8 percent of Cherokee households owned slaves, yet 78 percent of all slaveholders were of mixed descent.[27] In short, the small segment of mixed-blood Cherokees held a disproportionate amount of the personal wealth in the nation prior to removal. This small subset also held a disproportionate number of the political offices in the tribal government. Of the twelve men who signed the Cherokee constitution in 1827, eleven of them, Ross included, owned 22 percent of all the slaves in the Cherokee Nation.[28]

By the start of the nineteenth century, the process of acculturation among the Cherokees was well under way.[29] The tribe had largely become sedentary farmers, occupying tribal lands within the borders of numerous southern states. By 1802, Georgia had become so concerned with such a large band of Indians living within its borders that state leaders called for the federal government to extinguish the tribe's land title and extend Georgia sovereignty over the entire state. In exchange for a promise to do so, the state granted to the federal government all claim to its western lands—lands that would become the Mississippi Territory. However, the federal government could not just extinguish Cherokee land ownership, because that ownership had been guaranteed through a Senate-ratified treaty. The only way the United States could extinguish treaty-protected title to this land was to induce the tribe to agree to a new treaty.

The Cherokee government, led by Ross, refused the federal government's demand that the tribe sign a new treaty and trade its ancestral lands for a new home west of the Mississippi River. Feeling pressure from the Georgia government, President Andrew Jackson sought out a small group of wealthy, acculturated, mixed-blood Cherokees led by Major Ridge and his son John Ridge in hopes of persuading them to sign the new treaty on behalf of the entire Cherokee Nation. However, the Cherokee Constitution required the National Council's approval on all treaties. When the Ridges proceeded to sign the treaty without tribal authorization, the matter became a criminal affair as the group faced accusations of treason.

Although Ross and the Cherokee National Council protested the validity of the new treaty, the U.S. Army enforced it, driving the Cherokees out of Georgia along the infamous "Trail of Tears." It was the betrayal of the tribe by the small group who signed the removal treaty, rather than the institution of slavery (as some historians have argued), that caused the factionalism that developed in the Cherokee Nation and was the primary agent of discord in the tribe.[30]

When three of the signers were executed for their alleged crime, Stand Watie, John Ridge's cousin, blamed Ross for the killings. Even though the United States negotiated a peace between the two men in the 1840s, leading to a period of relative quiet, the animosity exposed itself again shortly after the start of the war. Both men were slaveholders, yet they each took a different position on the importance of slavery to the Cherokee Nation. The fact that slaveholders so dominated leadership positions within the tribe actually complicates our understanding of the tribe's role in the Civil War rather than clarifying it. Ross's commitment to tribal self-rule caused him to waver on his commitment to slavery, as he was willing to sacrifice the latter for the perpetuation of the former. Watie, who was determined to fight for the continuation of both simultaneously, took exception to Ross's stance. For Watie, the primary focus shifted from a defense of slavery to a struggle against his own tribal government. He waged war on anyone, including Cherokees, who demonstrated a lack of commitment to the institution of slavery or the Southern cause. Moreover, Watie's own men declared him principal chief after Ross was arrested by Federal troops in the summer of 1862 for his own protection and sent to Washington by Union officers to plead the Cherokees' case before the federal government. For Ross, the motivation was entirely about the protection of tribal autonomy, even at the expense of slavery.

Early slavery in the Cherokee Nation mixed European social models with traditional Cherokee social roles, creating an institution that, at least on the surface, resembled that of the southern United States while maintaining much of the tribe's familial focus. A census conducted prior to removal indicates there were 1,592 slaves belonging to 207 Cherokee households in 1835. Of those households, 168, or 83 percent, owned ten or fewer slaves. Only three individuals owned fifty or more. One of those men, however, owned one hundred slaves yet lived in a tiny log cabin himself, no doubt shunning the trappings of the material wealth associated with slaveholding.[31] Moreover, slavery among the Cherokee Indians was initially viewed through the lens of matrilineal kinship patterns, providing many early slaves with a more egalitarian experience than what slaves in white society experienced.[32]

However, slavery in the Cherokee Nation underwent an ideological change near the end of the eighteenth and into the nineteenth centuries as the tribe interacted increasingly with its European neighbors.[33] What began as a system based on Cherokee kinship and acceptance quickly degenerated into a race-based institution similar to that practiced in the southern United States.[34] By the turn of the nineteenth century, as an increase in Cherokee-white intermarriage influenced Cherokee attitudes toward their Black neighbors, many Cherokees adopted a new understanding of the changing social order based entirely on race.[35] In the years following removal, Cherokees reimagined and redefined the position of Blacks within Cherokee society. Moreover, the National Council began codifying these changing ideas of racial stratification, further delineating the emerging racial gap between Cherokees and Blacks.[36] Blacks in the Cherokee Nation, both slave and free, were barred from owning property and were no longer allowed to enjoy the privileges of Cherokee kinship unless they were connected to the tribe by bloodline.[37] That lineage became less likely, however, as most Cherokees, compared to their Creek neighbors, refrained from the Indian-Black intermarriage that helped change the face of the Creek Nation, for example, in the nineteenth century.[38]

By 1842, Cherokee slaves recognized the growing severity of the institution and sought opportunities to resist. In the early morning hours of November 15, about two dozen slaves belonging to Joseph Vann, a mixed-blood Cherokee and the wealthiest man in the Cherokee Nation, locked the Vanns inside their home, stole horses, supplies, and firearms, and escaped, headed for freedom in Mexico. John Ross immediately challenged the National Council to "adopt such necessary & prompt measures as will insure the apprehension" of the runaways, to uncover the depths of the conspiracy, and "to prevent any further similar outrages from being committed."[39] The council acted quickly, most likely because Vann was one of them, being a member of the National Committee from the Saline District at the time.⁴⁰ The council authorized Ross's nephew John Drew to head a military force and arrest the slaves. Drew chased them through the Creek Nation where the runaways killed two men. They were ultimately captured just north of the Red River and returned to Vann. Those accused of the murders were sent to Fort Gibson while the National Council decided their fate.⁴¹

Changing attitudes toward race did not end with emancipation. In February 1863, the National Council formally ended slavery in the Cherokee Nation yet made no accommodation for the former slaves' well-being. By war's end, many former slaves had become refugees, living in the squalor of refugee camps alongside Indian families or struggling to survive while roaming the hills of the Cherokee Nation. Unwilling to accept responsibility for the newly freed people, the U.S. government used the punitive postwar treaty of 1866 to compel the Cherokees to acknowledge their racist past and adopt all Blacks living in the nation prior to the war into the tribe with full rights of tribal citizenship. The tribe spent much of the next century in reluctant compliance, hoping for the issue to pass with time. However, one important element of the 1866 treaty kept the issue of freedmen citizenship on the front burner of Cherokee politics. The treaty granted citizenship not only to the tribe's former slaves but also to all their descendants. This opened the door of tribal membership to thousands of African Americans who had no blood lineage connection to the Cherokee tribe. Nearly a half century of judicial battles followed before a U.S. district court cleared the way for full citizenship for all descendants of former Cherokee slaves. The Cherokee Nation would finally capitulate on February 22, 2021, when the tribe's Supreme Court upheld the supremacy of the postwar treaty of 1866 and granted full citizenship to all former Cherokee slaves and their descendants.

Although the racial attitude behind the institution of slavery in the Cherokee Nation mirrored that of the Southern states, it had a lesser footprint than in the Confederacy. The wave of secession that ripped through the United States in 1860 and 1861 occurred on three levels. The first level took place after the election of the Republican president, Abraham Lincoln, in November 1860, when seven states, led by South Carolina, voted to leave the Union rather than face the abolitionist platform of the new administration. Slaveholders in these states held such power and influence that secession came almost immediately. In each of these states (Texas being the exception), slaves constituted at least 43.7 percent of their respective populations, indicating that slavery was spread across the entire state, giving slaveholders control over state politics.⁴² The second wave of secession did not occur until after the attack on Fort Sumter, South Carolina, in April 1861, motivating four additional states—Virginia, North Carolina, Tennessee, and Arkansas—to join the parade of secession. Slaveholders in these states did not possess the same influence as did their counterparts in the Deep South, yet they managed to drag their states into the Confederacy after Lincoln's call for volunteers provided them added impetus. Slaves in these upper South states made up between 24.8 percent and 40.2 percent of their respective populations, each less than the Deep South states, indicating a more limited influence over state politics.

Finally, the third level of secession never occurred, yet it is most important to our understanding of slavery in the Cherokee Nation. The four remaining slave states—Missouri, Kentucky, Maryland, and Delaware—had slave-friendly constitutions, yet slaveholders did not have enough power and influence to lead their states into secession, even after the added motivation of Lincoln's call for volunteers. Slaves in each of these states formed less than 24 percent of their respective populations, indicating an institution that was spread too thinly to have overriding influence on state politics. In 1860, there were 2,511 Cherokee slaves, or less than 12 percent of the tribe's population, a number that politically aligned the Cherokee Nation more with the border state of Maryland than with the Confederate states of Georgia, Texas, or Arkansas.[43] The institution of slavery in the Cherokee Nation was, most likely, unable to effect the kind of influence on the Cherokee government necessary to push the tribe into an alliance with the Confederate States. It is important to note that the Cherokee's bicameral legislature was modeled after those of U.S. states. Moreover, the system of checks and balances was also similar, so the process of secession would have had to follow virtually the same political path for the Cherokees as it did for Southern white governments. If slaveholders in those states with lower percentages of slave populations could not compel secession, the Cherokee slaveholders in a nation with similar density and a similar governmental structure most likely could not have done so either. Slavery in the Cherokee Nation certainly influenced tribal politics, but apparently it was not widespread enough to draw the tribe into the Confederacy on its own merit.

The existence of slavery among the Cherokee people has often misdirected understanding of the Civil War in Indian Territory by convincing historians that the tribe participated in the war to defend the institution, much like its white Southern neighbors. However, slavery among the Cherokees was not as widely engrained as in the Deep South. This book explores the real motivation behind the Cherokee Nation's alliance with the Confederacy and slavery's role in that decision. Cherokee leaders under Ross's guidance joined the Confederacy because they believed it provided them the best chance to protect their autonomy, allowing them to decide the future of the institution for themselves. Unlike slaveholders in the Southern states, many in the Cherokee Nation, including slaveholders, identified with an issue that was to them more pressing than slavery: the perpetuation of tribal self-rule. I argue that tribal sovereignty was paramount to Ross and much of the Cherokee Nation during the nineteenth century, more so than the defense of slavery.

In 1849, Calhoun's Indian office, now known as the Bureau of Indian Affairs, was transferred from the Department of War to the newly established Department of the Interior.[44] This placed Indian policy under the watchful eye of a different cabinet member, one who worked directly with the White House to formulate and implement the president's Indian policy. The military continued to handle U.S.-Indian relations. Historian Francis Paul Prucha refers to the U.S. Army as "a child of the frontier" because much of its development occurred while protecting settlers from Indians and enforcing U.S. Indian policy.[45] Moreover, superintendents and agents merely acted as the eyes and ears of the Indian commissioner, who reported directly to the new secretary. Often these men made suggestions to the commissioner, but the burden of Indian policy remained firmly with the president in Washington.

Ross also recognized that Indian policy originated in Washington and wasted little time communicating with agents, superintendents, or even the commissioner of Indian affairs during much of his time as principal chief. An evaluation of the primary collection of Ross's written communication reveals his strong faith in the process of constitutional law.[46] Prior to the Supreme Court's landmark decision in *Worcester v. Georgia* (1832), in which the Court upheld the sovereignty of Cherokee land ownership, Ross communicated frequently with the Cherokee agent in Tennessee, Hugh Lawson Montgomery, on matters concerning U.S.-Cherokee relations. He spent four months in Washington in 1829, according to the allowances of the Treaty of Holston, presenting the Cherokee grievances before Congress in the wake of Georgia's attack on Cherokee sovereignty and visiting primarily with the House of Representatives and the secretary of war, John Eaton, a Jacksonian Democrat from Tennessee. Following *Worcester*, however, Ross came to view the Cherokee tribe as an autonomous nation and began to interact with the United States as if he was a foreign dignitary. He turned away from the agents in the field and returned to Washington, where he visited directly with President Jackson and Secretary of War Lewis Cass, seeking enforcement of the Court's decision.

Ross's predilection for direct interaction with Washington instead of with the agents and superintendents demonstrates an important aspect of the chief's political ideology. Ross believed the Cherokee tribe was an independent nation with political autonomy and a strategic military alliance with the United States; therefore, he rarely communicated with agents and superintendents about treaty concerns. He relied on the lower-level Indian bureau simply to satisfy the government's treaty requirements. From his election in 1828 to the forced removal in 1838, Ross made seven trips to Washington and presented his arguments before Congress no fewer than fifteen times. Moreover, he wrote twelve formal letters to the president and thirty-eight to the secretary of war. During that same span, he wrote to the commissioner of Indian affairs only twice. His insistence on dealing directly with top officials in Washington rather than with the Indian bureau is a practice he continued throughout his career as principal chief.

Ross did, for a season, correspond more frequently with lower-level officials of the Indian bureau: upon arriving in Indian Territory at the terminus of the "Trail of Tears." His object was to secure the provisions, tools, and monies promised the tribe so that the people could transition to their new home with as little difficulty as possible. Between 1839 and 1846, he penned no fewer than forty-three official letters to the agents in Tahlequah (32), the superintendents in Fort Smith, Arkansas (11), and the commissioners of Indian affairs in Washington (5). However, in matters of national importance, he still interacted directly with the highest levels of the federal government. During the tribe's first eight years in Indian Territory, Ross made the 1,200-mile journey to Washington five times to visit with Presidents Martin Van Buren, John Tyler, and James K. Polk and their respective secretaries of war. Moreover, he presented Cherokee grievances before Congress no fewer than three times during those visits.

As the Cherokee people settled into their new homes in Indian Territory, Ross's greatest concern was the need to establish the protection protocols of the U.S. Army as outlined in the removal treaty of 1835. In this regard, he communicated most often with General Matthew Arbuckle, who was in command at Fort Gibson in the Cherokee Nation and who was most responsible for providing that protection. The relationship between Ross and Arbuckle is best described as strained, as the general struggled to keep the peace between the newly arrived Cherokee emigrants and the "Old Settlers," who had emigrated west as many as twenty years earlier and had an established tribal leadership.[47] Nonetheless, in a letter dated May 14, 1839, Ross reminded Arbuckle of his obligation: "The peaceful inhabitants of this Nation can only call upon your military authority for protection. And I trust you will take proper steps to prevent all unlawful acts of violence from being perpetuated upon the property & persons of the Cherokees . . . by citizens of the U. States."[48] The fact that the removal saga had arisen because of the intrusions of Georgia's citizens prompted Ross to immediately issue the demand for the military protection promised in their new home.

While the Cherokees were making the difficult transition to Indian Territory, the United States embarked on an era of unprecedented territorial expansion. The annexation of Texas in 1846 brought U.S. citizens to the southern border of Indian Territory. In addition, the vast Mexican land cession at the end of the Mexican-American War in 1848 pushed the nation's western border all the way to the Pacific Ocean. The new opportunities brought a wave of white settlers into the West looking for fortunes in land or gold in California. Moreover, the Kansas-Nebraska Act of 1854 invited settlers to the northern borders of Indian Territory as the nation placed a priority on answering its "slave question" rather than on solving its "Indian problem."

During this same time, from 1847 to 1856, Ross had virtually no contact with Washington as he led the Cherokee Nation in a period of peace and increasing prosperity.[49] However, as the tribe established roots in Indian Territory, the regions around them were undergoing great change. The aggregate white population of Texas, Arkansas, and Kansas immediately prior to the forced removal hovered around 100,000. By 1860, however, that population had increased to 1.2 million.[50] The population of Kansas alone grew from 8,500 as late as 1855 to over 100,000 five years later as white citizens from the northern and southern states converged on the territory to influence the slavery vote.[51] No longer could the Cherokee Nation enjoy the peace and prosperity of its new home in solitude. The growing mass of white settlers on their borders created a dark and ominous cloud that hung over Indian Territory as white America converged, once again, on the Cherokee Nation.

By the start of the Civil War in 1861, the Bureau of Indian Affairs found itself incapable of administering the nation's Indian policy as this wave of white settlers put added pressure on federal treaty obligations.[52] Unfortunately, the Civil War years saw the U.S. government turn the bulk of its attention toward the Southern states in rebellion and all but abandon its obligations to the Indians in the West. The election of Abraham Lincoln in November 1860 brought a new administration to Washington and a rapidly changing political climate.

Moreover, the rapid secession of Southern states between December 1860 and May 1861 nearly incapacitated large portions of the Indian bureau as many of its agents and superintendents resigned their posts and joined the Confederacy with their home states. Elias Rector, the Southern superintendent since 1857, resigned to join his home state of Arkansas, where his cousin, Henry, was the governor.[53] Rector was immediately named Confederate superintendent of Indian affairs in Indian Territory. Robert J. Cowart, the Cherokee agent and a slaveowner from Georgia, also resigned, leaving the Cherokee Nation without a federal agent outside Washington.[54]

The withdrawal of Federal troops from Indian Territory in the spring of 1861 precipitated the Cherokees' involvement in the war, especially after Confederate Texans moved in to occupy Indian country, completely severing the tribe's communication with the U.S. government. The prewar agent to the Choctaws, an Arkansan named Albert Pike, also resigned, and became a special Confederate commissioner to Indian Territory, charged with securing the cooperation of the various tribes. Pike immediately began a vigorous campaign to lure the tribes into an alliance with the new Confederacy. Ross's desire to remain loyal to the Cherokees' treaties with the United States and avoid an alliance with the Confederacy set the stage for an epic showdown with Pike in the spring and summer of 1861. However, the United States' inability to protect the Cherokees in accordance with their treaty obligations forced Ross to reconsider that neutrality and succumb to an alliance with Pike and the Confederate States.

At the start of the war, Ross would have no contact with Rector's replacement as agent, William G. Coffin. Moreover, the first two replacements for Cowart, John Crawford and Charles W. Chatterton, resigned almost immediately when presented with the daunting task of having to care for the growing number of Indian refugees who left Indian Territory to avoid the horrors of the war. The next choice, Justin Harlan of Iowa, whose brother, James would serve as secretary of the interior at the end of the war, spent the remainder of the war in Kansas helping Coffin provide as much aid as possible to the refugee Indians. The new secretary of the interior, Caleb Blood Smith, and the new Indian commissioner, William Palmer Dole, quickly recognized the error of the troop withdrawal and began calling on the new president to return the troops to Indian Territory and reestablish the prewar treaties.

One year into the war, President Abraham Lincoln did just that, hoping to persuade the Indian nations away from the Confederacy and back into a relationship with the U.S. government. Although destined for failure, the Indian

Expedition of 1862, the first attempt to return Union forces to Indian Territory, arrested Ross for his own protection and, upon hearing his story, sent him to Washington to share it with Lincoln. Ross stayed near his wife's family in Philadelphia and made the trip to the nation's capital a half-dozen times, where he had at least two face-to-face meetings with Lincoln. The first took place in September 1862, when Ross asked the president to consider the circumstances behind the Cherokee-Confederate alliance and to include his people on the list of tribes who had remained loyal to their treaties.

The request came at a time when Lincoln's attention was greatly divided between the Emancipation Proclamation, violence between Dakotas and whites in Minnesota, and the changing landscape of the war itself. The second meeting took place in 1863 after Lincoln had considered Ross's request and investigated the nation's treaty relationship with the Cherokees. Commissioner Dole accompanied Ross to the second meeting. Both men came away convinced that Lincoln believed the United States had abrogated its treaty obligations by abandoning Indian Territory, had forgiven the Cherokees for the unavoidable alliance with the Confederacy, and had promised to reinstate the tribe to its prewar status as soon as control of Indian Territory could be secured. Ross was so convinced of this that he turned his attention away from the president and began lobbying for assistance to the starving people of Indian Territory.

However, the United States failed to commit the necessary manpower to regain control of Indian Territory in 1862 or 1863. Union forces trying to secure this control after 1862 comprised primarily Indian troops. In fact, the federal government rarely used regular troops outside the main theaters of war. Volunteer soldiers administered the nation's Indian policy in the West while regular troops fought Confederates. These volunteers often worked with little to no oversight from Washington, and with even less training and discipline.[55] Perhaps the most important example occurred in late 1864 at Sand Creek, Colorado, when Colonel John Chivington led a cavalry regiment of Colorado volunteers in a massacre of peaceful Indians that sparked an Indian uprising across the plains. The nation's treaty-making process proved inadequate to handling the issues that arose among the Plains tribes, mostly because the United States continued its tradition of abrogating those treaties whenever it saw fit. The Cherokee Nation had always responded to abrogation in the halls of justice. Somehow, the United States expected the less acculturated tribes of the Plains to be just as diplomatic.

The government's attempts to force rapid acculturation on the Sioux, Cheyennes, Arapahoes, and others following the Civil War proved to be futile, if not incendiary. The government could, in a sense, bully the Cherokees into a new treaty whenever necessary without fear of violent reprisal, but the Plains tribes were not so diplomatic. They often responded to abrogation with violence. The process of making treaties with the Sioux, Cheyenne, Arapaho, Kiowa, Apache, and Comanche tribes would only work if the United States adhered to its obligations with what Prucha calls honor and dignity.[56] Unfortunately, honor and dignity, although implicated as part of the treaty-making process, rarely found their way into the actual dispensation of U.S. Indian policy.

This book shows how the interaction between John Ross and the U.S. government led directly to the dismantling of the country's prewar Indian policy of treaty making and its replacement with a less defined policy of impatience and violence. Before his death, Abraham Lincoln acknowledged the government's treaty responsibilities to the Indians, in particular the Cherokees. His willingness to admit that the nation had abrogated its treaty obligations in 1861 paved the way for the restoration of the prewar treaties with the Cherokees, reaffirming the nation's policy of treaty making. His assassination, however, brought immediate change to Indian policy as the new president, Andrew Johnson, ignored the actions of his predecessor, declared the Cherokees disloyal, nullified the prewar treaties, confiscated tribal lands once protected by those treaties, and established new reservations in Indian Territory for the removal of many Great Plains tribes.

The postwar process of dismantling Indian policy consisted of two important steps. First, the United States needed to reacquire land from the tribes in Indian Territory as a home for some of the Plains tribes to be relocated out of the path of white "progress." Second, the treaty-making process, dating back to the colonial period, had to be formally abolished so the government could compel Indians to follow the commands of the federal government. Many in the federal government believed that the practice of treaty making would never succeed with the tribes in the American West. The Indian policy that emerged in the years immediately following the Civil War has been described as "radically reformist."[57]

The primary agent of change for Indian policy in the postwar years was a Seneca named Ely Samuel Parker. Parker served as adjutant on the staff of General Ulysses S. Grant during the Civil War and became heavily involved in Indian policy in the postwar years. His interactions with Ross and the Cherokee Nation at the Fort Smith Council in September 1865, convened to deal with the pro-Confederate tribes of Indian Territory, convinced him of the need to change the prewar policy. By 1871, Congress, largely on Parker's recommendation, formally ended treaty making. However, to the detriment of U.S.-Indian relations, it failed to proffer any reliable alternative.[58]

Ross's behavior during the council led Parker to believe that treaty making filled the Indians with a false idea of independence. He and the other commissioners watched Ross and the other Cherokees resist the dictates of the council at Fort Smith. The last thing the United States needed, in Parker's opinion, was the Indians of the Plains, primarily the Sioux, Cheyennes, and Arapahoes, believing that they, too, had autonomy and, therefore, were not required to follow any nontreaty mandates forced upon them. To Parker's mind, tribes were not independent nations; rather, they were wards of the government and should be compelled to do whatever the government commanded. Parker's suggested dismantling of Indian policy found strong support in Washington, especially from President Grant, and helped directly alter U.S.-Indian relations as a result of the Fort Smith Council.

While politicians argued over how best to approach Indian relations on the Plains after the Civil War, the U.S. Army asserted itself as the enforcer of U.S. Indian policy. Robert Wooster argues that the military busied itself with trying to construct its own policy for dealing with the Indians once the rebellion in the South was thwarted.[59] The absence of a unified government policy blurred the line between the jurisdictions of the War Department and Department of the Interior, and the Indians were left to suffer the consequences.

Parker's influence on Indian policy continued after the Fort Smith Council into the postwar years. The Peace Commission of 1867, as well as the Board of Indian Commissioners that formed later, helped advance Parker's policies of forced acculturation on reservation lands held only with possessory rights. The conflicts that emerged during this period of confusion dominate our memory of U.S.-Indian relations. The U.S. Army's failure at Little Bighorn and the massacre at Wounded Knee Creek occurred because the United States opted not to define the military's role in the last quarter of the nineteenth century, allowing confusion to rule the day.

In this book, I follow the perspective of Ross and the Cherokee Nation, and, by so doing, produce a clearer narrative of the events in Indian Territory during the Civil War and their effect on postwar Indian policy. Removing the events that occurred between 1861 and 1865 from the Civil War context allows for a new story to emerge, a story of tribal sovereignty and U.S. Indian policy. The events in Indian Territory are more rigidly connected to the events at Little Bighorn and Wounded Knee than to the battles at Gettysburg and Antietam. While the Civil

War rightly dominates the narratives of the era in Arkansas, Missouri, and in much of Texas, the events in Indian Territory have a much broader connection to larger themes of American history.

I argue that the Civil War era in Indian Territory—more specifically, the Cherokee Nation's position in the war—is more a narrative of U.S. Indian policy than one of the Civil War. After the war, many within the U.S. government sought to change that policy so it could better deal with the nomadic Plains tribes. However, their inability to offer a working alternative led to the disasters of late-nineteenth-century Indian relations. I also argue that the administration of Andrew Johnson manipulated the postwar treaty negotiations at the Fort Smith Council in order to undo the prewar treaties, allowing the subsequent administration of Ulysses S. Grant to abolish the policy of treaty-making as part of a wider dismantling of U.S. Indian policy. And, finally, I show that the assassination of Abraham Lincoln at the close of the war was the pivotal moment—the tipping point—at which this dismantling began. The assassination did not cause the change in policy; rather it allowed the Johnson administration to undo the prewar treaties on the grounds that the tribes had been disloyal to the United States by signing new treaties with the Confederacy at the outset of the war. Johnson's abolition of the prewar treaties led to broader changes in U.S. Indian policy.

This book connects Abraham Lincoln more directly to U.S. Indian policy beyond Minnesota than has been imagined previously. His intervention on behalf of Ross and the Cherokee Nation reflects his belief in the supremacy of constitutional law. Chief John Ross and the Cherokees rightly claimed that the United States abrogated the treaties by abandoning three forts in Indian Territory in 1861. This withdrawal left the defenseless Indians without the ability to resist Confederate pressure to either ally with or declare themselves the enemy of the Confederacy. Lincoln admitted to the breach and declared his intent to restore Ross and the Cherokee Nation to their prewar treaty relationship with the United States, despite the tribe's alliance with the Confederates. His willingness to accept Ross's explanation for the Cherokee-Confederate alliance, and his plans to restore the prewar treaties endorsed the treaty-making policy. Unfortunately, the bullet that killed the president at Ford's Theatre also killed his planned restoration. The new administration soon began transforming U.S. Indian policy from dispossession by treaty to assimilation by the army.

The Johnson administration ignored the federal government's prior treaty abrogation. This blatant disregard for the nation's responsibility and its willingness to act devoid of honor and dignity fulfilled a historical theme that is interwoven throughout U.S.-Indian relations, with Lincoln as a notable exception. The assertion that Lincoln's support of Ross and the Cherokees was merely a wartime measure, similar to his actions in Louisiana with the Ten-Percent Plan, has no merit in that the United States had no wartime objective in Indian Territory.[60] The Union Army's activities in Indian Territory were simply a matter of Indian policy and not a matter of fighting the Civil War. Historians can only guess how different Indian policy might have looked in the late 1860s and 1870s had Lincoln been its primary author.

Cherokee Civil Warrior tells the story of how the U.S. government used the Cherokee Nation first to erect federal Indian policy in the 1830s and then to dismantle it at the end of the Civil War. Chapter 1, "Removal and the Struggle for Sovereignty," begins with the Removal Era of the 1820s and 1830s for three reasons. First, we learn how far the United States was willing to go to sidestep its treaty obligations and bully Indian nations in its negotiations with them. In what has been described merely as removal, the federal government instituted a policy of oppression, tyranny, and racism disguised as diplomacy. By ratifying many fraudulently acquired treaties, often with tiny factions of Indian tribes, the U.S. government propped its "policy of removal" behind the veil of constitutional law. When Principal Chief John Ross and the Cherokee Nation protested this very policy on the same constitutional grounds, the Indians quickly discovered that constitutional law was only as good as the ethics of the white men administering it.

Second, I begin with the Removal Era for what it reveals about the development of Ross's political ideology. He quickly realized that white governments were too often duplicitous in their interactions with indigenous people. When the Supreme Court ruled in the tribe's favor in *Worcester v. Georgia* (1832), he learned that constitutional law supported the autonomy granted the Cherokees through the treaty-making process. It was white politicians who could not be trusted to uphold that law when it came to Indian policy. In Ross's mind, all the Cherokees needed was a U.S. president who was willing to uphold the Constitution and treat the tribe in the manner prescribed by their treaties with the federal government.

Finally, the Removal Era of the 1820s and 1830s allows us to understand how historians have long overplayed the significance of the small Cherokee faction led by John Ridge in the 1830s and Stand Watie in the Civil War era. Ridge led a tiny group of fewer than eighty Cherokees who supported the Treaty of New Echota (1835). The group represented less than one-half of 1 percent of the tribe's total population. Even though Ridge tried for weeks to raise support for immediate removal, he did not have enough influence within the tribe to garner more than the fraction who voted in favor of the treaty. Historians have referred to Ross as the leader of the other "faction" of the Cherokee Nation. Use of the word "faction" here delegitimizes the political acumen of the Cherokee people who adopted a national constitution and elected Ross as their principal chief. Ross never led a faction. He led the constitutionally elected Cherokee government with the approval and support of the Cherokee people who elected him principal chief for ten consecutive terms beginning in 1828 until his death in 1866. Moreover, the inclination of historians to overplay the significance of Ridge has translated to Indian Territory and found its way into narratives of the Civil War. Ridge's cousin, Stand Watie, who was never able to raise more than three hundred men (and many of those were not even Cherokees), held far less political influence than historians have granted him. In fact, his true position in Cherokee history has been misunderstood until now. This book shows how Watie's incessant raids against pro-Ross Cherokees during the Civil War led to more death and destruction than occurred at the hands of Andrew Jackson during the horrific "Trail of Tears." Stand Watie should now assume his place as the biggest enemy of the Cherokee Nation during the Civil War, if not the entire nineteenth century.

Chapter 2, "Secession and the Preservation of a Nation," defines Indian sovereignty in early-nineteenth-century American politics. As Ross and the Cherokee Nation interacted with the federal government, they soon realized that tribal sovereignty actually had two definitions, one denoted by the Constitution and the other intended by white politicians. The U.S. Constitution as the supreme law of the land held Indian treaties on the same plane as treaties with other sovereign nations. However, many white politicians had no intention of allowing Indian nations to retain and exercise the same sovereignty as those foreign powers. Consequently, white politicians developed a system of making unequivocal promises to indigenous peoples through treaties in order to attain the objectives of the day in a peaceful manner, only to renege on those promises later whenever those objectives changed. The result was a nation full of Indian tribes that believed they held a level of autonomy and hoped the federal government would one day honor the promise to protect that autonomy. Ross and the Cherokee Nation had to learn the tribe's place within these competing definitions and how to navigate the grievance process when the tribe believed its rights were infringed.

Chapter 2 also discusses how Ross used what he learned of the federal government's ideas about Indian sovereignty to navigate the Cherokee Nation through the frightening process of secession in the days following the withdrawal of U.S. forces from Indian Territory in April 1861 and the consequent invasion of the territory by Confederate troops from Texas. His idea of tribal autonomy was built on the solid foundation of constitutional law, yet he struggled with the fear that white governments would not honor Indian self-rule. The intense pressure applied by white Confederates placed Ross on tenuous ground, as he had to negotiate the idea of not only protecting his people from the Civil War but also protecting them from a new white government with no intention of returning the loyalty it expected of the Cherokees.

Chapter 3, "Autonomy and the Confederate Alliance," discusses how Ross came to believe that the best way to protect the Cherokee people from the Civil War was by joining the Civil War. However, the decision to align with the Confederate States was not an easy one. Ross not only struggled with how best to protect the Cherokee people; he also believed that all Indians would be better protected by standing in unity. As the war began, Ross's allegiance to the Confederacy was quickly tested when Rebel forces, both white and Indian, attacked Opothle Yahola, as he and his followers sought simply to remain neutral in the coming war. The unmitigated attacks on innocent men, women, and children, often referred to (although not here) as the first battles of the Civil War in Indian Territory, alerted Ross to two realities: that war in Indian Territory was going to be a bloody affair and that neutrality was not a safe option. Chapter 3 also discusses the apparent reluctance Watie displayed to become involved during the political debates over secession. Significant evidence suggests that Watie only entered the war after the Cherokee Nation committed itself to an alliance with the Confederate States. However, when that commitment began to waver, Watie and his small force began a vengeful campaign to punish all Cherokees who did not fully and openly support the Confederate cause. Unfortunately for the Cherokee people, most of them found themselves in Watie's crosshairs.

Chapter 4, "Abraham Lincoln and the Indian Expedition," introduces Abraham Lincoln into the narrative and places him in the context of Indian policy rather than the Civil War. His decisions to acknowledge the United States' prewar treaty abrogation and to return troops to Indian Territory have largely gone unnoticed by historians who continue to evaluate the events through the narrower lens of the war. The broader interpretation through the lens of U.S. Indian policy allows the examination of the Indian Expedition of 1862 for what it really was: an attempt to restore the Cherokee Nation to its prewar diplomatic status according to the tribe's treaties with the United States. Lincoln's efforts to return

Federal troops to Indian Territory marked a pivotal moment in the history of U.S. Indian policy in that the president sought to acknowledge the nation's treaty relationship and responsibilities to its indigenous people by admitting that, by withdrawing Federal troops, the United States had abrogated its treaty obligations to the tribes of Indian Territory. His decision was in line with the opinions of many within his administration who frequently encouraged the president to do just that. The Indian Expedition was not a military maneuver but a movement of Indian policy, and the U.S. Army treated it as such. The story of the Indian Expedition has been widely misinterpreted as part of the Civil War, when in reality it had very little to do with the war at all.

Chapter 5, "The Fort Smith Council and the Dismantling of U.S. Indian Policy," discusses the unexpected transition from one administration to another following the assassination of Abraham Lincoln as the Civil War drew to a close in April 1865. The new administration had little sympathy for the tribes in Indian Territory and ignored the previous administration's attempts to reestablish the prewar Indian treaties. The Johnson administration's inability—or unwillingness—to follow its predecessor and admit to the prewar abrogation led to a series of punitive postwar treaties between the victorious United States and what Johnson believed were the disloyal nations of Indian Territory. However, Ross and the Cherokees refused to accept such a notion of disloyalty and resisted the new arrangement, claiming that the prewar treaties should remain in place because the United States had abrogated them in the first place. Lincoln had understood; why could Johnson not do so as well? Ross's aloofness toward the presidentially appointed commissioners at the Fort Smith Council in September 1865 angered many within the administration who viewed Ross as a hindrance to Cherokee loyalty and therefore U.S. Indian policy. The commission's unprecedented decision to depose Ross as principal chief found strong support from one of its members who would go on to have great influence on Indian policy in the years after the war. Ely S. Parker was appalled by Ross's attitude and soon helped dismantle U.S. Indian policy using Ross's intransigence as a motivation.

By excluding the events in Indian Territory leading up to the Fort Smith Council from our narratives of U.S. Indian policy, we dismiss their relevance to the changing landscape of U.S.-Indian relations in the post–Civil War years. Removing the Fort Smith Council from a formative role implies that Congress alone took the lead in the abolition of treaty-making with Indian nations by ending the practice through legislation in 1871. Legal historian Stuart Banner suggests that, having already appropriated several million dollars in additional funds for the rash of treaties signed immediately following the Civil War, the House of Representatives—with support from many in the Senate—agreed to end the practice of treaty making as a money-saving measure.[61] Prucha asserts that antitreaty fervor in the United States was nothing new in 1871 and points to Parker's tirade in his first annual report as Indian commissioner two years earlier as evidence. Prucha claims that jealousy in the House of Representatives over its continual exclusion from the administration of Indian affairs is what finally brought about the change.[62]

The fact that the measure to abolish treaty making was attached as a rider to the Indian appropriations legislation of 1871 indicates there was no such widespread support in either chamber, much less the House of Representatives. Scholars of U.S. Indian policy Vine Deloria Jr. and Raymond J. DeMallie argue that historians have assumed that Congress thoroughly debated the proposition in each house.[63] Such debate never occurred. The addendum was written and developed in a conference committee, away from open debate on either floor. Weeks of work in the House and eventually in the Senate over the appropriations bill led to the need for the committee to hammer out the differences between the two versions. The addendum was added only after the extended debate over Indian appropriations had occurred. To reject the addendum at this point would have been to reject the entire appropriations act. This late proviso angered some legislators who saw it as a "threat to transparent legislating."[64] Deloria and DeMallie assert that many legislators acted as if they were entirely unaware that a change had actually been made.[65] Clearly, Congress as a body cannot be credited—or blamed—with having led the charge to end the process of treaty-making with Indian tribes in the United States. There were no doubt enough supporters within Washington to push the bill through. However, a full analysis of the historical record, beginning with the Civil War in Indian Territory, not exclusive of it, indicates that no one pushed harder or with more influence than Ely Parker.

Parker's attack on tribal autonomy should not be misread as an attack on indigeneity in general. A champion of Native communities, Parker worked to provide "less disruptive methods" for encouraging assimilation, believing that the Indians would "choose to assimilate into mainstream culture and society" if only they understood how inevitable the demise of their own lifestyles was. Furthermore, he saw the obvious benefits of avoiding confrontation with the U.S. military by succumbing to that inevitability. Parker believed that assimilation was the only means by which Native societies could avoid extinction. His plan was to abolish the treaty-making process with all Indians and encourage assimilation by providing them with "the right tools, incentives, and opportunities" to make it happen.[66]

The Civil War era in Indian Territory is where histories converge. It is where narratives of the Civil War connect with broader themes of Native American history, of the history of U.S. foreign relations, and of westward expansion and Indian removal. It tells a tale of empire, of the vanishing frontier, and of contested borderlands. If we are to understand how the events in Indian Territory are interconnected with these broader themes, we must first resist the temptation to view them only through the lens of the Civil War simply because of the time frame in which they occurred. By restricting our perspective to just that one theme, we suppress all others. But by placing Ross and the Cherokee Nation at the center of our story, each of these themes becomes lucid. We find that the Civil War era in Indian Territory represents the place of intersection—the point of transition—between colonial America and the American West, between the Civil War and the Indian Wars, between the Louisiana Purchase and the Battle of the Little Bighorn, and between Indian removal and the massacre at Wounded Knee. Moreover, the story of U.S. Indian policy becomes a traceable timeline that runs directly through the Cherokee capitol at Tahlequah and through Ford's Theatre on a spring evening in 1865.

By viewing the events that occurred in Indian Territory between 1861 and 1865 from the perspective of Ross and the Cherokee Nation, and by refocusing the narrative away from the context of the Civil War, I provide a new understanding of the era in Indian Territory. The Civil War in Indian Territory becomes a narrative of perspectives. The Union Army, which previously abandoned Indian Territory because it did not fit its objectives, returned to occupy space in the Cherokee Nation simply as a matter of Indian policy. White Confederates from Texas viewed that occupation as a stepping-stone to a possible invasion across the Red River and placed themselves in a defensive posture within the Creek Nation. Arkansas Confederates hoped to secure help from the Indians in driving Unionists from the state, and Missouri Confederates sought simply to regain control of their home. Kansas politicians and military officers most often concerned themselves with the increasing number of Indian refugees who sought to escape the horrors of Indian Territory. These competing and conflicting perspectives fill the pages of the abundant records of the Civil War. Historians have had to shuffle through them, sort the various perspectives, and determine the proper order of their narratives. Add to them the growing number of Indian sources, which provide still other perspectives, and these narratives become increasingly more difficult to write. However, removing the narratives from the context of the Civil War actually brings a consonance to the story.

What Major Read perceived to be gross insubordination and disloyalty on the part of Watie and his fellow Cherokees that warm spring day at Pleasant Bluff actually had nothing to do with the war he and the other North Texans were fighting. The Indians most often waged their own war against racism, oppression, and treaty abrogation. Regardless of how brave and gallant the Native soldiers were during the American Civil War, the enemy was hardly ever whom it appeared to be. Efforts to expel white soldiers from Indian Territory and retain control of tribal lands proved futile. The enemy was not dressed in blue or gray. He was dressed in racism and oppression and fought from every corner. While Ross and the Cherokee Nation took solace in the fact that Lincoln joined their side, they were not prepared to defend themselves from the biggest attack that came only after the fighting had stopped.

CHAPTER 1

REMOVAL AND THE STRUGGLE FOR SOVEREIGNTY

The man known only as "the Ridge" stepped inside the dimly lit schoolhouse, his large frame filling the door. His piercing eyes slowly adjusted to the filtered light streaming through the lone window as he surveyed the scene before him. The schoolroom, carved out of an old blockhouse, had become the hiding place of his old friend, now a fugitive from Cherokee justice. Low muffled groans from above alerted him to the hiding place of his injured prey. He quickly climbed the ladder to the loft above, looked sadly at the wounded man crouched before him, and with one vicious swing of his hatchet, finished the job.[1] The Ridge was part of a squad of executioners charged with carrying out the traditional law of blood revenge on a tribal chief named Doublehead. In 1806, Doublehead had ceded Cherokee lands in Tennessee and Kentucky to the United States by signing a treaty without the consent of the Cherokee National Council. Traditional Cherokee law required the council's consent on any land cession, and the punishment for such a crime was death.[2] Two decades later, the Ridge helped perpetuate the law after it found new relevance in the first decades of the nineteenth century.[3]

Following the Revolutionary War, white Americans turned their faces toward the interior of the continent and, in unprecedented waves, set out to explore the hinterlands of the new nation. Disregarding the political boundaries established through treaties between the indigenous peoples and the new U.S. government, white settlers and profiteers blatantly encroached on tribal lands. In 1788, Chief Doublehead's brother, Old Tassel, approached one group of white intruders who had built a small village on Cherokee land. Even though he approached the settlers under a flag of truce, he was murdered by the intruders. The United States admitted, with embarrassment, its failure to protect the Cherokee people according to the dictates of the Treaty of Hopewell, signed at Hopewell, Georgia (1785). Secretary of War Henry Knox wrote to George Washington, following the latter's inauguration as the first president of the newly constituted United States: "The disgraceful violation of the Treaty of Hopewell with the Cherokees requires the serious consideration of Congress. If so direct and manifest contempt of the authority of the United States be suffered with impunity, it will be vain to attempt to extend the arm of government to the frontiers."[4] The letter helped induce the president to invite the Cherokees to reenter negotiations for a new treaty with the now more powerful federal government under the Constitution. In the new treaty, signed at Holston, Tennessee, on July 2, 1791, the United States formally declared its sovereignty over the states in matters of Indian policy by amending the protection clause of the Hopewell treaty. In Article Two of the Holston treaty, the Cherokees again acknowledged that they were under the protection of the United States alone. However, the article concluded with the new amendment that states "that the said Cherokee nation will not hold any treaty with any foreign power, individual state, or with individuals of any state."[5]

The declaration of sovereignty contained within the Treaty of Holston was as much a message to the states as it was to Native tribes. No longer would the United States sit by idly and watch individual states abrogate federally negotiated treaties with impunity. Article Eight made this quite clear. "If any citizen of the United States shall settle on any of the Cherokees' lands, such person shall forfeit the protection of the United States, and the Cherokees may punish him or not, as they please."[6] If the states would not recognize the sovereignty of the federal government when it came to Indian matters, then the federal government would ask the Indians to do it for them. This new restriction on white behavior was not included in the Hopewell treaty, and its inclusion here implies a significant shift in U.S.-Indian relations. The federal government had declared its sovereignty over the nation's Indian affairs, and it had persuaded, if not bribed, the Cherokees to formally recognize it.

The Treaty of Holston ceded something to the Cherokees that they had not previously had: a guarantee from the United States of perpetual land ownership. Article Seven stated, "The United States solemnly guarantee to the Cherokee Nation, all their lands not hereby ceded."[7] The Creeks, who lived primarily south of the Cherokees, had received a similar guarantee in their new treaty with the U.S. government as well, negotiated in New York (then the U.S. capital) in 1790.[8] Because of the Creeks' proximity to Spanish-owned Florida, however, they did not surrender their right to treat with foreign nations.[9] The new treaties with the Creeks and Cherokees became necessary because of the encroachments made on their lands by white southerners. While the new constitutional government was extending its own sovereignty over the nation's Indian affairs through these new treaties, the tribes were being granted something they held to be of equal value. The new treaties provided the Indians with what Francis Paul Prucha calls a "protected existence." In short, the Native nations had been formally granted control over their own borders to go along with the political autonomy they held within them. "This recognition of independence," Prucha asserts, "meant more to Indian groups than did their lands, and tribes eagerly sought treaties in order to gain political recognition."[10] With the Treaty of Holston, the Cherokees secured this recognition in exchange for an acknowledgment of federal sovereignty over Indian matters. Now, all the Cherokees needed to do to enjoy the benefits and privileges of this newfound independence was to trust the U.S. government to protect them from the numerous state governments staring greedily at tribal lands.

It took hardly more than a decade for the United States to begin to show signs of wavering in its commitment to the Cherokee people, forcing the tribe to reevaluate how it interacted with the federal government. In 1802, the state of Georgia formally asked the U.S. government to extinguish the title to tribal lands within the state's borders, hoping to satisfy the land needs of a growing population. Georgia agreed to cede its claim to its western lands—soon to become Mississippi Territory—to the United States in return for a promise to remove the Indians from Georgia lands as soon as it could be peacefully and practicably arranged.[11] The Georgia Compact of 1802, as it has come to be known, was never a legally binding document, yet it frequently drove state and sometimes federal policy over the following three decades. Georgia and the United States agreed to grant each other title to lands that neither of them had the moral or legal right to grant. Carl J. Vipperman argued that "neither party owned clear title to the princely domains they bargained away, for all of it was still in Indian possession."[12]

In the early nineteenth century, the United States asserted itself as the self-proclaimed broker of indigenous homelands by using Senate-ratified treaties to entice tribes to "cede" lands to the federal government in exchange for political recognition and protection. This process often achieved the government's early objectives but stymied future plans by blocking federal access to tribal lands now secured by federal treaties. If the government was to accomplish its later objectives, it would need to persuade the tribes to sign a new treaty or devise a way to sidestep an existing one.

This chapter discusses how the U.S. government, under the leadership of Andrew Jackson in the 1820s and 1830s, laid the foundation for manipulating the

American legal system in order to sidestep existing treaties with the Cherokee Nation, negotiate a new treaty with only a few Cherokees, and compel the entire tribe to comply with its requirement to migrate west of the Mississippi River along the "Trail of Tears." As Cherokee principal chief John Ross navigated the tribe through this gauntlet of duplicitous attacks on tribal sovereignty, he developed an understanding of nineteenth-century white American politics and racism, quickly learning that the promise of the former was often undone by the premise of the latter. Moreover, Ross's approach to the Confederate and Union governments during the American Civil War has its roots in the harsh lessons of the Removal Era. What he learned about traditional Cherokee law and U.S. constitutional law during his negotiations with federal and state governments helped shape his political views and prepared him to lead the Cherokee Nation into the maelstrom of the 1860s. Ross attempted to keep the tribe united at a time when Cherokee political thought was evolving away from the traditional tribal custom of consensus. Unfortunately, that unity would not be realized in either the Removal Era or the Civil War Era. Doublehead would not be the last to be held accountable to the law of blood revenge.

Increased pressure from white settlers caused the Cherokees to reconsider their political organization. Chiefs from towns across the Cherokee Nation who had previously handled local issues and crises with autonomy now gathered collectively in council to discuss the growing concern.[13] Acting in this manner, the Cherokees ceded small tracts of land over the next few years, hoping to satisfy the white man. However, in 1817, acting secretary of war George Graham commissioned Tennessee governor Joseph McMinn, General David Meriwether, and Andrew Jackson, then commander of the Tennessee militia, to negotiate a large-scale land exchange with the Cherokee people.[14] A small group of Cherokee headmen agreed to trade tribal lands in Tennessee, Alabama, and Georgia for lands along the Arkansas and White rivers in Arkansas Territory, west of the Mississippi River. Perhaps as many as three thousand out of the twenty thousand or so Cherokees emigrated to Arkansas and established themselves in the West, looking to escape the constant threat of intrusion by and interaction with white society.

Within months, those Cherokees who remained in the eastern United States—slaveholders and nonslaveholders alike—had announced a "fixed and unalterable determination . . . never again to cede one foot more of land."[15] The significant cession alerted the Cherokee people to the need to become a more centrally organized body, unified enough to fend off future attempts to acquire tribal land.[16]

That same year, 1817, the tribe organized its first standing committee, designed to "manage the affairs of the nation." By 1820, the Cherokee Nation had been divided into districts from which elected officials would serve on a national council, and in 1822, the Cherokee Supreme Court was established.[17] The increasing threat to Cherokee landholdings prompted the Cherokees to formally adopt a constitution in 1827. Undoubtedly, the Cherokee people acknowledged the need to remain united in defense of their homeland, and the vehicle of unity they chose was a republican-style government. The United States had guaranteed the tribe ownership of their land in the Holston treaty and had promised to protect their right to enjoy it. The Cherokees were more prepared than ever to hold them to it.

The new Cherokee governmental model, as laid out in the new constitution, blended a federal-style republican form of government, modeled after that of the United States, and a deeply traditional model based on consensus. The constitution divided the Cherokee Nation into eight districts and called for elections to be held in each. Two delegates from each district were to be elected to serve on the Committee, under the leadership of a president pro tem. All appropriations were to begin in the Committee. In addition, each district was to elect an additional three delegates to serve on the Council, under the leadership of the Speaker. The two houses, the Committee and the Council, were together to be called the General Council; however, the Cherokees soon began referring to the General Council as the National Council.[18]

The Cherokee constitution also called for the National Council to select five of its members to serve alongside the principal chief and the assistant chief as part of an executive council. The executive council was to convene under the direction and discretion of the principal chief and was authorized to conduct tribal business when time constraints precluded the assembly of the entire National Council.[19] In constructing the constitution, the Cherokee people retained aspects of their traditional law of consensus. While the U.S. Constitution vested its treaty-making power in one person (the president), the Cherokee constitution required all treaties to be negotiated and approved by the National Council alone. The National Council could authorize a delegation to conduct the actual negotiations, but any treaty had to be returned to the council for final approval. The Cherokee constitution outlined a highly organized governmental model based on that of the United States but still tied to traditional Cherokee law.[20]

Under the new constitution, the tribe elected thirty-eight-year-old John Ross as principal chief in the first national election held in 1828. Ross was a mixed-blood Cherokee of Scottish descent who had found favor with both full-blood and mixed-blood segments of the tribe. Ross frequently relied on the wisdom and leadership of the executive council during his long tenure as chief. Moreover, he often took things a step further in his quest for consensus by calling a general assembly of the Cherokee people in order to lay an issue before them, explain his stance, and encourage tribal unity. These assemblies had no political authority, yet Ross relied on their feedback because he believed unity was essential to defending the Cherokee homeland.

In response to the increasingly organized Cherokee Nation, many Georgia citizens became uneasy with the idea of such an "organized Indian republic" existing within the borders of their own state. Cries increased for the United States to fulfill the Georgia Compact.[21] A group of Cherokee leaders from Turkey Town, a Cherokee village located in northeastern Alabama, argued that the tribe had abandoned the hunt and the "pursuit of vagrant habits" at the encouragement of President Washington, and had adopted a better life as "cultivators of the soil." They went on to claim that "we are now assaulted with menaces of expulsion because we have unexpectedly become civilized and because we have formed and organized a constitutional government."[22] Many Cherokees came to realize that their politics had no bearing on whether or not they were welcome in white society. By the early nineteenth century, the racial and ethnic biases of many white Americans had openly expressed their disdain for the very presence of Native Americans.

By the mid-1820s, the topic of Indian removal hit the floor of the U.S. House of Representatives when that body instructed its Committee on Indian Affairs "to inquire into the expediency of organizing all the Territories of the United States, lying west of the State of Missouri and Territories of Arkansas and Michigan, into a separate Territory to be occupied exclusively by the Indians; and of authorizing the President of the United States to adopt such measures as he may think best, to colonize all the Indians of the present States and Territories permanently within the same."[23] The next January, President James Monroe told the House that the object of his Indian policy was the removal of all tribes to the new territory west of the Mississippi River, under terms that "would be satisfactory to themselves and honorable to the United States."[24]

In the face of increased efforts to force the Cherokees to cede the remainder of their lands, Ross exhibited three fundamental political beliefs that became the foundation for his response to the arrival of the Civil War in Indian Territory in the 1860s. These three principles coincided with three significant events that took place in 1828, prior to removal.

First, the discovery of gold on Cherokee land in July 1828 brought a flood of white treasure seekers into the territory, causing Ross to call on the federal government to honor its promise to protect the tribe from just such an intrusion.[25] The gold was discovered on Cherokee lands lying within the borders of the state of Georgia. Title to the land had been granted to the Cherokee Nation via Senate-ratified treaties; therefore, the Cherokee Nation believed the gold belonged solely to them. Ross quickly called on Washington to provide the protection promised in the tribe's treaties with the United States and remove the intruders from the nation.[26] In compliance with treaty obligations, the War Department dispatched troops to the area to drive out the prospectors. Georgia's governor, George R. Gilmer, protested the intrusion of federal troops on state soil. President Andrew Jackson responded quickly, removing the troops and promising Gilmer he would not interfere with state law.[27] Georgia had waited—impatiently at best—for the United States to fulfill its obligation under the Compact of 1802. The discovery of gold in the Cherokee Nation escalated the tensions between the Cherokees and Georgia and intensified the state's desire to drive the Cherokees out. It also amplified Ross's cries for the federal government to uphold its treaty obligations and protect the tribe from intrusion.[28] Ross's insistence that the government provide the promised protection, the first of his fundamental beliefs, became a recurring theme in Cherokee-U.S. relations during the nineteenth century. While the need for protection would change from one decade to the next, Ross's demand that the federal government provide it never wavered.

With Jackson's promise of nonintervention in hand, Gilmer had carte blanche to deal with the Cherokees as he wished. He admitted to Senator J. M. Berrian that "the state considers itself entitled to all the valuable minerals within the soil of the Cherokee Territory," regardless of who held the title to the land.[29] "It may become necessary," he claimed, "for the State to protect its property by taking possession of the gold country."

The second event, which occurred on December 20, 1828, involved Georgia's legislature passing a series of laws extending its jurisdiction over Cherokee lands. In response, Ross called on the nation to remain united in defense. This need for unity became the second of Ross's fundamental political beliefs. Set to take effect on June 1, 1830, the extension initiated an all-out attack on Cherokee sovereignty.[30] Gilmer planned to prevent everyone, not just the Cherokees, from plundering Georgia's gold.[31] No longer would Georgia sit back and wait on the federal government to uphold the Compact of 1802. As Robert W. McCluggage asserts, it became "clear that the interest of the Indians was being subordinated to the politics of expediency."[32] The extension of Georgia law into parts of the Cherokee Nation prohibited Cherokees from mining gold, speaking against removal, or even conducting the business of tribal government.[33] Gilmer especially warned the Cherokees to "cease operating the mines."[34] The longer the state of Georgia delayed, the more gold would be taken from them.[35] The Georgia law also declared that all Cherokee laws would become null and void on June 1, 1830. The following December, the Georgia legislature authorized the organization of a mounted guard unit consisting of sixty men to enforce state laws, and, more important, protect the state's claim to the Cherokee gold mines.[36] The Georgia Guard immediately began driving Cherokees from their own mines.[37]

In his annual message in 1829, Ross warned his people of the need for unity. "A crisis seems to be fast approaching," he told them, "much, therefore, depends on our unity of sentiment and firmness of action."[38] Despite the rising pressure on the Cherokees to emigrate west, tribal leaders remained united in their defense of tribal land and sovereignty. Even the Ridge, who was now known as Major Ridge following a stint under Andrew Jackson in the Tennessee militia, supported Ross in his stand against removal. Ridge and his son John, who later seemed to turn their backs on Ross and the National Council, traveled throughout the Cherokee Nation encouraging citizens to support the chief and to cling to their homelands.[39] Following the arrest of eleven missionaries by Georgia authorities for living and working among the Cherokees without a state license, Ross and the Cherokees appealed to the U.S. Supreme Court for relief. While the Court listened to arguments as to whether Georgia law should supersede Cherokee law within state boundaries, John Ridge and his articulate cousin Elias Boudinot traveled through the northern states, drumming up moral and financial support for the Cherokee plight. On January 12, 1832, John Ridge wrote an angry letter to Ross from Philadelphia: "General Jackson is bad and the people are willing to maintain him, not for the love of him, but the love of their party."[40] Neither Ridge nor Ross trusted Jackson. As long as the president refused to comply with the treaty obligations to protect the Cherokees from intrusion, the Cherokees faced constant pressure from the state of Georgia to cede their lands and emigrate west. Ridge did share encouraging news, however. "It affords me pleasure to state," he wrote, "that the prospects of a great and vigorous expression of indignation from this city [Philadelphia] against the cruelties of Georgia and the policy of the U.S. is now flattering." He also told Ross of having met with Matthew Cary, a prominent lawyer and publisher, and proclaimed him "as strong a friend as we have."[41] The need for unity became a fundamental belief for Ross as he led the

Cherokee Nation through the crises with the Georgia and U.S. governments. During the Civil War era, Ross's cries for unity would resonate throughout Indian Territory and, ironically, would help usher in the dismantling of Cherokee sovereignty in the postwar years.

The third event in 1828 that helped develop Ross's political beliefs was the election of Andrew Jackson to the presidency in November, bringing to the White House Jackson's disdain for tribal ownership of state land. It is here that Ross exhibited perhaps his strongest fundamental political belief: an undying faith in the process of constitutional law. In a letter to the Cherokee agent, Ross referred to the tribe's treaties with the United States as proof of Cherokee land ownership.[42] He knew that the Constitution referred to a Senate-ratified treaty as "the supreme law of the land." When Jackson, who resented having to deal with what he called "half-breeds and renegade white men" in negotiating with Indians, recalled the federal troops from the Georgia mines, thus denying the tribe the protection promised in the treaties, Ross pointed back to the treaties as evidence of Cherokee sovereignty over its land.[43] Jackson refused to listen and continued to buoy the Georgia claims. Ross then turned his energy to Congress.[44] The basis for Ross's faith in the legal process was founded in the tribe's first treaty with the fledgling United States government in 1785. Article Twelve of the Treaty of Hopewell states, "That the Indians may have full confidence in the justice of the U. States, respecting their interests, they shall have the right to send a deputy of their choice, whenever they think fit, to Congress."[45] Ross's strongest fundamental political belief was in the right to share his grievances directly with Washington. Whenever he felt that Cherokee rights were under attack, he asked the Cherokee National Council to invoke Article Twelve and authorize a delegation—usually led by himself—to travel to Washington and seek redress. While some might question Ross's absence from the Cherokee Nation during its most trying times, he was actually interceding for his people in accordance with the tribe's treaties and with the backing and support of the Cherokee people.

In slightly more than a year following the adoption of their constitution, the political climate had grown cold and ominous for the Cherokees. Long described by historians as a politically fractured tribe, torn between traditionalists and assimilationists, proremoval and antitreaty factions, the Cherokees actually presented a united front. Principal Chief John Ross stood at the head of a unified nation, supported by his future enemies Major Ridge; Ridge's son, John; and his nephews, Elias Boudinot and Stand Watie. The division within the tribe that would come to dominate the narratives of the Cherokee Nation during the Civil War years would not appear for another two years and, even then, would not be nearly as significant as historians have believed.

The case of the missionaries imprisoned under Georgia law in October 1831 made its way to the U.S. Supreme Court. The ruling in *Worcester v. Georgia* came down in March 1832 in favor of Cherokee sovereignty. The Court declared that the extension of Georgia law into the sovereign Cherokee Nation was unconstitutional and demanded the missionaries be released. Ross declared a celebration throughout the nation. To him the victory came not in the rebuke of the Georgia intrusion but in the proclamation of Cherokee sovereignty.[46] Boudinot called it "glorious news," while John Ridge claimed the decision "acknowledged every right for which we have contended."[47]

While on tour through the northern states, John Ridge stopped in Washington to discuss the Court's decision with the president. Jackson told him that he had no intention of interfering with Georgia law despite the Court's ruling.[48] Ridge later expressed his disgust with Jackson, whom he called a "chicken snake."[49] At this point, Ridge joined Ross in his strong belief in the process of constitutional law, though he realized that Jackson would most likely try to sabotage the Court's ruling. Ridge asked Ross to remain vigilant, "to keep up the hearts of our people."[50] While he believed that the Supreme Court's decision would motivate the Senate to honor the nation's treaties with the Cherokees, Ridge had also been told by the secretary of war that the government planned to negotiate a treaty with any group of Cherokees calling themselves a majority.[51] However, both Ross and Ridge independently expressed the belief that the Senate would never ratify such a treaty if it was not duly authorized by the proper Cherokee authorities.[52] In response to Jackson's noninterference confession, John Ridge called on Ross to encourage the Cherokee people to remain united. At the time of the Supreme Court's ruling in *Worcester*, Ridge appeared to be one of Ross's staunchest supporters, and Ross continued to rely on him as a voice for the National Council. Whatever caused the split between the two leaders had not yet occurred.

Sometime after visiting with Jackson, Ridge began entertaining the possibility that the Cherokees might be forced to emigrate, and that the tribe should be prepared to do so. In a letter dated April 6, 1832, less than one month after the Court's ruling, John Ridge confessed to his cousin Stand Watie that he believed the only way for the Supreme Court's decision to be upheld was to cut off the "snake's" (Jackson's) head and "throw it down in the dust."[53] Filled with anger, he wrote, "I feel disgusted at an administration who have trampled our rights under foot to offer new pledges from their rotten hearts."⁵⁴ When discussing the secretary of war's suggestion that the government would sign a treaty with any "faction or fraction of our nation," Ridge wrote, "We shall live to tread on the necks of traitors."⁵⁵ John Ridge was so adamant about honoring the tribe's constitutional authority that three years earlier, as clerk of the National Council, he had helped pass his father's new law based on the traditional law of blood revenge. The new law, designed to merge traditional tribal law with the modern constitution, was passed by the National Council in October 1829.⁵⁶ The Ridges made it clear that anyone who signed a treaty ceding away tribal lands without the council's authorization was guilty of treason and should be punished by execution.⁵⁷

On April 3, 1832, John Ridge bemoaned to Ross the possibilities of Jackson's success in the November election, claiming that if Congress did not get involved and coerce him into upholding the Court's decision, reelection was almost assured; and if reelected, "then he will be above control."⁵⁸ Historian Grant Foreman argued that, prior to the 1832 election, both Ross and Ridge exerted such a strong influence against removal that it was "too powerful to overcome."⁵⁹ If John Ridge was so vehemently opposed to a removal treaty with the United States during the spring of 1832, what could have persuaded him to change his discourse only a few weeks later? During Ridge's visit in the days after the Supreme Court's historic ruling, Jackson claimed to have noticed a wavering in his once committed foe.⁶⁰ The president's perception must have been accurate, for Ridge immediately sought the advice of U.S. Supreme Court associate justice John McLean, who doubted that the president would support any plan short of removal. McLean offered the Cherokees two suggestions. First, he advised the Cherokees either to apply for statehood and avoid such conflicts in the future, or to simply agree to a removal treaty.⁶¹ Rumors floated around Washington that John Ridge had begun capitulating and was on the brink of agreeing to removal. Word got back to Ross, who flew into a rage. Of course, Ridge denied the accusations on the ground of his years of loyal service to the Cherokee National Council and people.⁶² However, John Ridge's cousin Elias Boudinot came to believe that removal was the only thing standing between the Cherokee Nation and collapse. As editor of the *Cherokee Phoenix*, the tribe's newspaper, Boudinot offered both opinions in the pages of the paper to allow the widely literate Cherokee population to choose for themselves which side of the issue to take. For Ross, this prevented consensus and was therefore inappropriate. Boudinot, who had expressed his divergent opinion, resigned his position.⁶³

Following Jackson's reelection in November, John Ridge seemed to have succumbed to the inevitable. He saw no other recourse for the Cherokee Nation. On February 2, 1833, while Ross and an authorized delegation were in Washington invoking Article Twelve of the Treaty of Hopewell, John Ridge wrote Ross invoking the traditional Cherokee right to question the council's direction. "I have the right," he began, "to address you as the chief of the whole Cherokee Nation." He asked Ross to consider the possibility that removal might be inevitable. Upon the realization "that we cant [sic] be a Nation here," he continued, "I hope we shall attempt to establish it somewhere else!"[64] While Ross adhered to his unwavering faith in the honor of the U.S. government, Ridge adopted a more practical approach to the problem. Ross dug in his heels, believing that Cherokee sovereignty was directly tied to tribal land ownership and that the two were inseparable: to give up the land would be akin to surrendering tribal autonomy.[65] Ridge, on the other hand, believed that the two could exist independently. He argued that protecting tribal sovereignty was the highest priority and that the nation could exist as an autonomous body west of the Mississippi River.[66] For Ross, giving in to the demands of the federal government now would set a precedent of capitulation that could never be redressed. If the United States was allowed to force its will on the Cherokee Nation, the Cherokee Nation could no longer claim to be sovereign.

These antonymic viewpoints brought both men to Washington in February 1835: John Ridge to investigate the possibilities of securing a favorable treaty on behalf of the Cherokee people, and Ross to formally remind the government that the Cherokee National Council had not authorized Ridge to negotiate such a treaty. While there, Ross responded to Jackson's offer of $5 million for Cherokee lands in the east with his own counteroffer of $20 million.[67] Moreover, he proposed ceding tribal lands only if he could obtain permission from Mexico to relocate the tribe outside the United States, perhaps in Texas.[68] Ridge believed that Ross was merely delaying constructive negotiations until after the election of 1836, when Jackson might be replaced with a more Indian-friendly president.[69] In late February, Jackson and Ridge held a private meeting at the White House. Included were the Reverend John F. Schermerhorn, whom Jackson had commissioned to secure a treaty from the Cherokees, and Benjamin F. Currey, who was commissioned to enroll Cherokees for voluntary emigration west. During the meeting, Jackson attacked Ross and his motivations, declaring that he no longer had any intention of communicating with the chief.[70] In response, Ross submitted his proposal of $20 million directly to the Senate. The offer came one day after the chair of the Senate Committee on Indian Affairs, Hugh Lawson White of Tennessee, had recommended that the Senate do whatever necessary to secure a treaty with the Cherokees. Ross's offer was deemed so outrageous, however, that the Senate amended White's proposal and set a limit of $5 million.[71] Schermerhorn set out to convince the Ridge delegation to accept the offer.

On March 7, Secretary of War Lewis Cass wrote to Ross informing him he would no longer engage in written discourse with the chief.[72] Jackson had long believed that John Ridge was more willing to negotiate about Cherokee lands than Ross would ever be, and now that Ridge had proven him correct, he refused to recognize Ross as an official diplomat from the Cherokee Nation. Jackson had sensed a wavering in Ridge's resolve and quickly pounced, believing Ridge to be the one "most likely to negotiate a removal treaty."[73] The president ignored Ross's imploring. He had already ignored the Supreme Court's ruling in *Worcester*, so his refusal to honor the dictates of the Cherokee constitution was not surprising. Besides, he believed he had enough support in the Senate to ratify even a treaty with a minority faction.[74] The president had been battling Cherokee unity since taking office, and now he had the opportunity to defeat it by isolating Ridge and using him to obtain the coveted removal treaty.[75] Ridge hoped to secure the treaty for the protection of Cherokee sovereignty, even if it meant ceding tribal lands in the eastern United States. He planned to present it to the National Council for official approval once secured. Jackson did not care who approved it so long as he obtained a signed treaty; now that he had Ridge in one pocket and potential ratification in the other, he knew that a treaty of removal would soon cross his desk.

On March 14, John Ridge and his delegation agreed to take a preliminary treaty back to the Cherokee Nation in hopes of getting it ratified by the National Council.[76] Jackson, having grown weary of dealing with Ross, sent the treaty with Ridge as a final ultimatum for the Cherokee Nation. He informed the tribe through Ridge that there would be no other treaty offered than the one now presented.[77] Ridge called a meeting at his home in April to discuss the terms. However, no more than a hundred Cherokees attended, far too few to take any formal action. Ridge, who had expected more than a thousand, was no doubt disappointed.[78]

At this point, another opportunity arose. Hoping to attract a larger crowd, Schermerhorn announced plans to discuss distribution of the annual annuity payments given to the tribe as partial restitution for the lands ceded to the United States in 1817, at a special meeting three months later. He suggested dividing the funds equally among the citizens as opposed to delivering the entirety of the payment to Ross for depositing in the national treasury. Ross promised a large attendance if he could obtain a promise that the issue would be placed before the people for a vote.[79] Schermerhorn agreed. The Cherokees turned out en masse and voted overwhelmingly to allow Ross and the National Council to distribute the funds as they saw fit through the tribal treasury.[80] The people had elected Ross to be their principal chief, and this latest vote of confidence simply affirmed their trust in his leadership.[81]

Seizing the opportunity to broach the subject of removal before a larger crowd, Ridge presented the treaty to those gathered for the annuity vote. However, there was little, if any, willingness among those gathered to accept its provisions. Moreover, when he later presented it at the national assembly in October, the Cherokees once again rejected it. When Schermerhorn announced the date for the official treaty council to convene at New Echota, Georgia, in December, he did so with the realization that he had not added a single Cherokee to the ranks of the treaty party.[82] Most Cherokees continued to follow Ross's leadership and resisted removal entirely.

Although historians assign a certain political influence to John Ridge and his protreaty faction, in reality, he was politically impotent without the support of white governments in Georgia and the United States. Even with the backing of the United States, only about three hundred people, hardly 2 percent of the Cherokee population, attended the council at New Echota in December 1835, and less than half of 1 percent of the population, a total of seventy-nine people, voted in favor of the treaty.[83] The Cherokee people were against the Treaty of New Echota, and John Ridge did not possess the political clout to change their minds. The fateful treaty, signed on December 29, 1835, has been heralded by historians as the wedge that divided the Cherokee Nation into two rival political factions. Use of the word "faction"—which connotes a small group—in reference to Ross and his supporters delegitimizes the political acumen of the Cherokee Nation and assigns a more significant political prominence to a miniscule group of rivals than actually existed.

Historians propel John Ridge to a position of influence equal to that of John Ross while ignoring the political authority of the voting Cherokee public.[84] The truth is, the United States used John Ridge and a handful of other Cherokee people to accomplish what Andrew Jackson and many white officials wanted. By assigning labels to the two groups of Cherokees and claiming an equal distribution of power, influence, and authority between them, historians have produced a much tidier narrative than the historical record supports. The two groups have been granted a level of equality that never existed, and the influence assigned to Ridge and his tiny band of supporters has been imagined. In reality, John Ridge's significance rests solely in Andrew Jackson's manipulation of the so-called Treaty Party. Ridge was simply a puppet of the white government.

The Cherokee people, in compliance with their own constitution, had elected Ross principal chief. Moreover, the Cherokee National Council, duly elected in accordance with the same constitution, authorized Ross to act as the nation's representative in negotiations with the government in Washington. Clearly, Ross possessed influence and authority that Ridge did not. While historians recognize the Treaty of New Echota as a fraudulent document and acknowledge the small size of the Ridge-led faction that signed it, they delegitimize the Cherokee people by elevating Ridge and his followers to a position of political influence they did not possess. This delegitimization plays out again in narratives of the Cherokee Nation during the 1860s. Stand Watie has received much the same historical treatment for his actions during the Civil War and, just as with the Ridge family in the 1830s, has been granted a political influence that he did not possess. The Confederate government's backing provided Watie with the only real influence he had.

The governments of Georgia and the United States ignored Cherokee sovereignty as they exerted pressure on the Indians to relinquish their homelands. In doing so, they also rejected the Cherokee Nation as an autonomous political body. Major William M. Davis, an enrolling officer assigned to encourage individual Indians to agree to emigrate, accused Schermerhorn of purposely trying to divide the Cherokees so he could more easily obtain a removal treaty.[85] Georgia governor Wilson Lumpkin had promised Ridge, Boudinot, and "their friends" state protection "under any circumstance" while they sought to secure a removal treaty.[86] Three months prior to the signing of the treaty at New Echota, Ridge thanked Lumpkin for this protection under the Georgia Guard. "I do sincerely believe," he wrote, "that this Guard is necessary to be continued in this country until the treaty is consummated."[87] Elias Boudinot, writing to his brother Stand Watie, confessed that the federal government had promised to protect their rights as long as they agreed to a treaty. Jackson's decision to limit his diplomatic interaction to Ridge and his followers reveals how far the administration would go to obtain a signed treaty of removal from the Cherokee Nation. Ridge cheerfully wrote to his father that "the United States will never have anything more to do with John Ross."[88] Though overstated, John Ridge became the only remaining point of contact between Andrew Jackson and the Cherokees east of the Mississippi River.

Jackson's disregard for the Cherokee Nation manifested itself in his attack on tribal sovereignty. The treaties between the Cherokee Nation and the United States provided specific safeguards for that sovereignty, and even though the Supreme Court upheld the authority of those treaties, Jackson chose to ignore the constitutional mandate to honor the federal government's responsibility toward the Cherokee Nation. Jackson also succeeded in manipulating constitutional law by calling on supporters in the Senate to ratify the fraudulent treaty of New Echota in the face of growing public opposition within the United States. Historians trumpet the narrowness with which the treaty passed the Senate's scrutiny by emphasizing the one-vote margin achieved for ratification.[89] However, the fact that ratification requires a two-thirds majority of those Senators voting exposes the widespread treachery in the upper house. The Senate, therefore, shares the responsibility for the "Trail of Tears" that history has bestowed on Jackson alone.

If a Senate-ratified treaty becomes the "supreme law of the land," according to the U.S. Constitution, did the ratification of the fraudulent treaty of New Echota remove the fraudulence?[90] Jackson, who had a reputation for ignoring the legality of Senate-ratified Indian treaties, did not care. He believed that once the new treaty was ratified, the people of the United States would accept it, regardless of who in the Cherokee Nation had signed it. Ross argued vehemently against it, though he feared that the government would enforce it. He contended that the treaty was unauthorized and, therefore, should not be ratified.[91] But to the federal government, there was no question of its authenticity, and once it was ratified, the United States enforced it.[92] In 1838, President Martin Van Buren, Jackson's successor, dispatched General Winfield Scott to oversee the forced removal of the Cherokee people. Ross's argument that the treaty was worthless became moot when the army arrived to compel compliance.

In a scathing letter to the secretary of war, Major Davis assigned to Schermerhorn full responsibility for the treaty's fraudulence. He accused the commissioner of attempting to mislead the president by presenting the treaty as having been "made with the *whole Cherokee nation*" (italics original). Davis believed that if the Senate ratified the treaty, it would become law. He attempted to warn Cass, who had already ceased communication with Ross, that the only way the federal government could enforce such a treaty would be by "the strong arm of force."[93] Davis deplored the fact that there were fewer than one hundred voters representing nearly seventeen thousand Cherokee citizens, and that none of those voting on Schermerhorn's treaty had been authorized to do so by the National Council.[94] He also accused Schermerhorn of trying to conceal the fraudulence by taking the treaty to other towns to gather additional signatures. Schermerhorn announced a meeting in the mountains of western North Carolina and prepared a feast for the more than five thousand Cherokees who lived in the vicinity. No one came.[95]

Davis was not present at the signing of the Treaty of New Echota, but he had inferior-grade officers who were. They quickly reported the irregularities to Davis. Lieutenant M. W. Bateman of the 6th U.S. Infantry reported firsthand that only seventy to eighty Cherokees voted. He claimed to have counted only 203 people present during the final session, including women and children. Lieutenant Jonathan L. Hooper of the 4th U.S. Infantry, commandant of federal troops in the Cherokee Nation, agreed with Bateman as to the crowd's size. He claimed that there were never more than three hundred Cherokees present at any one time during the week. Dr. C. M. Hitchcock and James C. Price concurred.[96] James J. Trott, an observer of the events at New Echota, later told Ross that there were only about one hundred Cherokee men present who favored the treaty.[97] Unbeknownst to Davis, the Jackson administration had authorized the acquisition of the fraudulent treaty; therefore, his charges fell on deaf ears in Washington. The duplicitous Jackson presented the treaty to the Senate on March 5, the day Davis penned his missive to Secretary of War Lewis Cass. Breaking with tradition, Jackson did not send a copy to the House of Representatives. This gesture was usually a way of informing the House that certain appropriations might be needed to carry out the stipulations should ratification occur. In this case, Jackson opted to limit the treaty's visibility, at least until he could get it through the Senate.[98] He needed to disguise the fraudulence long enough to get the treaty ratified.

Instead of surrendering to Jackson's Indian policy and removing quietly westward, Ross stepped up his appeals to Washington for redress. In the months following the treaty, he collected 15,665 signatures on a petition presented to the Senate.[99] Despite his efforts, the Senate ratified the treaty on March 18, 1836. Jackson signed it into law on March 23.[100] The Treaty of New Echota allowed the Cherokees two years to prepare to emigrate. The Ridge family did not wait that long, avoiding the tragedy of the "Trail of Tears" by emigrating early.[101] Because of their utility in securing the treaty, they were allowed more "leisure and facilities" in gathering their belongings, were protected along the route, and arrived in Indian Territory with considerable wealth.[102] Moreover, the members of the Ridge faction were reimbursed for their expenses in negotiating the treaty, while Ross and the authorized delegation, who traveled to Washington on multiple occasions, were denied the same courtesy.[103] Vipperman asserts that the Cherokees' failure to meet the removal deadline is what led to the tragedy of the forced march to Indian Territory.[104] Ross and the Cherokees would, no doubt, disagree.[105] Had the authorized delegation negotiated the treaty, the bulk of the tribe would not have resisted emigration as it did. Of the twelve thousand Cherokees who were forced along the "Trail of Tears" in the winter of 1838–39, as many as four thousand died, including Ross's wife, who was buried one morning in a shallow grave in central Arkansas.[106]

The transition of the Cherokee government to Indian Territory was slowed by the reluctance of the "Old Settlers," those Cherokees who had voluntarily emigrated prior to the Treaty of New Echota, to acknowledge the new tribal authority above their own established leadership. Many of the recent emigrants blamed the Ridges and their followers for not only working against Ross and preventing the tribe from achieving consensus, but for negotiating and signing the unauthorized Treaty of New Echota. For about three hundred newly arrived Cherokee emigrants, the Ridges had gone too far. Prior to emigration, Ross had blocked a plan to execute John Ridge, Major Ridge, and Elias Boudinot for their crime under the blood revenge law Major Ridge himself had helped revive.[107] However, following the "Trail of Tears," Ross was not able to stop it. The three were executed on the morning of June 22, 1839, for their efforts to circumvent the Cherokee National Council by negotiating and signing the treaty of New Echota. Ironically, the leaders of the Ridge family had been executed under the terms of the very law Major Ridge had helped revitalize. Ross's son, Allen, stayed with the chief to prevent him from discovering the plot.[108]

The three hundred plotters passed sentence on only three men: John Ridge, Major Ridge, and Elias Boudinot.[109] Even though Stand Watie initially feared for his own life, there is no evidence that he was ever one of the intended targets.[110] Watie would seek retribution for the executions of his family members, and between 1839 and 1846 several Cherokees died in an undeclared civil war.[111] Following a fifteen-year interlude, Watie's anger would be rekindled by the start of the Civil War, and the violence he demonstrated toward the Ross-led Cherokee government has been misunderstood. Historians have traced the origin of the Ross-Watie conflict, one that has come to define the mid-nineteenth-century narratives of the Cherokee Nation, to the Treaty of New Echota. In reality, the division between Watie and Ross occurred because of the executions of Watie's family members. Other than the fact that his signature appears on the treaty, there is no evidence Watie participated in the negotiations. As late as November 25, only five weeks before the signing of the Treaty of New Echota, it appears that Ross had never even met Watie. Elias Boudinot wrote to Ross and suggested his younger brother as a potential substitute to accompany the chief to Washington. Boudinot had decided to stay behind and attend Schermerhorn's meeting at New Echota in December. He wrote of Watie, "Though probably not particularly known to you, from his modesty, yet he is a man of sterling sense and integrity, and you will be pleased to find him so."[112] The twenty-eight-year-old Watie accompanied Ross to Washington to petition Congress for redress. Watie's signature was added to the treaty on March 1, 1836, in Washington, but only after the U.S. Senate made a few minor alterations to the original agreement.

The events surrounding the signing of the Treaty of New Echota laid the foundation for historical narratives about the Cherokee Nation during the Civil War era. However, unless we understand how those events helped develop Ross's political motivations, our narratives will be incomplete. In fact, the development of Ross's political beliefs was one of the most significant outcomes for the Cherokee Nation during the 1830s. His vociferous demands that the federal government provide the protection promised to the tribe would change little over time and would drive Cherokee-white relations on numerous occasions throughout the nineteenth century. Initially, the intrusion of white settlers and profiteers on Cherokee land in Georgia brought Ross to Washington to demand the protection promised in the tribe's treaties. Upon the Cherokees' arrival in Indian Territory, the proximity to nomadic raiders of the plains created a new concern for the tribe.[113] Finally, with the start of the Civil War in 1861, the need for protection would force Ross to make a difficult decision as the invading Confederate Army became, perhaps, the Cherokees' most dangerous enemy to date.

Ross's belief in the need for tribal unity would also be a major theme of Cherokee policy during the Civil War. As external forces threatened tribal sovereignty, Ross encouraged his people to remain united in defense of their way of life. The need for unity would become paramount as the Civil War arrived in Indian Territory, leading Ross to extend his appeal to the other tribes in the vicinity. The arrival of the Confederate Army posed a threat to all the tribes, and Ross tried to keep them together. Even after deciding to align with the Confederacy, Ross reached out to his counterparts in other tribes and asked them to consider the same course "that the united Brotherhood of the Indian Nations might be preserved and perpetuated."[114]

The most important of Ross's political beliefs to develop during the removal crisis, however, was his faith in the process of constitutional law. Even though the federal government often refused to extend due process to the Indians, Ross continued to rely on the system. The Supreme Court decision in *Worcester* only strengthened Ross's resolve. In addition, the Treaty of Hopewell guaranteed the Cherokees the right to petition Congress for redress in the event tribal interests were encroached upon, and Ross exercised this option readily. His frequent trips to Washington during the removal crisis reflected his belief that Congress would ultimately do the right thing and uphold the government's responsibilities to the Cherokee people. All he needed to do was remain vigilant on behalf of his people. The onset of the Civil War and the invasion of Indian Territory by the Confederate Army prevented Ross from petitioning Washington for assistance for the first year of the war. However, as soon as he had the opportunity to travel to the White House, he visited President Abraham Lincoln and entreated him for relief. Ross's faith in the process of constitutional law seemed to pay off when Lincoln expressed his interest in honoring the government's treaties with the Cherokee Nation. However, an assassin's bullet in the spring of 1865 did more than just disappoint the Cherokee Nation. It radically altered U.S. Indian policy in the years following the Civil War.

Ross and John Ridge appear to have been on opposite sides of the major issue facing the Cherokee people during the Removal Era of the 1820s and 1830s. The two men came together at the head of the nation as the governments of Georgia and the United States commenced an attack on tribal sovereignty. President Jackson, noticing a weakening in Ridge's resolve, drove a wedge between the two men, isolating Ridge politically from Ross and the remainder of the tribe. Ridge's involvement in the fraudulent Treaty of New Echota cemented his fate; he, his father, and his cousin were executed in 1839 in accordance with Cherokee law. The political division between Stand Watie and John Ross was not so clearly tied to New Echota. Watie had little involvement in the treaty, and his hatred for Ross stemmed more from his belief that the chief was somehow responsible for the execution of his family members. Even though the two men came together in peace in 1846, the relationship remained strained until the start of the Civil War, when it again turned to violence and murder.

Finally, a new analysis of the events surrounding New Echota reveals that John Ridge was politically impotent on his own. As a cog in the wheel of Cherokee government, Ridge contributed to tribal leadership in that he authored laws and helped bring growth and unity to the Cherokee Nation. However, on his own, he proved to be less influential than historians have assumed. Without the backing and support of the two white governments, Ridge would have remained impotent.

He was more a marionette of Jackson's political whims than an influencer of Cherokee history. Stand Watie would find himself in a similar position during the Civil War. Until the Confederate Army arrived and propped him up with a colonel's commission, Watie remained quietly in the background of Cherokee influence. While his followers bemoaned the Cherokee-Confederate alliance as a threat to their new position within the Confederacy, Watie appeared to welcome it, believing that Ross had finally pivoted to his way of thinking.[115] However, when Ross showed signs of wavering in his commitment to the Confederates, Watie began a campaign to punish any and all members of his own tribe for supporting the chief. The influence of the Ridge-Watie faction has been misunderstood. By elevating this minority to a level of unrealistic and illegitimate influence, historians delegitimize the strength and resolve of the Cherokee Nation under the leadership of John Ross. That strength and resolve would be crucial if the Cherokee Nation was to survive the horrors of the Civil War.

CHAPTER 2

SECESSION AND THE PRESERVATION OF A NATION

On August 1, 1838, after the Treaty of New Echota and prior to the forced removal west, the Cherokee National Council drew a line in the Georgia sand, refusing to be held accountable for a treaty it viewed as fraudulent, despite its ratification by the U.S. Senate. The council resolved that the treaty was null and void and reaffirmed the tribe's outright title to the land. The "Resolutions of 1838" also declared the Cherokee Nation to be a "distinct national community" possessing all the "attributes of sovereignty," a political community, moreover, that would exist in perpetuity. In short, the Cherokees wished to remain where they were.[1] However, their claims of unmitigated sovereignty and outright defiance did not reach Washington in time to prevent, or even delay, the arrival of Winfield Scott and the U.S. Army to compel the emigration west along the "Trail of Tears." Even if the resolutions had reached Washington in time, the federal government was in no way prepared to recognize Cherokee sovereignty. In fact, the Supreme Court was still searching for consonance with its own definition of tribal sovereignty. This judicial struggle has left a legacy that helps historians better understand nineteenth-century Indian relations in ways John Ross and his contemporaries never could.

In his 1839 annual report, Thomas Hartley Crawford, who served as commissioner of Indian affairs in the Van Buren, Harrison, and Tyler administrations from 1838 to 1844, acknowledged having received a copy of the resolutions only after the completion of the forced march. Nonetheless, he chose to address the question of tribal sovereignty. "The Government exerts control over all within the territorial limits of the United States," he wrote. "It is an attribute of sovereignty which cannot be controverted and could not be yielded without destroying the vital principal."[2] According to this logic, tribal sovereignty in the United States exists only at the discretion of the federal government. The Constitution serves as the "supreme law of the land," defining relationships and responsibilities within the nation. A treaty, also legally binding on the United States, relinquishes a portion of that sovereignty, granting it to another entity and thus weakening the United States proportionally.[3] In theory, a treaty stipulation requiring the United States to protect the interests of the Cherokee Nation requires government action. The government must act in accordance with the treaty or be guilty of abrogation. However, the sovereignty of the United States is supreme, which means that the nation may change the treaty relationship at its own discretion. When John Ross and the Cherokee Nation repudiated the Treaty of New Echota on the grounds that the Cherokee National Council had not approved it, the United States invoked its sovereignty by ratifying and enforcing the treaty anyway. As part of its sovereign rule, the United States had granted the Cherokees the right to govern themselves under their own constitution; however, that constitution did not obligate the United States to action or inaction. In other words, it did not need the approval of the Cherokee National Council to secure a treaty with a minority faction. The United States claimed the power to do so based on its supreme sovereignty.

From Commissioner Crawford's perspective, sovereign power belonged solely to the United States, and any rights retained by the Cherokee Nation existed only at the discretion of the federal government. John Ross, on the other hand, believed, at least prior to removal, that the Cherokee Nation retained full sovereignty and was limited by the cessions of powers it had voluntarily made to the United States. As was the case with *Worcester v. Georgia* (1832), the question of tribal sovereignty echoed in the halls of America's court system throughout the nineteenth and twentieth centuries, and even into the twenty-first. Chief Justice John Marshall laid out his doctrine of first discovery in *Johnson v. McIntosh* (1823), in which he reasoned that title to the land ultimately belonged to the European discoverer.

Marshall's doctrine was based on the same principle as Crawford's notion of supreme sovereignty. Prior to European arrival, the indigenous peoples held sovereignty over the land with full, uncontested rights to its occupancy and utility. When Europeans arrived, they assumed for themselves that sovereignty and began dividing, granting, and assigning the land as they wished. Marshall asserted that other Christian nations of the world recognized each other's claims. Moreover, for the Native tribes to have retained sovereignty over European claims, they would have had to contest those claims successfully. Because they did not, or could not, contest them, the European discoverer assumed the supreme sovereignty once held by the Indians.[4]

The Marshall Court, however, appeared to contradict its own opinion less than a decade later when, in *Worcester*, it recognized Cherokee sovereignty over land shared with the state of Georgia, even though Georgia claimed sovereignty under the discovery doctrine. Instead of contradicting its previous opinion, however, the Court actually validated the nation's treaty-making process with Indian tribes. Georgia had vested certain powers in the new federal government by ratifying the Constitution in 1788. The Constitution gave the president power to enact treaties as long as two-thirds of the senators concurred. Furthermore, any duly ratified treaty became "the supreme Law of the Land," according to Article VI. When the federal government used those powers to grant ownership title to land to the Cherokees via the Holston Treaty in 1791, it granted a portion of Georgia territory to the Indians. Many in Washington questioned whether the federal government had the authority to give away land belonging to an individual state. Others simply disagreed with the Court's opinion and threw their support behind Georgia's governor—among them President Andrew Jackson, who vehemently refused to enforce the ruling.

Prior to removal, Ross viewed the relationship between the Cherokee Nation and the United States as a contest between dueling sovereigns, each vying for a larger chunk of the political pie.[5] The Supreme Court's ruling in *Worcester* supported this opinion by endorsing Cherokee sovereignty over Georgia land and reaffirming the federal government's treaty-making process with Native Americans. However, when Congress refused to question Andrew Jackson's inaction following the ruling, the president quickly recognized the gift of political impunity. With neither branch of government stepping up to intercede on behalf of the Cherokees, the executive office continued unabated in its quest to drive the tribe across the Mississippi River despite its sovereignty.[6] The fact that the United States acted with impunity in its creation, ratification, and consummation of the fraudulent Treaty of New Echota helped the Supreme Court redefine Indian sovereignty at the turn of the twentieth century when it recognized the federal government's adverse-possessory right in *Lone Wolf v. Hitchcock* (1903) to abrogate Indian treaties at will.[7] The absence of any oversight in U.S.-Indian relations gave the United States the right to define the relationship itself. In short, the government could freely abrogate an Indian treaty so long as no one stopped it from doing so.

By signing the Treaty of New Echota, John Ridge and his small faction surrendered the Cherokees' claim to sovereignty by implicitly admitting to the United States that the tribe was incapable of securing that sovereignty on its own.[8] The Resolutions of 1838 were an eleventh-hour attempt by Ross and the National Council to hold onto that sovereignty. However, the enforcement of the treaty at the hands of the U.S. Army nullified the resolutions and brought major change to Cherokee-U.S. relations. No longer could the Cherokee people hope to be counted among the sovereign nations of North America. The forced removal did more than carry the tribe away from its roots as an autonomous, independent nation; it forced the Cherokees to recognize their relationship with the federal government as suzerain.[9] Ross's idea of dueling sovereigns died somewhere along the "Trail of Tears."

The Treaty of New Echota changed U.S.-Cherokee relations in that it ceded lands promised to the tribe in perpetuity through a ratified treaty with the United States. In short, it showed Ross and the Cherokee people what the Supreme Court would see in *Lone Wolf*—that ownership of tribal lands was never fully guaranteed. A treaty relationship with the United States was tenuous if the federal government could abrogate those treaties at will. Ross realized that this shaky treaty relationship was all the tribe had remaining. He also realized that any remnant of Cherokee sovereignty existed only in the pages of the tribe's treaties with the United States; if the Cherokee Nation wanted to retain its last vestige of autonomy, it must do whatever necessary to protect that treaty relationship.

Although a treaty with the United States often meant an extinction of rights, Francis Paul Prucha has identified three benefits provided to the tribes by Indian treaties, benefits that Ross would deem extremely valuable as the Civil War years approached. First, the treaties provided outright political recognition of an Indian nation. Prucha argues that many tribes valued this recognition above any other concession, often trading for less land to acquire it.[10] Second, tribes were given a level of autonomy over their own land.[11] Ross viewed retaining sovereignty to the extent that the tribe could rule over its own landholdings as a key component of the treaties. He believed that Cherokee land ownership was critical to retaining tribal identity and nationality.[12]

The third benefit of having a treaty with the United States was the protected existence that came with it.[13] For the Cherokee Nation, the idea of federal protection had already proven to be meaningless because of the government's refusal to uphold that part of the tribe's treaties in their interactions with Georgia citizens in the 1820s. "Georgia struck at the heart of the treaty system," claims Prucha, "for it denied the Indians' title to the land, their sovereign jurisdiction over the territory they claimed."[14] The need for protection only increased with removal to Indian Territory, as a new threat to the Cherokee people appeared in the form of the Comanche, Apache, and Kiowa tribes of the southern plains. The sedentary agrarian lifestyle of the Southeastern tribes contrasted with that of the nomadic Plains Indians, putting the placid Southeastern tribes at risk of attack from their more aggressive neighbors.[15]

As the Cherokees made their way west, President Martin Van Buren, Jackson's successor, announced the next phase of federal Indian policy. If the nation's Indians were to be transplanted west of the Mississippi, the United States would have to extend its military arm into the plains to provide the protection promised in most treaties. For many of the tribes, particularly the Cherokees, the fear that the president would do no more to protect them in their new homes than he had when they were in their original ones caused tension among them as they emigrated into lands already occupied by other, more aggressive tribes.[16] Fort Smith, in western Arkansas, was built in 1817 to protect early Cherokee emigrants, but was closed in 1824 with the construction of Fort Gibson in the Cherokee Nation and Fort Towson in the Choctaw Nation to the south. With the removal of the main Cherokee population, Van Buren ordered Fort Smith reopened. These posts quickly became the center of government activity in the territory as Indian agents moved in to join U.S. troops in implementing Indian policy. In 1841, Van Buren's successor, John Tyler, suggested that a series of new forts be built throughout the southern plains, designed to protect white traders, travelers, and settlers, as well as the Indians. Fort Scott in southeastern Kansas and Fort Washita in south-central Indian Territory were constructed in 1842. Fort Arbuckle would be added eight years later to protect the stream of travelers headed to California in search of gold.

Although he was most immediately concerned with the threat emanating from the plains, Ross kept a cautious eye on two developing situations closer to home. First, at the time of the New Echota treaty on December 29, 1835, Indian Territory was somewhat isolated from white society. However, within six months of the treaty's signing, Texas won its independence from Mexico, and Arkansas achieved statehood, bringing a fresh flood of white Americans to the very borders of Indian Territory just as the Cherokees were shaking off the dust from the "Trail of Tears." Ross's experiences in Georgia reminded him of the constant threat posed by a proximal white society. On May 14, 1839, Ross wrote to General Matthew Arbuckle, who commanded the 7th Infantry Regiment at Fort Gibson. "The peaceful inhabitants of this Nation can only call upon your military authority for protection," he wrote, "and I trust you will take proper steps to prevent all unlawful acts of violence from being perpetrated upon the property & persons of the Cherokees . . . by Citizens of the U. States."[17]

The second threat arose within the Cherokee Nation in response to the executions of Major Ridge, John Ridge, and Elias Boudinot in June 1839, hardly three months after the tribe's arrival in Indian Territory. Ross feared that the federal government would continue to favor those who had agreed to removal at New Echota. A few weeks after the killings, Ross wrote again to Arbuckle, calling for impartiality. He reminded the general that the U.S. government had presented the fraudulent treaty as if it applied to all Cherokees. If the treaty applied to all Cherokees, he argued, then the promise "to protect the Cherokees from domestic strife" also applies to all, not just those who signed the treaty.[18] Ross hoped the federal government would do in Indian Territory what it had refused to do in Georgia. President Jackson had proven duplicitous. Perhaps, Ross suggested, future presidents would acknowledge that duplicity and vigilantly protect the tribe's right to self-government.

As the Cherokees were settling into their new homes, Ross had a moderate amount of formal communication with the Indian bureau, including agent Montfort Stokes. Although Stokes had been the governor of North Carolina from 1830 to 1832, during the height of the tribe's struggles with Georgia, there is no evidence of extended interaction between him and Ross prior to removal. However, his presence as Cherokee agent in Indian Territory did not encourage Ross. Stokes, a Jacksonian Democrat who had supported removal, became the Cherokee agent in Indian Territory at the conclusion of Jackson's presidency. The idea that Stokes, a former governor and U.S. senator, would accept an appointment as Indian agent a thousand miles from his home is perhaps indicative of how much these positions were coveted by white politicians, who often became wealthy in the process through the administration of government contracts.

Upon arrival in Indian Territory, the emigrants found that the provisions promised by the government were being held at depots located conveniently for the white traders but inconveniently for the Cherokees. Moreover, much of the beef that awaited them had already begun to rot. Although filled with the diplomatic platitudes of the day, Ross's letter to Stokes betrays his anger. "I deem it my duty," he began, "to request that you as the agent of the United States (*to whom we should apply*) will cause Provisions to be immediately furnished to this portion of the Emigrants at some convenient place" (parenthetical original; italics added).[19] It is safe to say that the only reason Ross wrote to Stokes is that the former governor was the one with control of the provisions and the responsibility to distribute them. He then asked Stokes to replace the beef with fresh bacon. "Fresh Beef that poor . . . is unhealthy and unfit for use." He concluded, "I cannot suffer myself to believe the Government of the United States will require the Cherokees to be subsisted on provisions of such description."[20]

By 1851, the string of forts seemed to have secured the peace along the southern plains, and the tribes in Indian Territory were progressing rapidly toward "civilization," at least according to Luke Lea, the commissioner of Indian affairs from 1850 to 1853, in the Millard Fillmore administration.[21] The bureau, confident that its Indian policy was working, now turned its attention to the upper plains and the Sioux and Chippewa tribes. The plan was to replicate the success in Indian Territory among the more nomadic tribes of the plains. The burgeoning success of the plan to civilize the Southeastern tribes now in Indian Territory convinced the United States that its decision to remove the Indians had been the correct one, even though it had come under heavy attack from all corners of the country. However, the federal government's offer to cover the costs of removal, to support the tribes with provisions for the first year upon arrival, and to provide generous annuity payments moving forward seemed to satisfy most critics. Coupled with the apparent success of the federal policy, the latter half of the 1840s was one of relative quiet in terms of U.S.-Indian relations, outside regional conflicts.[22]

The mid-1850s disrupted the peace and quiet in Indian Territory as the United States rumbled toward Civil War. The Kansas-Nebraska Act of 1854 brought a violent political contest to the very border of the Cherokee Nation, creating an issue for the Cherokees akin to the struggle with Georgia twenty-five years earlier. While historians have discussed the significance of the Kansas-Nebraska Act in the context of the Civil War, it had other immediate implications for Ross and the Indians of the region. The opening of Kansas and Nebraska territories to white settlement caused the United States to secure treaties with the Indians of those regions in order to clear the land for white emigrants.[23] The tribes involved, including the Osages, Shawnees, Delawares, and Quapaws, either voluntarily migrated or were quickly removed to new homes in Indian Territory. The idea of another round of Indian removal to satiate an expanding white population did not sit well with those tribes already in possession of the territory. Moreover, white settlers often crossed the border into Cherokee territory, creating uncertainty among the tribe as memories of Georgia still haunted those old enough to remember. On October 28, 1854, the Cherokee National Council authorized a delegation to Washington to petition the government to acknowledge the rights of the Cherokees and to reaffirm the tribe's ownership of its current land.[24] The quiet of the 1840s had been disrupted by the aggression of the 1850s, and the situation in Kansas would soon erupt in violence, helping to drag the United States toward Civil War.

The new governor of the Kansas Territory, Andrew H. Reeder, did little to keep the peace. Slavery supporters and abolitionists were already taking sides when he arrived, yet he turned his attention away from the major issue of the day and became embroiled in land speculation and sought to establish the new capital on land he had recently purchased. In the summer of 1855, the Kansas territorial legislature petitioned President Franklin Pierce to remove Reeder from office, and the president fired Reeder on August 16.[25] However, the political climate had already soured to the point of bloodshed. In May 1856, proslavery men shot the antislavery sheriff in the back in Lawrence.[26] The abolitionist John Brown and his men arrived too late to assist the antislavery faction but took revenge a few days later on Pottawatomie Creek, killing as many as five proslavery men.[27] The fact that Americans had proven their willingness to kill other Americans over the issue of slavery alarmed the nation. In October 1859, Brown led a group of abolitionists in the seizure of the federal armory at Harper's Ferry, Virginia, hoping to arm area slaves and incite an insurrection.[28] Nine months later, abolitionists were accused of burning the town squares in Dallas and Denton counties in North Texas on the same sultry July afternoon, leading to a series of vigilante hangings across the region.[29] The fear of Kansas "Jayhawkers" crossing the Red River and inciting a slave revolt in North Texas like the one attempted by Brown spread as quickly as the fires.[30] The only thing sitting between the "Texas Troubles" and "Bleeding Kansas" was Indian Territory. Civil war was coming to the United States, and the Cherokee Nation found itself caught in the middle.

The passage of the Kansas-Nebraska Act has long been heralded as an instigator of the American Civil War. It asked the residents of Kansas to decide the fate of slavery in their own territory and, by extension, settle the key political debate of the nation. However, the legislation attracted proslavery and antislavery extremists from around the country and allowed them to join the debate. The act had at least two significant effects on the Indian population south of the Kansas border. First, opening Kansas Territory brought white Americans once again to the very border of the Cherokee Nation. The primary purpose of the Treaty of New Echota was to move the Cherokee people away from white Americans. However, this new onslaught three decades later, included a new wave of white settlers who ignored the physical limitations of the Kansas border and invaded Cherokee Nation lands. These intrusions prompted the delegation to Washington to remind the government once again of its responsibility to protect the Indians from just such an invasion.[31] Second, many of the new arrivals in southeastern Kansas were avid abolitionists, and the fear of an attack on Cherokee property rights—which included ownership of slaves—swept over Ross and the National Council. The thought of outside agitators dictating Cherokee policy angered Ross, who demanded the United States honor its obligation to protect the tribes' right to slavery.[32]

The constant change within the Indian Bureau, however, only added to Ross's consternation. Between the signing of the Kansas–Nebraska Act in 1854 and the summer of 1860, there were five Indian commissioners, one of whom served in an interim capacity. In June 1860 Ross bypassed the Indian Bureau and sent a letter directly to the Secretary of Interior Jacob Thompson demanding that the Buchanan administration act to protect the Cherokees' right to decide for themselves the fate of slavery in their own territory. Ross believed that Thompson, from Mississippi, and current Indian Commissioner Alfred B. Greenwood, from Arkansas, were both "disposed to protect the Cherokees against the abolitionists."[33] The pair of proslavery southerners ordered new Cherokee agent Robert Cowart of Virginia to enforce the treaty as soon as he could reach Indian Territory and assume his post. However, within a few months, all three men, including the southern superintendent, Elias Rector of Arkansas, would resign their positions and join their home states in secession. In short, the secretary of the interior, the commissioner of Indian affairs, the southern superintendent, and the Cherokee agent—the entire hierarchy of the Indian bureau from the Cherokee perspective—resigned in early 1861 and joined the Confederacy. Once again, Ross would have to plead his case before an entirely new administration.

As Ross understood the treaties, the United States was obligated to protect at least four political and personal rights of the Cherokees. First, the federal government had granted the Cherokee Nation fee simple title to the land and had promised to protect their right to possess the land. Moreover, the United States was obligated to prevent or remove any and all intruders from the tribe's territory. Based on the Cherokees' experiences in Georgia, this had the potential of becoming a major issue for the tribe. Second, the federal government agreed to protect the Cherokees' right to govern themselves, both individually and as a national body. The threat of abolitionists crossing the border from Kansas and interfering with the Cherokees' rights to formulate and institute their own governmental policies prompted Ross to lead another delegation to Washington in 1860.[34]

The third way the federal government promised to protect the Cherokees was in their right to personal safety, from both internal and external enemies. This was crucial to the Cherokee people in the early years after emigration. However, the relative peace of the previous decade enabled the Indians to turn their attention to other matters. Fourth, the United States had obligated itself to protect the Cherokee people's right to personal property. Ross insisted that this stipulation meant the federal government must work aggressively to protect the Cherokee people's right to own slaves. The growing abolitionist controversy on the northern border of the Cherokee Nation caused many Cherokee slaveholders to feel that their slaves might be taken or, worse, incited to rebellion. Ross secured a promise from Secretary Thompson to protect the tribe's human property as well.[35]

While Ross was calling for the United States to honor its treaty obligations to the Cherokee Nation, he also reminded the Cherokee people of their own duties. He called for all the tribes in Indian Territory, not only the Cherokees, to remember their obligations. "Our duty is very plain," he wrote. "We have only to adhere firmly to our respective treaties."[36] Before the presidential election of 1860, he spelled out what he called his nation's three responsibilities. First, the Cherokees were to remain firm in the defense of their rights as defined by the tribe's constitution and protected by their treaties with the United States. Second, he called on his fellow Cherokees to resist any interference in the internal affairs of their nation. Any instigation from any source, whether white or Indian, would endanger the tribe's standing with the federal government. Finally, he urged the Cherokee people to join him in clinging to the treaties with the United States and trusting the government to provide the security and protection promised in those treaties.[37] Two months after the attack on Fort Sumter, Ross summed up the tribe's responsibilities for David Hubbard, a former congressman from North Carolina and future Confederate commissioner of Indian affairs: "It is their duty to keep themselves if possible disentangled and afford no grounds to either party to interfere with their rights." To Ross, the most important responsibility of the Cherokee Nation was to protect its limited sovereignty by remaining loyal to the treaties and staying out of the white man's war.[38]

As much as the events in Kansas pushed Americans toward civil war, the election of Abraham Lincoln in November 1860 did much more, as the election became a metaphoric Rubicon for many Southern states. Fearful that the antislavery platform of the newly elected Republican party meant the end of slavery in the United States, on December 20, 1860, South Carolina kicked over the first domino, voting to secede from the Union. Before the second domino could fall, Cyrus Harris, governor of the Chickasaw Nation, informed Ross that the Chickasaw legislature had formally requested a meeting of the leaders of the Chickasaws, Choctaws, Creeks, and Cherokees to consider a formal alliance, either in neutrality or in support of secession. This meeting would be held January 17 at the General Council grounds in the Creek Nation.[39] In reply, Ross urged Harris to refrain from any action that could be misconstrued as a treaty between the tribes.[40] Such an act would violate the stipulation, added to the Holston treaty in 1791, that prohibited the Cherokees from entering into any treaty, even with another tribe of Indians.[41] Ross explained,

> Our relations to the United States, as defined by our Treaties, are clear and definite. And the obligations growing out of them easily ascertained. And it will ever be our wisdom and our interest, to adhere strictly to those obligations, and carefully to guard against being drawn into any complications which may prove prejudicial to the interests of our people, or imperil the security we now enjoy under the protection of the Government of the United States as guaranteed by our Treaties.[42]

By the time of Ross's reply to Governor Harris, five states had joined South Carolina in secession, and the three states bordering Indian Territory were debating their course of action. Arkansas and Missouri had called secession conventions to meet in the coming weeks, while Texas had passed a declaration of secession and was awaiting a statewide referendum on the matter.[43] The growing tension between North and South caused Ross to shy away from even a resolution of unity with the other tribes of Indian Territory. "Should any action of the Council be thought desirable," he wrote to his nephew, William P. Ross, who headed a delegation to attend Governor Harris's meeting, "a resolution might be adopted, to the effect, that we will in all contingencies rest our interests on the pledged faith of the United States, for the fulfilment of their obligations." He added a stern warning: "We ought to entertain no apprehension of any change, that will endanger our interests." If the other tribes would simply remain loyal to their own treaty responsibilities to the United States, he argued, all of them would be united through *nudum pactum*, a bare promise, an agreement without consideration.[44]

Less than a week after Ross's reply to Governor Harris, while Arkansas voters were considering whom to send to the secession convention, Ross received a letter from Arkansas governor Henry Rector.[45] Rector, the cousin of former southern superintendent Elias Rector, warned Ross of the newly elected president's intent to turn the "fruitful fields" of the Cherokee Nation into a land filled with "abolitionism, free-soilers, and Northern mountebanks." He reminded Ross of the commonalities between the Cherokee Nation and the slaveholding states of the South. Rector predicted that by March 4 there would be no fewer than thirteen states separated from the federal government and urged that the Cherokee Nation join them in defense of slavery.[46] On the same day Rector penned the letter to Ross, Congress granted statehood to Kansas as a free state. In his reply to Rector, Ross reiterated his loyalty to the tribe's treaties with the United States and asserted a strong faith in the federal government's pledge to protect the political and individual rights of the Cherokee people. Moreover, Ross rebuked the governor for his insinuation that the Cherokee people would ever permit the rise of an abolitionist spirit among them.[47] To Ross, the fear of abolitionism was hardly about slavery. It was mostly about the ability of the tribe to make its own decision concerning the institution's future.

On February 23, the day following Ross's reply to Rector, Texas voters approved secession, joining South Carolina, Mississippi, Alabama, Georgia, Florida, and Louisiana in leaving the Union. However, on March 21, the Arkansas convention adjourned without having agreed on a secession decree. Governor Rector seemed to have overestimated the support for secession in his own state. Moreover, the state of Missouri met in convention to discuss secession and voted to remain in the Union instead. The crisis in the Cherokee Nation seemed to have abated as its nearest neighbors, Arkansas and Missouri, opted to remain loyal to the United States, or at least to delay the decision. The Cherokee Nation could almost exhale as Indian Territory entered a placid, three-week interlude.

In the meantime, the Indian convention suggested by Governor Harris had taken place at the Creek Agency, about eleven miles up the Arkansas River from Fort Gibson, without representatives from the Chickasaw or Choctaw tribes. Apparently, Ross's temporizing spirit in response to Harris's invitation angered the Chickasaw leader, who had hoped the tribes would take formal action in response to the controversy growing around them. Ross encouraged unity, patience, and neutrality and convinced the Creeks and Seminoles to join him. He bluntly refused to endorse any agreement that might jeopardize the tribe's treaty relationship with the United States. Instead, the Cherokees, Creeks, and Seminoles agreed "to do nothing, to keep [quiet] and to comply with" their respective treaties. To Ross, perhaps the most significant outcome of the meeting was the decision to "be found acting in concert and sharing Common destiny."[48] In the face of uncertainty, Ross believed that the unity of all Indians—not just within the tribes but between them as well—was vital to the survival and perpetuation of indigenous nationality in Indian Territory. He argued that unity and harmony were the only means by which Cherokee rights might be maintained in the current political climate. To that end, Ross worked diligently over the next few months to keep the tribes of Indian Territory united without a formal treaty.[49]

The brief interlude enjoyed by Ross and the Cherokee Nation ended abruptly before dawn on April 12, 1861, when Confederate forces opened fire on the federal garrison at Fort Sumter, South Carolina, launching the American Civil War. In response, President Abraham Lincoln issued a call for 75,000 volunteers from the states to help put down the rebellion. Within days, Virginia joined the parade of secession, refusing to go to war against its southern neighbors. On the same day as Virginia's secession, the U.S. War Department issued a simple order that would resonate throughout Indian Territory and the American West for the next 150 years. On April 17, 1861, the U.S. Army ordered Lieutenant Colonel William H. Emory, in command of Federal forces in Indian Territory, to march "with all the troops in the Indian country west of Arkansas" to Fort Leavenworth, Kansas.[50] The decision had been made to concentrate regular troops for distribution to what the army considered more important theaters across the nation. On the surface, the order was simple and within the realm of routine military operation. However, withdrawing the troops from Indian Territory could never be a simple or routine decision.

Surprisingly, the significance of the abandonment of the forts has largely been downplayed over time as historians focused on other events.[51] However, few events had more impact on Indian Territory during the Civil War era than this fateful decision, and the manner in which it was handled by the War Department provides evidence that the U.S. Army anticipated that impact to some degree. Historians have overlooked the fact that the order to abandon the forts in Indian Territory was issued by the general-in-chief of the army, Winfield Scott, who had enforced Cherokee compliance with the Treaty of New Echota in 1838.[52] Scott had developed a strong dislike for the Cherokees in the 1830s, calling them "miscreants" because they refused to comply with federal demands to prepare for emigration and resisted what they believed was a fraudulent treaty. This no doubt alerted him more than two decades later to the potential of an uprising in response to the evacuation of the Federal forts in 1861.[53] At the outset of the

Civil War, Scott believed he had larger concerns than Indian Territory. He sought to strengthen the defenses in and around the nation's capital with as strong an army of regulars as possible, particularly with a growing Confederate Army in Virginia.[54]

The manner in which the order was delivered provides the strongest evidence of Scott's concern. Instead of sending the order through normal channels—as he did similar orders for other troop evacuations—he had the order hand delivered by Lieutenant William W. Averell, who traveled in civilian clothing and under an assumed name.[55] Averell's mission was to deliver the communique directly to Emory at Fort Arbuckle in the Chickasaw Nation and return immediately to Washington.[56] Troop withdrawals occurred in numerous locations throughout the West, so the forts in Indian Territory were not the only ones affected.[57] However, the manner in which these orders were delivered indicates a level of significance that the others did not have. The secrecy of Averell's mission suggests that Scott was concerned about how the nations in Indian Territory would respond to the withdrawal. Possibly he thought that removing the forces quietly would not garner as much attention and would therefore allow him to make the move with little backlash from the Indians.

Perhaps a secondary motivation behind the secrecy of the troop withdrawal was General Scott's penchant for making controversial decisions without seeking appropriate permission. In October 1860, as rumors of secession spread in the weeks before the presidential election, President James Buchanan had blocked Scott from ordering troops into the South to reinforce a half-dozen southern forts. Yet, following the secession of seven states in response to the election of Abraham Lincoln, Scott ordered the troops at Fort Moultrie to move across the harbor in Charleston, South Carolina, to occupy what he believed to be the more impregnable location of Fort Sumter, and he did so without consulting the new president. The move was viewed by many South Carolinians as preparation for war.[58] Scott's decision to relocate the troops in Indian Territory to Fort Leavenworth was carried out in a similar manner. The general wished not only to avoid the protests of the tribes being abandoned but also to remove the troops without the interference of Lincoln's secretary of the interior, Caleb B. Smith, or his commissioner of Indian affairs, William P. Dole. Immediately upon learning of the withdrawal, Dole fired off a letter to the War Department requesting that the troops be returned to prevent an abrogation of the federal treaties.[59] But, by the time the letter reached Washington, it was too late. Confederate forces had already occupied the abandoned forts.

Averell placed the order in Emory's hands on Thursday, May 2, just east of Fort Arbuckle. The troops spent the next day making preparations and then marched out of the post on Saturday, May 4, headed for Fort Leavenworth.[60] Two days later, Arkansas formally seceded from the Union, prompting Ross to call a meeting of the Cherokee Executive Council to discuss the new developments. He invited his nephew-in-law John Drew.[61] The meeting was to convene at Ross's home at Park Hill, south of Tahlequah, on Tuesday morning, May 14, 1861.

On May 9, a group of citizens from Washington County, Arkansas, wrote to Ross, asking him to clarify his stance on the impending conflict. "Not knowing your political status in this present contest as the head of the Cherokee Nation," they wrote, "we request you to inform us by letter . . . whether you will co-operate with the Northern or Southern section."[62] Ross did not immediately answer. No doubt he hesitated to reveal his position before discussing it with his executive council. On May 11, one week after Emory marched out of Fort Arbuckle, Commissioner Dole wrote the chiefs of the Five Tribes to introduce them to the newly appointed federal superintendent of the Southern District, William G. Coffin. Dole informed the tribes of his letter to Washington requesting that troops be returned to Indian Territory as soon as possible to protect the Indians from outside agitation. However, Confederate Texas troops had already occupied the vacated forts, cutting off all communication between the Indians and the federal government. Dole's letter of reassurance never arrived.

On Monday, May 13, the Confederate War Department asked Douglas H. Cooper, a former Indian agent, to raise a mounted regiment of Choctaws and Chickasaws and to cooperate with General Benjamin McCulloch, who commanded Confederate forces in Arkansas and Indian Territory. Confederate secretary of war L. P. Walker promised Cooper that weapons would be sent to Fort Smith as soon as they could be acquired and that he could apply for them as soon as the regiment was full.[63] The Choctaws and Chickasaws had been openly supportive of the Confederacy, unlike the Creeks and Cherokees to the north. Ross had earlier informed Governor Rector of his desire to stay out of the war, but now that the situation had changed, there were those who wondered if Ross would lead the Cherokee Nation into secession along with its white neighbors. On May 15, Colonel J. R. Kannady, commanding officer at Fort Smith, warned Ross of ongoing efforts to gather abolitionists in Kansas to storm the borderlands between Arkansas and the Cherokee Nation. Kannady claimed that Kansas senator James Lane, an ardent abolitionist, was at the head of the planned invasion. The commander asked Ross if he intended "to adhere to the United States

Government during the pending conflict," or would "support the Government of the Southern Confederacy."[64] Again, Ross would not reply to Kannady until he had consulted with his executive council. After doing so, he issued his formal Proclamation of Neutrality on Friday, May 17, 1861.[65] However, it was actually something more than a proclamation for neutrality.

Ross used the proclamation to advise his people how to respond to the growing crisis in the United States. He began by admonishing them to remember "the obligations arising under their Treaties with the United States" and to remain faithful to those treaties.[66] He then instructed them to adhere to no fewer than six propositions that Ross believed must be upheld in order to eliminate any chance that the United States could accuse the Cherokees of treaty abrogation. First, if the Cherokees wished to retain their treaty relationship with the United States, they must maintain peace with all the states—those Northern states that wished to end slavery as well as the Southern states that had already invaded Indian Territory. Second, he urged his people to attend to their "ordinary avocations."[67] Ross believed that the Cherokees needed to go about their daily lives as if nothing had changed. This would demonstrate a level of trust in the protection promised by the federal government in its treaties.

Holding firmly to a position of neutrality was the overarching objective of the remaining propositions. The third proposition Ross issued to his people was that they avoid taking sides in the political debates of the day. He feared any engagement in "unprofitable discussions" or "partisan demonstrations" could be misconstrued as anything but neutrality. Fourth, Ross encouraged his people to be wary of those in their midst who might seek to persuade them with false or glorified reports of the political climate in and around the Cherokee Nation. The fifth proposition called on the people to cultivate harmonious attitudes within the tribe. Any dissension in the Cherokee Nation threatened to undermine tribal autonomy; the United States would most likely intervene to bring about peace, as the Polk administration had done fifteen years earlier following the killings of Major Ridge, John Ridge, and Elias Boudinot. Ross feared that a repeat in the current climate could prove fatal for Cherokee nationality and autonomy. Finally, Ross urged his people to follow him in a public show of neutrality, as he believed this was the only way the Cherokee people could demonstrate their loyalty to the treaties with the United States.[68]

Ross's response to Kannady, written the same day as his proclamation, set forth his reasoning for neutrality. He claimed that Cherokee rights of soil, property, and personal welfare, as well as the tribe's relationship to the federal government and individual states, "were defined by Treaties with the U.S. government prior to the present condition of affairs," and that those treaties had been in place long before any of the states voted to secede: "Those relations still exist." The secession of Arkansas did not obligate Ross and the Cherokee Nation to join in the rebellion. He wrote, "We do not wish to forfeit our rights."[69] Ross further reminded his people that there had yet to be a formal declaration of war and that hope existed for a peaceful resolution of the matter. If that occurred, he did not want the Cherokees to have committed themselves one way or the other.[70]

The day following his proclamation, Ross responded to the citizens of Washington County, Arkansas, enclosing a copy of his reply to Kannady as evidence of his stance. Ross refused to take sides, especially without a formal declaration of war. "What will then be our situation," he wrote, "if we now abrogate our rights, when no one else is, or can just now be bound for them?"[71] Again, Ross knew that Cherokee autonomy existed only within the pages of the tribe's treaties with the U.S. government. If he were to walk away from those treaties now, who would guarantee their rights for them? They could not walk away from one treaty without another to take its place.

Ross's home at Park Hill was less than thirty miles from the Arkansas state line, and his response to the citizens in Washington County could have been delivered within one day. Therefore, it is conceivable that the disappointing news from the Cherokee leader prompted the Arkansans to turn to another option. Writing the same day as Ross, two Arkansans, perhaps members of the group who inquired of Ross, sent a letter to Stand Watie, informing him of Lane's rumored attack and asking him to organize a regiment and help defend the borderland between Arkansas and the Cherokee Nation.[72] Watie's response, if given, has not survived. However, eight weeks later, on July 12, 1861, Ben McCulloch, Confederate commander of Arkansas and the Indian Territory, commissioned Watie a colonel in the Confederate Army and authorized him to raise a regiment of Cherokees.[73] The commission was a presumptuous attempt to entice the Cherokees out of neutrality, as there is no evidence that Watie immediately accepted the position. Upon the announcement, however, about three hundred mixed-blood Cherokees and Arkansans volunteered for the unit and, one month later, participated in the Battle of Wilson's Creek, Missouri. Interestingly, Watie was not among them. His absence from his own regiment at the start of the war renders his service with the Confederate Army a bit questionable.

History remembers Watie as an eager participant who seized the opportunity to lead a regiment in defense of slavery and the Southern cause. The amount of scholarship dedicated to him far outweighs that of other Cherokee leaders. Moreover, in 1995 the U.S. Postal Service issued a commemorative stamp in his likeness. However, Watie's political stance was not nearly as clear-cut as has been remembered. Both men valued tribal autonomy, yet they disagreed vehemently about what its defense should look like. Ross believed that tribal self-rule was constantly on tenuous ground and that it had to be secured at all costs, even at the expense of slavery. Watie believed that the two were interrelated. In his mind, to give up slavery to appease the federal government was to surrender Cherokee self-rule. Ross recognized that Cherokee autonomy was only as secure as the tribe's relationship with the United States, and if slavery endangered that relationship in any way, Ross believed, it had to be sacrificed.

Watie's political stance at the start of the war has been shrouded by his legendary status as a staunch proponent of the Confederacy. Watie's political posture actually carried very little influence within Cherokee political circles. He apparently had little success adding additional soldiers to the 300 initial volunteers in the regiment he would ultimately lead. By the end of 1863, the size of his force had not grown at all, but his reputation had become overblown. Watie was often given credit for leading his men into battles even though the records are clear about his absence.[74] Union officers often reported having heard rumors of Watie being in command of a force between 500 and 1,000 strong. One report claimed the number to be about 3,000 men.[75] However, Union colonel M. LaRue Harrison encountered what he realized was Watie's entire force near Cane Hill, Arkansas, on December 21, 1863. The small size of the force, still about 300, came as a surprise to Harrison, who reported to headquarters, "I believed Stand Watie's force has been greatly exaggerated."[76] Moreover, in his testimony before the Bureau of Indian Affairs following the war, Albert Pike, Confederate commissioner to the Indians west of Arkansas, downplayed the size and significance of Watie's small band of followers. In his estimation, the Ross-led Cherokees always had the strength and numbers to destroy Watie and his pro-Confederate followers.[77]

In late 1862, Confederate leaders called on Watie to use his influence within the tribe and increase the number of men in his unit. Confederate general William Steele doubted "the propriety of organizing a brigade for Colonel Watie." He complained that Watie had been operating around Fort Gibson with an imaginary force that seemed to be scattered around the territory. He argued that Watie's men were allowed to roam freely and that they often took more than their share of rations from Confederate stores.[78] A quick analysis of the service records for Watie's Confederate Mounted Volunteers reveals about 1,400 enlistees.

However, many of the names are citizens of Arkansas who no doubt enlisted with the unit to satisfy the requirements of the Conscription Act of April 1862, yet never joined the unit for actual service. Many more names appear only once, at registration, and never appear again. Moreover, nearly three dozen names on Watie's regimental rolls are found later on the rolls of those serving alongside other Cherokees in the Union Army as part of the Indian Home Guard.[79] Apparently, the legend of Stand Watie, like many legends, is out of proportion to reality.

In early June 1861, three men, all envoys of the new Confederate government, turned their attention to Ross in an attempt to bring the Cherokee Nation into the Confederacy. Albert Pike, David Hubbard, who would become the Confederate commissioner of Indian affairs, and Ben McCulloch each wrote letters to Ross outlining his personal and political beliefs as to why the Cherokees should align with the Confederates. While Hubbard and McCulloch made strong arguments for the perpetuation of slavery, Pike understood the Indian political viewpoint better than most other nineteenth-century Americans. The former pair did little to convince Ross to abandon his stance of neutrality. The latter constructed an argument so sound, so in line with Ross's mindset, that it might actually have pushed Ross toward a treaty of alliance with the Confederate States.

In their letters, both written on June 12, 1861, Hubbard and McCulloch warned Ross of the dangers of remaining neutral. Hubbard claimed that Northern aggressors would sweep in and take Cherokee land for white settlers while the Cherokees sat defenseless.[80] Perhaps few men in U.S. history better understood the possibilities of the government taking land from Native Americans than did Ross. Therefore, Hubbard's warning had little effect on the Cherokee chief. McCulloch argued that the Arkansans and Cherokees shared a "common cause against a people who are endeavoring to deprive us of our rights."[81] They both admonished Ross to join the fight to protect the rights of his people just as other Southerners were fighting to protect theirs. Neither Hubbard nor McCulloch understood Ross's concerns. They believed that the only way to protect Southern rights was to go to war and fight for them. However, Ross knew that for the Cherokees to protect their rights, they had to do the exact opposite. Going to war against the United States would abrogate their treaties and place their rights in jeopardy. While the Cherokees and Arkansans shared similar institutions, they differed ideologically. McCulloch's threat to enter the Cherokee Nation and defend its people from any approaching attack did nothing to push Ross toward an alliance. In fact, it further solidified his belief that war of any kind in the Cherokee Nation would not end well for his people.[82]

Pike, on the other hand, had worked as an agent with the Choctaws and Chickasaws prior to the war and understood the ideological differences between the Indians and the Arkansans. He realized that Southerners would take up arms to defend their rights and institutions; he also recognized that the tribes of Indian Territory viewed their treaties with the United States as the sole protector of theirs. For the Indians to align with the Southern states, the Confederacy would have to be willing to guarantee them their rights of land ownership, personal safety, and personal property, and it would have to do that through a treaty. In short, the Confederate States would have to replace the United States as the guarantor of Indian sovereignty. On May 20, just three days after Ross's Proclamation of Neutrality, Pike wrote to acting confederate commissioner of Indian affairs Robert Toombs and informed him of his plan to do more than just seek treaties of alliance with the Indians. "I very much regret," wrote Pike, "that I have not received distinct authority to give the Indians guarantees of all their legal and just rights under treaties." He reiterated that "it cannot be expected they will join us without them . . . [A]s I am not directed not to give the guarantees, I shall give them, formal, full, and ample by treaty."[83] Pike encouraged Toombs to oversee the ratification of any treaty he secured. Pike had recognized a key component of Ross's political posture: the fact that his loyalties lay with the U.S. government treaties guaranteeing the tribe some level of autonomy and protecting their rights of tribal land ownership and personal security and property. Ross had never been loyal to the Union. After all, the United States had treated the Cherokees with contempt and racial hatred in the 1830s. Pike believed the Cherokee Nation would come to an alliance with the Confederacy only if that government promised to provide the same securities to the Indians by treaty.

Pike was so convinced that his offer for a treaty of protection would sweep the Cherokee Nation into the Confederacy that he asked Ross to allow him to present it directly to the Cherokee National Council.[84] Instead, on June 27, Ross convened his executive council and showed members the letters from Kannady, Hubbard, McCulloch, and Pike, as well as his response to each. Moreover, he showed them a copy of his Proclamation of Neutrality from May 17 and asked the council to approve his neutral stance.[85] The council did just that. In his response to Pike, he sent copies of his correspondence with Hubbard to "show the position which I have felt constrained to assume." He concluded by telling Pike that the tribe did not feel at liberty to enter into a new treaty with anyone, much less the Confederate States. Ross politely and diplomatically declined Pike's invitation.[86]

Pike, however, recognized a contradiction. He believed that Ross's claim of neutrality was merely a disguise for his loyalty to the treaties with the United States. At first Ross did not believe he was being contradictory in his position; he thought that proclaiming his neutrality was the only way for the Cherokee people to safeguard their rights. In his eyes he could have remained loyal to the treaties and still maintained neutrality at the same time, at least until Pike confronted him on it.

Pike told Commissioner Toombs that if he could not secure a treaty with Ross, he would turn to a minority faction in order to accomplish his goals.[87] He knew that Ross's façade of neutrality would crumble if those tribes around him traded their treaties with the United States for new ones with the Southern government. Pike's treaties with the mixed-blood factions of the Plains tribes in the southwestern part of Indian Territory alerted Ross to the growing dangers of neutrality.[88] Pike's pressure on Ross began to chip away at the façade that Ross worked so diligently to construct, and when the political posturing turned to actual conflict in the summer of 1861, Ross was faced with arguably the most difficult decision of his life.

While Pike waited for Ross's response, he visited with and obtained treaties from the leaders of the Creeks (July 10) and the Choctaws and Chickasaws (July 12). While securing a treaty with the Seminoles on August 1, Pike fired off an incandescent response to Ross's refusal to allow him to speak before the National Council. "I do not propose now," he retorted, "to enter upon any further argument . . . nor to seek to open any further negotiation with the Cherokee Authorities." Pike was angry that his efforts to replace the tribe's treaty with one he considered to be better for the Cherokees had been rejected. He reminded Ross that he had offered, on behalf of the Confederate government, "ample protection by their troops, and that at any cost and at all hazards they would maintain the Cherokees in the possession of their country." He also reminded him that he had offered the tribe a promise of "perpetual possession" of their land in fee simple. He even promised to pay the tribe any and all annuity money still owed them by the U.S. government.[89] Pike's reasoning was sound. He implied that the new Confederate States had been ancillary participants in the treaties with the United States as part of the Union. Therefore, they felt obligated to uphold their stipulations under them. In short, the Cherokees had not agreed to those treaties with only the Northern states; the Southern states had a responsibility to them as well. Pike hoped his show of allegiance to the Cherokees would convince Ross that the Confederate government would never treat the tribe the way the U.S. government had.

In a brilliant maneuver, Pike called into question the sincerity of Ross's stance of neutrality by referencing the chief's letter to McCulloch on June 17. In it, Ross had told the general that the Cherokee people would never assume "an attitude of hostility toward the Government of the United States."[90] Conversely, Ross added, their nation would not welcome the presence of Confederate troops because it would "place in our midst organized companies not authorized by our laws, but in violation of treaty."[91] Pike pounced on this, accusing Ross of having set a double standard. If the U.S. Army was welcome in the Cherokee Nation, but the Confederate Army was not, how could Ross claim to be neutral? Pike had identified the chink in Ross's armor. The chief was not neutral at all. He was loyal to the treaties with the United States and therefore, in Pike's mind, loyal to the Union. Pike believed that if the Confederacy could convince Ross that the treaties would be guaranteed by, and secure in, the Confederate government, Ross would turn to an alliance with his Southern neighbors.[92]

As Ross mulled over his waning options, the nations around him prepared for war. General Scott's decision to abandon the forts in Indian Territory, though routine to the United States, represented the first in a train of events leading to disaster for the Five Tribes. The resulting chain reaction of events came quickly, and no matter how diligently Ross worked to halt the flow, the Cherokee Nation found itself in a valley awaiting an avalanche. Despite Scott's efforts at secrecy, the impact of the removal of Federal troops was felt immediately by the tribes in Indian Territory, which viewed the move as another abrogation of treaty obligations by the United States. The abandonment of Indian Territory left the Indians without the protection promised them—protection they cherished now more than ever. Furthermore, without that protection, the Indians were left to defend themselves from the onrush of Confederate forces as Texas troops quickly swept in and occupied the vacated forts, prompting many of the Indians to align themselves with the Southerners. Although the U.S. War Department expected an uproar from the Indians over the withdrawal, they never anticipated that the Indians would align themselves against the United States. The government believed that the Indians would remain loyal to their treaties and stay out of the war altogether.[93]

Despite the rapid alliances between Pike and the other Indian Territory tribes, John Ross and the Cherokee Nation refused to disregard their treaty obligations to the United States, even though the United States had abrogated their promises to the Cherokees. The withdrawal of Federal troops from Indian Territory placed Ross in a difficult position as he had to decide the best way to protect his tribe's existence. Ross realized that Cherokee sovereignty existed only in the tribe's treaties with the United States, and the evacuation of the forts left the chief with little hope of securing that autonomy. The days and weeks that followed were among the most difficult of Ross's life as he had to navigate the approaching storm of war as it descended upon his people. The decisions he made in the subsequent months were calculated to preserve Cherokee identity, and the risks involved made choosing his course difficult. Between April 1861 and September 1862, Ross held firm to the belief that the Cherokee people would be rewarded for their loyalty to the tribe's treaties with the United States, even if that loyalty was often disguised as rebellion.

CHAPTER 3

AUTONOMY AND THE CONFEDERATE ALLIANCE

As John Ross watched the last member of the executive council ride away from his home at Park Hill on the first weekend of August 1861, his thoughts turned once again to the latest letter he had received from Confederate commissioner Albert Pike.[1] He had taken time for a quick reading when it first arrived, but now he hoped to devote his full attention to its important lines. Over the years, Ross had won the admiration and respect of the Cherokee people for his steadfast adherence to the tribe's treaty responsibilities to the United States and for his tireless efforts in demanding that the federal government honor its obligations. The Cherokee Nation had had no contact with any agent or representative of the federal government since the previous April when the U.S. Army had pulled out of Indian Territory. Ross had thus been unable to seek redress. Since January, representatives of Southern governments had actively solicited his cooperation; so far, he had resisted their overtures, outlining his firm stance of neutrality, even after Confederate forces marched in and occupied the forts vacated by the United States. Pike had written to Ross earlier, asking permission to speak before the Cherokee National Council and offer the tribe generous terms of alliance. Ross refused to allow the meeting, leading to this latest epistle. However, this letter was different. Pike saw through Ross's veil of neutrality and recognized his loyalty to the tribe's federal treaties; therefore, he withdrew his offer for a treaty of protection with the Cherokees. Ross returned to his study to give the letter his full attention. No doubt, he noticed that Pike, by implication, had issued an ultimatum to the Cherokee people. What impact did the letter have on Ross's decision? Did Pike's letter of August 1, 1861, set in motion the events that led to Ross's treaty with the Confederate States? Or did it simply ignite the combustible climate that already existed in the Cherokee Nation? In actuality, the letter merely redirected Ross's thinking. His goal of securing tribal autonomy would never change. His decision in response to the letter would be calculated to benefit the Cherokee Nation, and it set in motion a series of events that would have profound and lasting impact not just on the Cherokee Nation but on all Indians across the United States.

Ross had convened the executive council on July 31 to discuss his growing concerns about the Cherokee Nation.[2] The council consisted of Joseph Vann, the assistant principal chief; James Brown, who had served the tribe for nearly fifty years, having served on the initial standing committee formed in 1817; William Porter Ross, the chief's nephew and a graduate of Princeton University; and John Drew, who filled in for Daniel Colston, who had recently died after having served in the tribal government for more than two decades. Ross's wish for unity among the tribes of Indian Territory disintegrated before his eyes as, one by one, the tribes aligned themselves with Pike and the Confederate government. The Seminoles were the most recent to capitulate, agreeing to a treaty on August 1—no doubt, prompting Pike's letter to Ross. With the Creeks, Choctaws, Chickasaws, and now the Seminoles in alliance with the Confederacy, and with Ross's determined stance of neutrality, Pike turned his attention elsewhere. Apparently, he was serious about terminating all negotiations with the Cherokees as he headed for the Wichita Agency at Fort Cobb to seek alliances with the Comanches, Wichitas, Caddos, and other tribes, leaving the Arkansas River valley behind.

The alliances with the neighboring tribes placed Ross in a difficult position. The executive council authorized a mass meeting of the Cherokee Nation at Tahlequah, set to begin on August 21, 1861. Ross hoped to unite the Cherokee people in defense of their rights and privileges as a nation under the treaties with the United States.[3] However, the changing political climate around him and Pike's threatening letter in front of him caused the chief to question the wisdom of continued resistance. He had remained hopeful, believing that cooler heads might prevail and war might be avoided. However, on a Sunday afternoon in mid-July, North and South met on the battlefield just north of Manassas, Virginia, along a small river named Bull Run. Not only had war begun, but the unthinkable happened. The Confederates under Pierre G. T. Beauregard defeated Irvin McDowell's Union Army, causing Ross to consider a new concern: what if the Confederate States won the war?

Ross's initial reading of Pike's letter revealed three explicit points. First, Pike acknowledged Ross's formal proclamation of neutrality. However, Pike also knew that neutrality for the Cherokees meant allegiance to their treaties with the United States. Second, in consequence, Pike formally withdrew the Confederate government's offer of protection. If Ross was going to use neutrality as a smoke screen, Pike was going to stoke the fire. Third, Pike suggested the two men sign a treaty of neutrality, formally declaring the Cherokees' intention to support neither side during the war. Knowing that the federal treaties prohibited such an agreement, Pike called Ross's bluff. If Ross signed such an agreement, he would have abrogated the treaties. If he refused, it would reveal his true loyalty to the United States.

Ross's concerns with the letter stemmed less from what Pike's words said than from what they implied. The two most alarming implications concerned Stand Watie. Referring to federal annuities, Pike declared that his informal offer to pay the tribe what the United States owed it was no longer available. In doing so, however, he promised that the money would be made available, on a prorated basis, to "those of your people who have declared themselves the friends of the South."[4] His recognition of Watie and his followers, no doubt, concerned Ross. If the Confederates were to provide Watie with the protection once promised to the Cherokee people, Ross's rival might be free to wage war on those Cherokees not loyal to the South. The second alarming implication furthered this concern. Pike warned Ross that the only two reasons the Confederates would advance into the Cherokee Nation were to repel a Union invasion or to protect those Cherokees loyal to the Confederacy. Ross understood the implication. The Cherokees would have to allow Watie to roam the nation without resistance. If the tribe or any of its members confronted him, the Confederates would move in to defend him.

As Ross studied the letter, the political climate around the Cherokee Nation continued to change. Not only was Indian Territory bordered on two sides by Confederate states, but the tribes within signed treaties of alliance with Pike. Pike's trip to the Wichita Agency at Fort Cobb portended further gloom as the Plains tribes were soon to meet with the Confederate commissioner to consider their own fate. Beauregard's victory in Virginia at Manassas greatly compounded the difficulty on two fronts: first, cooler heads were not going to prevail; and second, the unexpected victory by the infantile Confederacy further confused the Cherokee chief, who continued to place great trust in the treaties with the United States. The mass meeting of the nation would be upon him soon, and he pondered how best to keep his people united when he, himself, was beginning to doubt the practicability of remaining aloof from the Confederacy. Ross hoped that the tribes of Indian Territory could remain united in order to multiply their collective strength in defense of their homes. Now all the other tribal leaders were aligning their peoples with Pike and the Confederacy, leaving Ross as the lone holdout.

The Creeks had been the first to sign with Pike, on July 10, yet their tribe remained largely split over the issue. An elderly headman named Opothle Yahola openly advocated for neutrality in the war and loyalty to the treaties with the United States, much like Ross. Opothle Yahola was not the head of the Creek government and could not prevent his tribe from aligning with Pike. However, he quickly became the leader of a large group of Indians, many from other tribes, who also wanted to remain out of the impending war. The group gathered unceremoniously near Opothle Yahola's home and continued to grow in numbers during the late summer of 1861. By early autumn, the group's size caused consternation within the Creek tribal government, which reached out to Ross for assistance.[5] Ross and Opothle Yahola would correspond frequently as the war closed in on Indian Territory.

Unbeknownst to Ross at the time of Pike's letter, Union and Confederate troops skirmished in southwestern Missouri in an encounter that would culminate in battle along Wilson's Creek on August 10.[6] The battle, which included a small group of Cherokees, resulted in another resounding Confederate victory and seemed to convince Ross that the South would, in all probability, win the war.[7] He now found himself with a difficult decision. The mass meeting of the Cherokee Nation was to begin on August 21, and it appeared the Confederate States might win their independence. How should the latter affect the former? Was his stand of neutrality still the wisest option for his nation, or should he consider abrogating the treaties with the United States by signing a new one with the Confederacy? Given Pike's ultimatum, was a Confederate alliance even still on the table?

Ross appeared to have two options, both of which offered multiple scenarios. The tribe could either remain neutral or seek a treaty of alliance with the Confederacy. If the Cherokee Nation remained neutral, it would run the risk of being overrun by the Confederate Army during the war, possibly without any protection from the United States, and Stand Watie would be free to harass the Cherokee people at will, without any recourse. Moreover, a neutral position would prevent Ross from protecting the tribe from Watie's advances. If he reined Watie in, the Confederates would most likely interpret it as aggression on the side of the United States. Also, if the tribe remained neutral and could maintain that position throughout the duration of the war, a Confederate victory would render them the only nation south of Kansas not aligned with the new Southern government. Pike's letter explicitly stated, "If your treaties are with the North alone on one side, they are so on the other side also." It further warned, "If you owe to *them* alone allegiance, loyalty, and friendship, *they* alone can owe you moneys and protection" (emphasis original).[8] In short, John Ross could not expect to remain "neutral" through the war and then depend on treaties with the Confederate government afterward. Pike closed the letter with a tacit warning, "sincerely wishing that the policy of the Cherokee people may not prove disastrous to them, nor a cause of regret to their rulers hereafter."[9] If Ross wanted a treaty with the Confederate States, he had to agree to it now, or face the consequences if the South were to win the war.

However, if the Cherokee Nation remained neutral and the North won the war, the tribe would have proven its undying loyalty to the treaty relationship with the United States. If the tribe could hold out long enough for U.S. troops to return to Indian Territory, the Cherokees could join the war effort to secure that relationship. As it was, having had no contact with federal agents since the Confederate occupation, Ross questioned the federal government's intentions toward the Cherokees. Many questions remained, however. Could the Cherokee Nation survive the war as a neutral party with Stand Watie and his men roaming the territory? How probable was it that the United States would win the war? The first two battles were decisive Confederate victories. How likely was it for the United States to return to Indian Territory? If it abandoned it once, what would motivate a return?

Ross's second option was an alliance with the Confederate States. In this scenario, a Southern victory in the war would mean that the treaties of the Cherokee Nation would now be guaranteed by a different white government. There would, in one sense, be no change. However, if the United States won the war, would Ross ever be able to convince the federal government that he had desired loyalty all along, but been forced to choose an alliance with the South out of self-preservation for the Cherokee people? Also, if the United States were to recapture Indian Territory, could the Cherokees then prove their allegiance by abandoning the Confederacy and joining the United States upon reentry?

Which option gave the Cherokee Nation the best hope for perpetuating tribal autonomy? Had the United States not abandoned Indian Territory, the decision would have been a simple one. The tribe would no doubt have remained loyal to the treaties and most likely have helped fight the Confederacy. Now it appeared to Ross that Missouri would be joining its Southern brethren in secession, increasing the danger on the Cherokee border. Moreover, it looked as if the South would prove victorious, and Pike's letter implied disaster for a "neutral" Cherokee Nation if that scenario were realized. To Ross, an alliance with the Confederacy seemed the only viable option. If the South were to win, the Cherokee Nation would be protected. If the United States were to win, Ross would have to convince the federal government that its abandonment of Indian Territory had left the Cherokees no other alternative. Either option proved more palatable to Ross than enduring the war without the protection of the North or South, and it appeared that the United States was not offering its protection any time soon. It is not known exactly when Ross decided to negotiate a treaty of alliance with the Confederate States. Speculation places it between the Battle of Wilson's Creek on August 10 and the date of the mass meeting of the Cherokee Nation on the 21st. Regardless of when it was made, Ross now faced the task of convincing the Cherokee people that the decision to abandon neutrality and align with the Confederacy was best for their nation.

The shift from neutrality to an alliance with the Confederacy should not be considered a reversal for Ross, as many historians suggest, but rather a lane change as the chief sought to navigate the tribe through the horrors of the Civil War. The decision's significance can be understood only by viewing it through the lens of Ross's long-term goals for the Cherokee Nation. Pike's letter provides the framework through which we can understand Ross's actions. Ross's long-standing goal was always "to preserve the existence of the Cherokee tribe with as much self-government as possible"; he just needed to decide the best route to take to accomplish that goal.[10] His first choice was to remain neutral out of loyalty to the treaties. However, when the lane of neutrality was blocked by Pike's ultimatum, he chose the next best available lane, an alliance with the Confederate States. If a better option presented itself before the war ended, Ross would not hesitate to take it.

On Wednesday, August 21, as many as 4,000 Cherokees descended on the council grounds at Tahlequah at the bidding of their principal chief. Ross hired cooks and purchased enough beef at five cents per pound to feed the crowd, hoping to make the attendees' stay as comfortable as possible.[11] Ross's address, delivered in the town square, consisted of two parts. He spent the first half explaining why he had initially settled on neutrality. He explained that the United States had never asked the Cherokees to enter the war, and that the tribe had no reason to go to war against the Union now. He declared that Cherokee soil had not been invaded, nor their peace molested, and that the treaty relationship with the United States was still in place.[12] In the second part of the address, he expressed his concern that there was growing unrest within the nation and that the tribe must have unity in order to survive. "Union is strength, dissension weakness," he advised. "In time of peace together! In time of war, if war must come, fight together! As Brothers live, as Brothers die!" He then called on the Cherokee people to remember what he considered the most important thing: Cherokee autonomy allowed the tribe to enjoy laws and rights of their own choosing. "Here they must be enjoyed or nowhere else," he exclaimed. "When our nationality ceases here, it will live nowhere else. When these homes are lost, you will find no others like them." He confessed to his audience that he believed the South might win the war and, if it did, that the permanent division of the United States into two separate governments "is now probable," he argued. Without expressing the various scenarios at play within his decision, he asked permission to "adopt preliminary steps for an alliance with the Confederate States."[13] Those Cherokees in attendance approved his request.[14]

W. S. Robertson, a missionary in the Creek Nation who was present at the mass meeting, claimed that many of the Cherokee men left the meeting confused, believing that the nation had reaffirmed its stance of neutrality.[15] Actually, the tribe had done just that. However, the crowd was reported later to have shown its support for Ross's efforts to negotiate an alliance treaty with the Confederacy if one could be agreed upon.[16] It is unclear why there was confusion. Did the men hear only the first part of Ross's address, or had Robertson simply misunderstood what he heard from the crowd? Moreover, Robertson claimed that there were only eighteen hundred men in attendance, not the 4,000 claimed by Ross. Did Ross exaggerate the support he received from the convention's attendees, or did Robertson underestimate the crowd's size? Did the chief hope to promote a greater sense of unity among the tribe by disguising the convention's lack of unanimity? Or did he hope to mislead the masses in order to advance an unpopular agenda?

The actual number of Cherokee men in attendance that day is irrelevant to the broader story of Ross's proposed Confederate alliance. Robertson's smaller crowd could easily have followed Cherokee tradition and acknowledged unanimity, even if there had been heated debate on the issue. The men reaffirmed the stance of neutrality and later authorized the chief to seek an alliance. Moreover, the turbulent political climate of the day could have lent itself in support of either man's estimate. The controversial topic could have attracted a larger crowd to Tahlequah for the important meeting, as Ross suggested. It also could have prevented many from attending out of fear and uncertainty of travel, supporting Robertson's claim. In short, the size of the crowd that day does not directly indicate the level of support for or against Ross's proposal. Cherokee tradition called for unanimity, and there is no evidence that the convention achieved anything other than that, regardless of the crowd's size. Moreover, the crowd had no legislative authority. Ross simply called the people together, hoping to create a sense of unity within the tribe.

Ross's first act following the meeting was to authorize his son-in-law John Drew to raise a regiment of mounted men to defend the Cherokee Nation from internal and external threats. Many of the initial volunteers in Drew's regiment belonged to the Keetoowah Society, a group of full-blood Cherokees who sought to remain loyal to tribal traditions and to honor the tribe's treaties with the United States because those treaties allowed them the autonomy to adhere to the traditional Cherokee way of life.[17] The Keetoowah Society had arisen within the tribe in opposition to the assimilationist mindset of the pro-removal faction led by the Ridges in the 1830s.[18] The society's desire to adhere to tribal tradition was so strong that it helped endear the Keetoowahs, an abolitionist society, to the leadership of slaveholder John Ross, who also sought to protect tribal autonomy and tradition by honoring the federal treaties. His opposition to removal in the 1830s and his marriage to a full-blood Cherokee allowed him to hold the society's loyalty.[19] During the war, this group would gain an unfair reputation for disloyalty to the Confederate cause—unfair, because the Keetoowahs intended to remain loyal not to the Confederate cause, but to Ross and the Cherokee government while they sought to protect the tribe's treaty relationship with the U.S.—or Confederate—government, whichever was in line at the time to secure it. Members of the Keetoowah Society wore crossed pins on their lapels as an identifier, leading Watie's followers to refer to them as "Pins."

Although the Keetoowah Society became active again in the Cherokee Nation under the encouragement of Baptist missionary Evan Jones, the organization is somewhat shrouded in mystery.[20] It is clear that the group comprised full-blood Cherokees and that it strongly supported Cherokee customs. Moreover, the group reemerged in the Civil War era in opposition to Cherokee slavery.[21] What is unclear, however, is how far Keetoowah influence reached across the tribe. The fact that many of the men in Drew's regiment were Keetoowahs in no way implies that they all were. While the society threw its support behind Ross and the Cherokee government, it is tempting to conclude that all Ross supporters were Keetoowahs. This is not practical. The Keetoowah Society influenced Cherokee politics during the 1860s. However, there is no evidence that Keetoowahs controlled tribal government during the war years. They did strongly support the Ross-led government, even if it meant joining the Confederate Army in defense of an institution they fundamentally opposed.

Following the endorsement of the National Council, Ross turned his attention to the treaty negotiations, informing Pike and McCulloch of the decision to seek an alliance with the Confederate States. He dispatched George W. Clark to McCulloch's camp with a letter addressed to the general.[22] At the same time, he sent C. R. Hicks and Joshua Ross with a note addressed to the chiefs and headmen of the Creek Nation. The men carried a letter for Pike and hoped to have a Creek guide escort them to his camp.[23] No doubt, the Creek leaders were surprised to learn that Ross had backed away from neutrality and was seeking an alliance with Pike and the Confederacy. When the note was shown to Opothle Yahola, the headman incredulously scribbled a note on the back of Ross's letter asking if the original was really from his own hand. "We don't know wether [sic] this is the truth or no," he wrote.[24]

In the meantime, William P. Adair and James M. Bell, alarmed by the results of the mass meeting, wrote Stand Watie. This intriguing letter, dated August 29, reveals perhaps more about Watie than historians have realized.[25] With near unanimity, historians describe Watie's entry into Confederate service as quick and decisive. However, the Adair-Bell letter appears to betray this interpretation in at least three ways. First, the letter makes no mention of any loyalty on the part of Watie and his followers to the Southern cause. It cites only a concern for their position within the Cherokee Nation. The bulk of Watie's followers during the war belonged to a secret society known as the Knights of the Golden Circle.[26] The Knights were a proslavery group based in Cincinnati, Ohio, that found its way into the Cherokee Nation when the issue of slavery among the Cherokees was threatened by abolitionists from Kansas. General Ben McCulloch, a prominent member of the Knights, helped encourage development of the society among the mixed-bloods and sought to buttress the group by authorizing Watie to raise a force of Confederates, because Ross and the tribal government had refused to. Therefore, by extension, the Knights rose in opposition to Ross and the Keetoowahs and presented a credible threat to the traditional leanings of mainstream Cherokee society. However, the pending alliance between Ross and the Confederacy would place Ross and the full-bloods in a position of favor with the Confederate government. The Knights, led by Adair and Bell, scampered to retain their fleeting influence with the Confederate States by imploring Watie to join them. If there was any loyalty to the Southern cause within the ranks of the Cherokee Knights of the Golden Circle, it took a backseat to the groups' concern for their own position of power within the Cherokee Nation.

The second way the letter calls into question the traditional image of Stand Watie is to show that Watie's influence within the Cherokee Nation, like that of his cousin John Ridge in the 1830s, has been overstated. The Adair–Bell letter makes it appear as if Watie's only influence was with Pike and the Confederate government, and only then if Ross remained neutral. If Ross and his followers became "the Treaty making power," the two men wrote, "you know our destiny will be inalterably sealed."[27] The men asked Watie to consider a face-to-face meeting with Pike in order to lobby for the security of their position of influence with the Confederate States, "to the end that we may have justice done us and our rights provided for and place us if possible at least on an honorable equity with this old Dominant party that has for years had its foot upon our necks." Why would the men ask Pike and not Watie to protect their influence within the Cherokee Nation? Most likely, it is because they realized that Watie had limited personal influence within the tribe and that, without the support of the Confederate government, they had little hope of gaining any.

Finally, the most significant way the Adair-Bell letter undermines the traditional image of Stand Watie is that it suggests the authors themselves, perhaps on behalf of the Knights of the Golden Circle, were the ones looking for power and influence and that they simply chose Watie to be the face of their movement. "We have selected you," they wrote, "for . . . the well known [sic] fact that you have had an honorable reputation abroad in the South for years and are well known by A. Pike." If Stand Watie was already the outspoken leader of the group, why were the men attempting to persuade him to intervene with Pike on their behalf? "If you will go, please come right away," they added. "If you can't go, please to send us a note and let us know but if possible you must go."[28] In an endorsement to the letter, Bell strongly encouraged Watie to consider their request. If the men did not act promptly, he warned, "we are done up. All of our work will have been in vain, our prospects destroyed, our rights disregarded, and we will be slaves to Ross's tyranny." He concluded with one final plea. "It wont [sic] do for you to hold back. Declare yourself ready to serve your country in what ever capacity *we may want you*" (italics added).[29] No doubt, the Knights of the Golden Circle tried to recruit Watie to be their front man.

Both Adair and Bell were members of Watie's regiment, having enlisted on July 12, 1861, more than six weeks prior to their letter. Thirty-year-old William P. Adair enlisted as the assistant quartermaster of the regiment with the rank of captain. Thirty-three-year-old James M. Bell was the captain of Company D. Why would these men write such a letter to the colonel of their own regiment?

Had Watie not fulfilled his responsibilities as leader of the troops? Newspapers of the day lauded Watie and his actions at the Battle of Wilson's Creek. However, two prominent Watie biographers admit that, even though some of his men participated, Watie was not present at the battle.[30] Moreover, Watie's force participated in the largest battle of the Civil War in Indian Territory at Honey Springs Depot in July 1863; once again, Watie was not present. He was "on detached services at Webber's Falls" at the time.[31] Why was Watie absent from both engagements while his men were present? Has the historical record credited Watie with more than he deserves? Perhaps the Adair-Bell letter reveals a side of Watie that historians previously failed to see. His activities during the war have been deemed heroic by contemporaries and historians alike, yet maybe the praise has been too adulatory. It appears that Adair and Bell knew a different Stand Watie than the one presented by history. Apparently, he was not even the leader of his own group, at least at the outset of the war.

Stand Watie's involvement in the Civil War is difficult to understand. The Adair-Bell letter suggests a reluctance on his part to enter the war, whereas history describes him as an avid, early volunteer for the Confederate cause. Was he the avid leader of the Knights of the Golden Circle, as historians suggest, or was he simply a well-known member of the group who was thrust into prominence by his more avid counterparts? Did Watie enter the war to defend slavery, or was he fighting for his place in Cherokee political circles? Most likely, both are true. Watie, like Ross, wanted to protect the future of the Cherokee people and to ensure that that future included slavery. However, his support for the Confederate war effort led him to resent those within his own tribe who were less committed to the defense of slavery. At times, it became difficult for some in Indian Territory to determine which war Watie was fighting: the war to defend slavery or a war against his own people.

As Watie was reading the letter from Adair and Bell, two Cherokee messengers were trying to locate Pike and deliver the letter from Ross informing the commissioner of the chief's desire to enter treaty negotiations. Once located, Pike received the news with satisfaction. The messengers returned to Park Hill with a note, written on September 3, expressing Pike's "liveliest gratification" and, more importantly, his willingness to "consider as not written my letter of the 1st August to the Principal Chief."[32] Pike's willingness to disregard his ultimatum to the Cherokees no doubt pleased Ross, who heartily complied with Pike's request to invite the chiefs of the Osages, Shawnees, Senecas, and Quapaws to the negotiations. Ross invited the leaders of the other tribes because he valued unanimity and cooperation. Regardless of which side he chose, he believed the Indians were stronger as a united people. Pike planned to arrive two weeks later, on the evening of the 24th, to begin the negotiations. In preparation, Ross called a meeting of the executive council to convene on the morning of September 23, the day before Pike's expected arrival.[33]

On September 19, Ross wrote to the Osage chiefs, declaring that "a dark black cloud . . . is lowering o'er our bright Southern sky, and it threatens to disturb and overwhelm the redman's peaceful Homes." He continued, "If you love your people, your Land and your Country, I beseech you not to fail to meet us around our great Council fire at Tahlequah to smoke the pipe of peace and shake the right hand of Friendship."[34] Ross asked them to arrive no later than September 25, if possible, because the negotiations needed to be wrapped up quickly so the Cherokee Nation could formally approve a possible treaty at their National Council, which was already scheduled to convene on October 7.[35] He wrote a similar letter to the chiefs of the Shawnee, Seneca, and Quapaw nations.[36]

On the same day he wrote the letter to the other tribes, Ross received the note from Opothle Yahola, written on the back of his own August 24 missive, inquiring whether or not Ross was, in fact, the author. Opothle Yahola had difficulty believing that his friend would abandon neutrality and turn to the Confederacy in such haste. "Brothers," Ross responded, "if it is your wish to know whether I had written the above note, or not—I will tell you that I did!"[37] He sent them copies of his address to the Cherokee people, dated August 21, in which he had explained his reasoning for the shift. "My advice and desire," he continued, "under the present extraordinary crisis, is, for all the red Brethren to be united among themselves in the support of our common rights and interest by forming an alliance of peace and friendship with the Confederate States of America." Ross's insistence on Indian unity had nothing to do with loyalty to the Confederate cause or, inversely, disloyalty to the United States. It was simply based on his belief that unity was in the best interest of all Indians.

The Quapaw delegation was the first to arrive in Tahlequah, on the evening of September 24. The next morning, Ross received a letter from his brother-in-law John W. Stapler informing him of the arrival of James M. Bell (coauthor of the Adair-Bell letter) and his company of Cherokees, who had been distributing information suggesting that the Cherokee Nation was divided in its support of an alliance with the Confederacy.[38] Bell was no doubt attempting to discredit Ross's leadership, hoping to prevent an alliance between the principal chief and the Confederate government. Stapler informed Ross that Watie was expected to arrive on the evening of the 25th. Bell's efforts to thwart the Ross-Pike alliance before Watie even arrived in Tahlequah further supports the argument that he and Adair were the leaders of the early Knights of the Golden Circle movement. Stapler further accused Bell of trying to incite a civil war among Cherokees supporting the Confederacy. He asked, "Does Ben McCulloch *tolerate* the above in Soldiers of *his army?*" (emphasis original).[39] He acknowledged, however, that he had overheard one of Bell's men justify the disruption by claiming that no official treaty had yet been signed by Ross and the Cherokees. There is no evidence that Watie was privy to Bell and his men's attempted disruption of the treaty negotiations. Once the treaty was finalized, Watie reportedly shook Ross's hand as a sign of unity.[40] At that moment, Ross and Watie were on the same side, both fighting for the perpetuation of Cherokee autonomy. Watie believed that that autonomy included the institution of slavery. Ross, however, would be willing to give up the institution of slavery for the continuation of Cherokee self-rule.

Ross and the Creek headman Opothle Yahola shared a similar political ideology at the outset of the war and, therefore, developed something of a kindred spirit. The fact that the principal chief of the Cherokee Nation was determined to remain neutral out of loyalty to the treaties with the United States gave Opothle Yahola a sense of legitimacy, if not a boldness to stand firm in the face of increasingly difficult circumstances. The headman's reputation in the Creek Nation caused many disaffected Indians from various tribes to gather at his farm, hoping with Opothle Yahola to escape the growing unrest. Creek chief Motey Kennard had viewed the elderly headman as a political adversary since removal. Having Ross as an ally in neutrality provided a sense of protection for Opothle Yahola and his growing band of followers. Ross's decision to lead the Cherokee Nation into an alliance with the Confederate States left thousands of neutral Indians, including those with Opothle Yahola, without any protection other than whatever unity could provide on the chief's farm. Ross's apparent defection also resulted in two unintended situations. First, it yanked Opothle Yahola out of a supporting role and thrust him unwillingly into the forefront of the neutral movement in Indian Territory. Second, the number of refugees gathering at his farm increased daily, forcing him to assume some level of responsibility for the mass of peaceful Indians. Opothle Yahola claimed to have selected the location for the farm because its seclusion would allow him and his family to "live in peace and quiet away from the scene of strife and confusion."[41] The number of peaceful people seeking to join Opothle Yahola in that solitude climbed to an estimated 6,000 to 8,000 Indians and Black people, as many slaves took the opportunity to escape and sought refuge and freedom.[42] Opothle Yahola's hope of being "at peace with all the red and white people" diminished further with each additional exile who arrived.[43]

Just like the Cherokees, the Creek Nation had also been divided over removal, and that division started to concern Kennard, who, in light of the swelling masses of people around Opothle Yahola, considered the headman a threat to the political stability of the Creek Nation.[44] On October 1, 1861, Kennard sent a letter to Ross seeking help with the growing concern. Kennard believed Ross's wisdom and influence would help persuade Opothle Yahola to abandon neutrality, as Ross had done, and to join the other Indians in a Confederate alliance. He told Ross that Opothle Yahola believed that most Cherokees were against an alliance and that the Cherokee Nation would not be joining Ross in that declaration. Kennard went so far as to blame the misconception on a Creek named Track Stimson, who allegedly helped spread the rumor of Cherokee disunity. He asked Ross to consider sending "wise delegates" to meet with Opothle Yahola and "give them a true statement of the condition of your people." The Creek leader warned that if no remedy could be found, "it will and must end in civil war."[45] Two days later, Kennard sent another letter to Ross, this one urging the Cherokee chief to intervene and stop a rumored attack by Opothle Yahola and his followers on the Creek regiment "in five days."[46] Ross responded immediately with plans to dispatch a delegation to Opothle Yahola to invite him to attend the National Council of the Cherokee people scheduled to take place three days later, on October 7. "In the meantime," he wrote to Kennard, "let me ask you and your friends to exercise prudence and forbearance and to avoid any collision unless it be forced upon you."[47] Ross believed strongly in the need for unity among the people of Indian Territory. He recognized the impatience in Albert Pike's letter of August 1 and did not wish for Opothle Yahola and his followers to fall prey to the Confederate commissioner's ultimatum.

While Ross concerned himself with the tension in the Creek Nation, Pike negotiated treaties of alliance with the Osages (October 2), the Quapaws (October 4), and the Senecas and Shawnees (October 4).[48] The Cherokee-Confederate treaty, signed on October 7, did more than simply replace the tribe's treaties with the United States; it offered the Indians a path to eventual statehood, should they choose it—and should the Confederate States grant it.[49] The next day, October 8, Ross sent his assistant chief, Joseph Vann, as the head of a delegation to visit Opothle Yahola and express to him once again the importance of communication and cooperation among the tribes of Indian Territory.[50] Even though the treaty negotiations were over, Vann had orders to invite Opothle Yahola to Tahlequah under promise of safe passage from Pike. Ross hoped the Creek headman could arrive in time to meet with Pike and Kennard and learn firsthand the truth about the Cherokee and Creek alliances.[51]

On October 11, three days after Vann's departure, Ross received a note from Opothle Yahola expressing his concern about rumors of Texas troops crossing the Red River headed into Indian Territory. Ross's reply reveals his frustration. "It makes my heart sad," he wrote, "to find the whole Country filled with false alarms." He proceeded to tell Opothle Yahola that the five regiments of Texas soldiers that crossed the Arkansas River near Fort Gibson were headed to Missouri when they heard rumors that the Creek headman and his crowd of followers were planning to attack Motey Kennard's Creek regiment, the rumor mentioned in Kennard's letter to Ross on October 3. When the force realized the rumors were false, they continued their journey to Missouri.[52] Ross took the opportunity to express his hopes that Opothle Yahola would receive Vann and the Cherokee delegation as soon as they arrived and would return to Tahlequah with them.[53] But Opothle Yahola was still distrustful of Kennard and the Creek government and refused to risk the journey. After failing to convince the headman to attend the meeting, Vann returned by way of the Creek Nation, where he met with Kennard and shared Opothle Yahola's refusal to entertain Confederate overtures, even if they were delivered by his friend John Ross. Opothle Yahola remained loyal to the treaties with the United States.

Kennard wrote to Ross thanking him for his efforts to bring peace to the Creek Nation. The Creeks learned that Opothle Yahola had written to President Lincoln asking him to return Federal troops to Indian Territory.[54] When they learned that the headman had rejected Ross's invitation, the Creek leadership expressed grave concern. "If they get aid from the North," Kennard wrote to Ross, "they will be our most formidable enemy." He declared that it has become "necessary for them to be put down at any cost." He continued, "Therefore so soon as we are reinforced . . . we shall proceed without further delay and put an end to the affair."[55] Ross was indignant. "Brothers," he retorted, "we are shocked with amazement at the fearful import of your words! Are we to understand that you have determined to make a Military demonstration, by force of Arms, upon Opothle Yahola and his followers, at the cost of civil war among your own People?"[56] Ross's dream of a united Indian Territory was unraveling. He urged Kennard to have patience, claiming that the cost of such an attack on Opothle Yahola and his followers "would be lamentable."[57] He sought to placate Kennard and the Creek leadership by expressing his faith in common sense. "We have no good reasons," he argued, "to consider the Mission of the Asst. Chief and his associates to Opothle Yahola as a hopeless failure."[58] Hoping to avoid any undue confrontation, Ross sent the letter to Drew at Fort Gibson, asking him to deliver it to Kennard. He wanted his forces to be aware of the situation in case there was a movement against the peaceful Indians. He also asked Drew to show the letter to Colonel Douglas H. Cooper, who was in command of Pike's forces while the commissioner was in Richmond seeking the ratification of the newly signed treaties. "I most sincerely regret," he wrote to Drew, "the state of confusion and excitement growing out of the Creek affair, which might have been amicably adjusted, without all the trouble it has created if a prudent and wise course had been pursued by the Creek authorities."[59] Ross feared that if the Creek Nation did not unite in cooperation with the other tribes, Cherokee forces would be left alone to defend the northern border of Indian Territory from invasion. Ross hoped to secure Opothle Yahola's alliance and turn his attention away from the Creek situation and focus the nation's resources on protecting its own territory.[60]

Ross's attempt to mollify Kennard had little effect. By the end of October, the Creeks grew weary of waiting. Kennard wrote to Colonel Cooper, informing him that the Creek general council had decided to go ahead with the attack on Opothle Yahola on Friday, November 8, "to put down if possible the hostile movements" of Opothle Yahola and his "Party."[61] Kennard further advised Cooper of the tribe's intentions to capture any free Blacks who might be among Opothle Yahola's followers and to sell them for the benefit of the Creek Nation. Cooper's response reveals his interpretation of the political situation. He told Kennard that he would not be prepared to move by the date suggested, as he hoped for reinforcements from Texas or Arkansas. Moreover, he informed the Creeks that he was not willing to call any engagement with Opothle Yahola a tribal war. He argued that because the forces involved were being paid by the Confederate government, "all captured property or property of person found in arms against the Confederate States and confiscated in consequence thereof, will be deemed and held as the property of said states."[62] Cooper's view of the situation was blinded by the North-South binary, while Kennard simply saw it as a matter of Creek politics. In reality, neither was correct. It was a matter of Indian sovereignty and failed U.S. Indian policy. Opothle Yahola sought the protection of the U.S. government as a requirement of the tribe's treaties. He took no side at all. Kennard and Cooper could not see that. They were both blinded by their own perspectives.

To understand the story of Opothle Yahola, his followers, and the tragedy that befell them, we must lay aside our narratives of the Civil War and view the events from the perspective of John Ross. Ross's initial stand of neutrality attracted Opothle Yahola and secured a line of communication between the two men. By allowing their correspondence to drive the narrative, a much different story develops than the one presented in modern scholarship.[63] Without Ross's perspective, we see the events only through the eyes of Kennard, who was blinded by fear, and the Confederates, who were blinded by the North-South binary. Cooper instigated an attack on Opothle Yahola to force the group to comply with the Creek-Confederate alliance. The only other alternative in his mind was to drive them out of Indian Territory toward their Union allies in Kansas.[64] Opothle Yahola wanted neither. His aim was to remain loyal to the treaties with the United States and await the return of Federal troops. Sadly, neither Kennard nor Cooper were willing to allow that. They believed that Opothle Yahola and his following represented a growing military opposition to the Creek-Confederate alliance, and the quicker that resistance could be put down, the safer they would be.[65]

By Monday, November 11, 1861, the waiting game ended. Cooper's Confederate Indians were reinforced by Lieutenant Colonel William Quayle and a detachment of the 4th Texas Cavalry that left North Texas on October 29 en route to northwestern Arkansas.[66] Ordered to assist Cooper against Opothle Yahola, the regiment promptly departed, moving rapidly in complete silence toward Cooper's camp, motivated by fear of a proximal enemy. The men arrived in camp on the North Fork of the Canadian River about midnight and found themselves surrounded by what appeared to be painted Confederate Indians who entertained their guests with a rousing war dance.[67]

After allowing the Texans a couple of days to rest, the regiment prepared to attack Opothle Yahola's neutral Indians. Drew's regiment of Cherokees received orders to proceed to Coodey's Bluff on the west side of the Verdigris River, about forty miles east-northeast of present Tulsa, and to await further orders. Drew marched out of Fort Gibson on Thursday, November 14, with five hundred Cherokees, leaving the remainder under the command of Ross's nephew Lieutenant Colonel William P. Ross. William wrote a letter to his uncle informing him of the movement of Drew's forces. Believing that the approach of winter made an engagement with Union forces unlikely, William hypothesized that the movement was against Opothle Yahola.[68] The chief responded with exasperation: "The steps taken by me for restoring confidence and reconciliation among the Creeks, in all probability may be defeated by the counteracting course since pursued by the chiefs and military authorities of the Creek nation!" Ross opposed placing Cherokee troops in the middle of an internal Creek affair.

> If we cannot exercise a salutary influence as mediators between the opposing parties—we should by all means avoid taking part in any measure calculated to widen the breach and bring about a conflict between them—let us therefore look closely to our Treaty and to do our duty that nothing short of open rebellion or resistance to the Govt. of the Confederate States or, the invasion of our Territory by any of our red allies, should ever induce us to apply the forces of arms against them![69]

Ross was angered, and saddened, by the idea of using Cherokee troops to attack Opothle Yahola and his neutral Indians, but he was quick to reassure his nephew that his disappointment was not aimed at Drew or the regiment. He expressed frustration over the idea of another white government, this one the Confederacy, getting in the way, causing his efforts to fail, as had happened to Cherokee efforts at "mediation between the U.S. Govt. and the Seminoles in Florida [in 1837]."[70]

The next morning, November 15, Cooper's forces crossed the river and headed toward Opothle Yahola's camp. The force consisted of six companies of Pike's 1st Choctaw and Chickasaw Mounted Rifles, D. N. McIntosh's Creek regiment, Chilly McIntosh's Creek and Seminole battalion, John Jumper's Seminoles, and a detachment of Sims's 4th Texas Cavalry under the command of Lieutenant Colonel Quayle.[71] The entire Confederate command numbered about 1,400.[72]

As soon as Opothle Yahola's scouts detected the approaching force, the entire group of women, children, and aged Indians fled toward the Cherokee Nation with Opothle Yahola leading the caravan. The able-bodied men of the group provided a screen of protection in the front and rear of the retreating column.[73] The Indians set fire to the dried grass around them, burning everything in sight and creating a screen of smoke to veil their escape. When the attacking Confederates entered Opothle Yahola's camp on the 18th, they found it had been so hurriedly abandoned that campfires were still burning.[74]

On that very day, November 18, while fleeing the approaching Confederates, Opothle Yahola sent an important message to Ross.[75] While historians argue that the retreat was a tactic to lure the Confederates into a trap, or that the movement was a premeditated attempt to flee into Kansas where the Indians could find solace among their allies in the North, the message reveals Opothle Yahola's true desire.[76] The message was delivered to James McDaniel, a captain in Drew's regiment at Coodey's Bluff, who immediately sent two men to Fort

Gibson with it. The men, Captain Porum Davis and Lieutenant Crab Grass (Cabbin) Smith, delivered the message to Ross's brother Lewis, who carried it to the chief.[77] The message was simply a cry for help. With Cooper bearing down on him, Opothle Yahola abandoned his camp and headed for safety, declaring his desire to accept Ross's invitation to discuss peace among the Creek people while obtaining sanctuary in the Cherokee Nation.[78] On November 20, Ross replied, "I am happy to hear this." He ordered McDaniel, Davis, and Smith to find Opothle Yahola and escort him safely into the Cherokee Nation "where I will meet him in view of holding a meeting with the proper authorities for an amicable adjustment to his difficulties."[79]

The timing and logistical difficulties of delivering the messages between Ross and Opothle Yahola were more than the Indians could overcome. Neither message reached its target in time to prevent one of the most unfortunate events of the Civil War west of the Mississippi River. The next day, November 19, one day before Ross received the plea for help, Cooper's forces located Opothle Yahola's new camp and attacked them at Round Mountain, while Drew's regiment waited at Coodey's Bluff nearly eighty miles away. Throughout the afternoon hours of November 19, the Confederates positioned themselves for what they expected to be a strong counterattack by Opothle Yahola's forces. However, once engaged, the skirmish lasted only fifteen minutes before the neutral Indians abandoned the field and retreated toward the Cherokee Nation, seeking refuge in the cliffs along Bird Creek. The retreat was not north to Kansas, as much of the historiography would have readers believe, but rather east-northeast, toward Drew's regiment in the Cherokee Nation.[80] Even Cooper realized that Opothle Yahola's flight took him in the direction of the Cherokee Nation where Cooper believed he had "taken refuge . . . by invitation of a leading disaffected Cherokee" (Ross).[81]

Puzzlingly, the event has been widely portrayed as the first "battle" of the Civil War in Indian Territory. It can hardly be such, given that it was not an engagement between two military forces. As many as three-fourths of Opothle Yahola's followers were women, children, and elderly people. Moreover, the group traveled with wagons, carts, buggies, oxen, sheep, cattle, and crated chickens—hardly the composition of a military force.[82] Besides, Opothle Yahola had no intention of using his warriors as a military force. His primary aim was to use them to protect the children, women, and the aged, and when that task was complete, they simply disengaged and left.[83] This does not sound like a fighting force. History has remembered the attack as part of the larger Civil War narrative and, in doing so, has shrouded one of the darkest days in Oklahoma history.

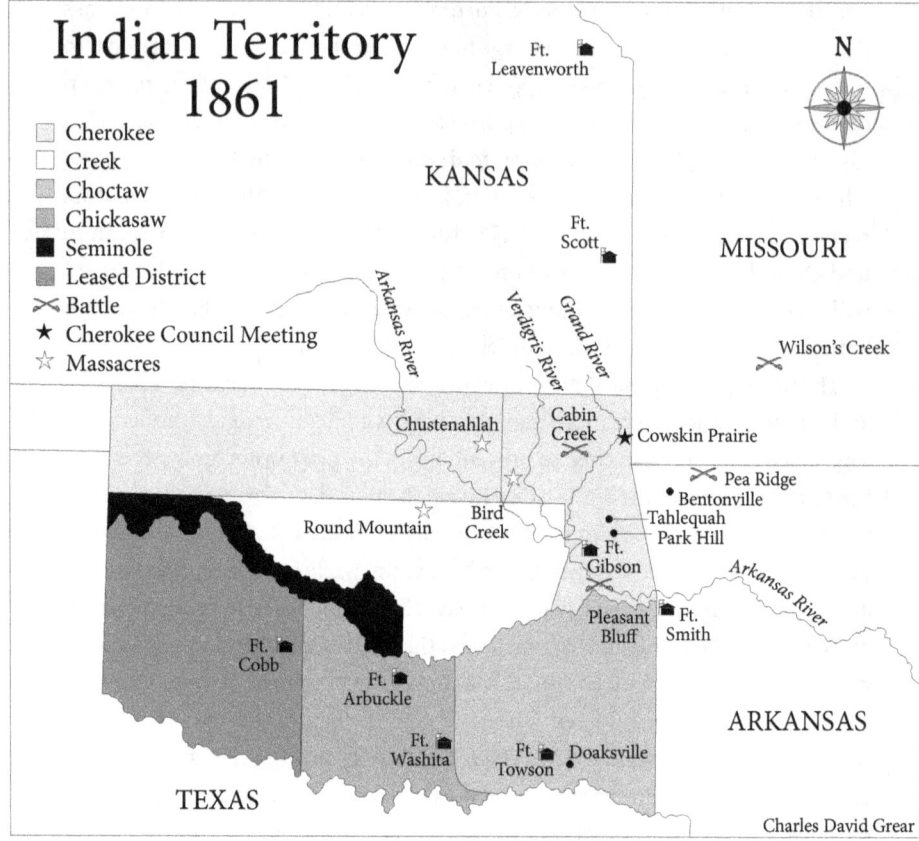

While Opothle Yahola and his followers were seeking refuge on Bird Creek in the Cherokee Nation, Cooper received intelligence that Union general John C. Frémont was preparing to invade northwestern Arkansas with about 20,000 men. McCulloch, gathering forces for a defense, ordered Cooper out of Indian Territory to Maysville on the Arkansas border.[84] Cooper quickly returned to his trains on the south bank of the Arkansas River at Concharty—or Concharta, as reported by Cooper—near present Bixby arriving on November 24.[85] While there, he received a second communiqué from McCulloch informing him that the feared Union advance had not materialized and that he should return his attention to the Creeks. Cooper gladly did just that. The fact that Opothle Yahola had entered the Cherokee Nation concerned him.[86]

After allowing his men and animals to rest and eat, Cooper ordered his force, consisting of 780 Indians, to Tulsey Town (present Tulsa) on November 29. At the same time, he ordered Colonel Sims and all available men of the 4th Texas Cavalry, then en route to Missouri, to return and join Drew's detachment at Coodey's Bluff. On arriving at Tulsey Town, Cooper received information that Opothle Yahola was preparing an attack with more than 2,000 of his Indians. Cooper quickly ordered Drew to march south and meet him. He ordered Sims to join them in the vicinity. Somehow, Drew misinterpreted the order and, instead of marching south, marched with 480 men to the southwest, directly toward Opothle Yahola's camp, stopping about six miles away on December 7. When Cooper arrived the next day, his first encounter with Drew's regiment, he learned of the message Opothle Yahola had sent two weeks earlier asking for peace. Cooper ordered Drew to send a messenger to the headman to inform him that the Confederates did not wish to shed any more blood, either, and that Opothle Yahola should meet with him the next day. Drew dispatched Major Thomas Pegg at the head of a delegation to deliver the message.[87]

When Pegg and the others arrived to deliver Cooper's message, they were refused permission to speak with Opothle Yahola. Instead, the warriors had painted themselves for war and were preparing their defenses for an attack.[88] If Opothle Yahola desired peace as vehemently as it appeared in the hastily written note, why did he not welcome this opportunity to have it? He had written the note two weeks prior and, by the time it reached Ross, had given up on the prospects of help arriving. Moreover, with Cooper's Confederate force bearing down on him, he had no choice but to prepare for battle. Captain McDaniel's decision to send the note to Fort Gibson, and the subsequent decision to send it on to Ross near Tahlequah, created too lengthy a delay. Opothle Yahola had cried out for help that did not come in time.

The next day, December 9, Cooper went on the offensive at Bird Creek, attacking Opothle Yahola and his band of neutral Indians.[89] Opothle Yahola hid himself among the bluffs surrounding Bird Creek, hoping to receive word from Ross that danger was averted. After four hours of heavy fighting, the neutral Indians retreated deeper into the hills along with their noncombatants. Based on reports, Cooper claimed to have killed 500 of the neutral Indians while only losing a handful of his own men.[90] Opothle Yahola's beleaguered followers retreated, unsure when the next attack would come. They were running out of ammunition, and the freezing temperatures began to take their toll on the women and children. The group had left most of their belongings behind as they fled the initial attack at Round Mountain. Their leader led them to the northeast, toward the Cherokee Nation, hoping to contact Ross and put an end to the nightmare that had befallen them. However, circumstances prevented Ross from responding to Opothle Yahola's cry for peace before belligerents arrived and attacked the neutral Indians again. Douglas Cooper was unable—or unwilling—to see the event as anything less than a battle between opposing forces aligned along the North-South binary, and the peaceful Indians with Opothle Yahola were expected to answer for Cooper's nearsightedness.

Not all Confederate-aligned forces, however, missed the reality of the situation on Bird Creek. The Cherokee regiment under John Drew knew of Opothle Yahola's attempt to seek peace in the Cherokee Nation, and before Cooper could initiate his attack on December 9, about 420 of the 480 men of Drew's 1st Cherokee Mounted Rifle regiment deserted their command. Of the 420 deserters, however, an estimated 300 crossed into Opothle Yahola's camp to join the neutral Indians and fight against the Confederate Indians.[91] Many of Drew's Cherokees, mostly members of the Keetoowah Society, sympathized with Opothle Yahola's followers after the call for peace failed to halt the aggression, and they switched sides to help defend them from an unnecessary attack. It is important to remember that Keetoowah loyalty lay with Ross and the tribe's treaties, not with the Confederate or the U.S. governments. Historians have had difficulty explaining the desertions.[92] However, Drew's men seemed to find nothing confusing about it. Following the attack, many of them simply returned to Drew's camp as if they had done nothing wrong.[93]

In the aftermath of the attack, William P. Ross and the remainder of Drew's regiment, which had marched out of Fort Gibson earlier to join its commander on Bird Creek, encountered some stragglers from Captain Pickens M. Benge's company, who told him of the attack and the mass desertions. William penned a hasty note to his uncle, informing him of the "rupture" of the regiment.[94] Initially, William learned that a number of high-ranking Cherokee officers had been "captured" by Opothle Yahola's forces about the same time that numerous Cherokees had switched sides. No doubt the officers had simply joined their men in the desertion. On hearing the news, Ross was both surprised and relieved: surprised to hear of the violence of the attack, and relieved to learn that many Cherokees had refused to participate in it. Despite the fact that the Cherokees were now under scrutiny by Confederate leaders, Ross refused to punish any of the men involved.[95] He had not aligned the tribe with the Confederacy to protect it from neutral Indians. He had joined the Confederacy to protect the Cherokee people from the Civil War.

Perhaps the greatest impact of the desertions and defections was the fact that the Confederate government came to view Drew's regiment as a useless fighting force. Moreover, Ross would now have to demonstrate his loyalty to the Confederates once again. It is unclear how much Drew empathized with the deserters. His correspondence with Cooper and Ross in the days following the desertions was understandably guarded. However, Cooper doubted Drew's sincerity. Although he acknowledged that Drew "suppressed" any visible signs of sympathy toward the deserters, he refused to trust the Cherokee leadership further. On December 10, the day after the attack, Cooper placed the Cherokee regiment under his own command and ordered them to Fort Gibson. His goal was to separate the Cherokees from Opothle Yahola and his followers as soon as possible in order to prevent any further cooperation. Moreover, he demanded a face-to-face meeting with Ross and Drew at Fort Gibson to address the issue of loyalty to the Confederacy within the Cherokee Nation. On the evening of December 20, Cooper crossed the Grand River and headed to the fort to confront the Cherokee leaders.[96]

Due to the disintegration of Drew's regiment, Confederate commanders sent Colonel James McIntosh, Benjamin McCulloch's cavalry commander, and about 1,400 Texans and Arkansans to Fort Gibson to help Cooper finish the attack. Uncertainty over whether Drew's men had permanently joined forces with Opothle Yahola led to the decision to renew the attack immediately. McIntosh arrived at Fort Gibson on the evening of December 20 and planned to resume marching in the early morning hours of the 22nd. Cooper was to proceed up the Arkansas River as soon as his ammunition arrived from Fort Smith to position his forces to the west of Opothle Yahola. McIntosh was to travel up the Verdigris River, placing the peaceful Indians between the two Confederate forces. McIntosh rode out on the morning of the 22nd, as planned. However, Cooper's ammunition was not expected to arrive until the next evening. Moreover, the lack of forage in the field discouraged the Confederates from delaying the attack, so Cooper ordered Watie and his men to join McIntosh by the 25th in his stead. When McIntosh discovered Opothle Yahola's guards before Watie's arrival, he decided to proceed with the attack without any support.[97]

Opothle Yahola's guards comprised mostly Seminole warriors, who occupied a rocky, tree-lined ridge beyond Shoal Creek, a tributary of the Verdigris. At the top of the ridge, commanding the right of the crossing, was the main body of Opothle Yahola's mounted defenders, about 1,700 men in all. The force acted as protection for the main body of peaceful Indians, including women and children, encamped in the hills beyond the ridge. McIntosh lined his forces for battle as if confronting Union troops.[98] Many if not most historians have viewed the events that followed from the perspective of the Confederate commanders who reported their activities to their superiors in the following days, a perspective that has dominated our memory of the events.[99]

After dislodging Opothle Yahola's guards from the tree-lined hillside, McIntosh sent the 11th Texas Cavalry to cut off the protectors from the main body, separating them from the women and children in camp.[100] In the following melee, McIntosh ordered the 6th Texas Cavalry to pursue those trying to escape. The Texans charged into camp, where they proceeded to ride up and down for as many as three hours, destroying everything and chasing everyone in sight. When the dust settled, McIntosh reported as many as 230 killed and 160 women and children taken captive in the name of the Confederate States. Moreover, the group captured thirty wagons, seventy yoke of oxen, five hundred horses, nearly two hundred sheep, hundreds of cattle, and all the personal property that the fleeing Indians were unable to carry away. In his report, McIntosh bragged that "the strong hold of Hopoeithleyohola [sic] was completely broken up and his force scattered in every direction destitute of the simplest elements of subsistence."[101] Even if the Confederates misjudged the intentions of the neutral Indians, received erroneous reports, or were simply blinded by the North-South binary, the attack on Opothle Yahola and his followers at Shoal Creek on December 26, 1861, was not a Civil War battle. It was nothing short of a massacre of peaceful Indians.

The next day, December 27, McIntosh ordered Watie and his small force to pursue the fleeing Indians and clean up any stragglers. Watie rode more than twenty miles, all the while harassing Opothle Yahola's beleaguered followers and capturing an additional 75 prisoners, along with 250 horses and more than eight hundred additional head of cattle. Watie admitted to killing another dozen peaceful Indians.[102] While Opothle Yahola and his starving and frostbitten followers eventually staggered into southern Kansas with various Confederate soldiers nipping at their heals, Watie, enraged that the Cherokee regiment had acted so poorly and that the chief acted so leniently in his punishment of what he perceived as treasonous Indians, initiated a reign of terror north of the Arkansas River. Over the next few months, he would be applauded by Southerners for his ruthless attacks on non-Confederate whites in southeastern Kansas, southwestern

Missouri, and northwestern Arkansas, as well as on non-Confederate Cherokees in the Cherokee Nation.[103] During the Civil War, Watie's brutal attacks created hardship for his numerous victims. Sadly, many of his victims were members of his own tribe, and for most of them, their only crime was loyal support of their elected chief and tribal government.

CHAPTER 4

ABRAHAM LINCOLN AND THE INDIAN EXPEDITION

The early morning calm was shattered by a distant shout, and soon an excited buzz swept through the camp. Many of the soldiers jumped to their feet while others emerged sleepily from their tents to survey the scene. Word spread quickly of the approaching wagons, causing a few of the men to mount their horses and ride into the woods. Officers barked orders to groups of men as the rest of camp sprang to life. The wagon train was still more than a mile away as soldiers hurriedly prepared to meet its advance. At about 10:00 on the humid spring morning, the head of the train came into view, causing other soldiers to rush out and greet it. Shouts echoed as the soldiers welcomed its occupants, many of whom were openly crying.

The wagon train had reached the object of a ten-day journey from Missouri into Indian Territory, and many of the soldiers in camp were glad to see it. The soldiers were members of the Federal Indian Brigade who had entered the Cherokee Nation from Arkansas a few days earlier. Now camped near the Cherokee capital of Park Hill, the soldiers had been awaiting the train's arrival. In the train were about a thousand families of refugee Indians, many of whom had been driven from their homes the previous summer with the final collapse of the Cherokee-Confederate alliance. The refugee families were returning to their homes in Indian Territory under the protection of Colonel William A. Phillips and the forces of the Indian Brigade. The soldiers, many of them Indians themselves, were sent to protect the returning refugee families as they tried to reestablish their homes. The arrival of the caravan was a day of great joy for many of the soldiers because their own families were among the returning refugees. Some of the soldiers, upon learning of the train's approach, did not wait for the train to enter camp. Instead, they mounted their horses and rode out to greet it, riding triumphantly back into camp with their loved ones. The reunions that took place that beautiful spring morning marked the first time many of the soldiers had seen their families in over a year.

White Union soldiers watched the reunions with great interest, describing the scenes in which fathers hugged their wives and children as "manifestations of joy."[1] The refugees had spent the previous winter in camps in Kansas and Missouri, often in horrible conditions. Their return to their homes after such an extended absence prompted one observer to suggest that the event should occupy a special place in the memory of the Cherokee Nation. It "will surely be an event in their history," he wrote, "that should not be passed over without mention."[2] Despite these prophetic urgings, history has done just that—passed over the event without mention. The return of Federal forces to Indian Territory and the repatriation of the refugee families represents one of the most important events to occur during the Civil War years in Indian Territory, and should be memorialized.

The ink on the Cherokee-Confederate treaty had hardly dried before the alliance began to crumble. The desertions and defections from John Drew's regiment forced Ross to have to prove his loyalty to Douglas H. Cooper, and over the next few weeks, that loyalty would be tested by Watie's wanton attacks on non-Confederate Cherokee citizens. Watie and his force of no more than 300 mixed-bloods and whites began a campaign to punish tribal members for their refusal to commit to the Southern cause, even before the disintegration of Drew's regiment in early December.[3] By the first week of January 1862, Ross had written to Cooper for a second time, asking for protection for Cherokee citizens from "the reckless proceedings" of Watie and his men.[4] Watie's vicious attempts to compel unanimity among the common Cherokees was more than Ross could take. He even appealed to Colonel James McIntosh for help.[5] Moreover, Watie's rising favor with Confederate leaders, coupled with the duplicitous actions of Drew's regiment at Bird Creek, placed the reputation of Ross and the Cherokee government on shaky ground. However, before the first quarter of 1862 ended, the Lincoln administration would initiate plans to return to Indian Territory and reestablish itself as the protector of the loyal tribes. For Ross, the challenge would become more difficult. He would now have to prove his loyalty to two white governments at the same time.

On February 25, 1862, as Drew's regiment marched to Fayetteville, Arkansas, to meet an expected Union advance out of Missouri, Ross wrote to Albert Pike, who commanded all Confederate forces in Indian Territory, and explained why he would not be accompanying his regiment. Ross could not afford to appear to waver on his commitment to the Confederacy. The desertions had damaged the reputation of the Cherokee leadership, and now Ross needed to repair it, especially with Watie and his men roaming the hills of the Cherokee Nation looking for any signs of disloyalty. However, the activities of Watie's men caused Ross's advisors to insist that he remain at Tahlequah for protection.[6] Ross had informed General McCulloch in June 1861 that he would, even at the advanced age of seventy, assist in the defense of any foreign invasion of Cherokee soil.[7] However, the dangers posed by Watie and his men rendered that impractical.

As Ross returned to Tahlequah, Drew and his regiment marched to Arkansas to take part in the most significant battle west of the Mississippi during the early months of the Civil War, a battle that would take place in Benton County at a place called Pea Vine Ridge, or simply, Pea Ridge. Confederate president Jefferson Davis placed General Earl Van Dorn in command of all forces in the Trans-Mississippi theater, and Van Dorn quickly went to work to reinstate Confederate control over the state of Missouri. He combined McCulloch's Arkansas troops with the Missouri forces of General Sterling Price and added the Indians from Indian Territory under newly commissioned Brigadier General Albert Pike.

Pike's brigade, consisted of Drew's and Watie's Cherokees, as well as a squadron of North Texans under the command of Captain Otis G. Welch, which had occupied Fort Arbuckle immediately following the Federal abandonment. On March 3, the force received orders to proceed toward Fayetteville and to report to newly promoted brigadier general James McIntosh near Elm Springs, Arkansas.[8] When Van Dorn learned that Union general Samuel R. Curtis was still more than fifty miles north of Fort Smith awaiting reinforcements, the decision was made to advance the next morning, hoping to catch the Federals before that support arrived. Pike left Indian Territory without the Choctaws, Chickasaws, or Creeks of his regiment, as they refused to fight the Federals in Arkansas. He overtook Watie's Cherokees at the Arkansas state line on Tuesday, March 4. The next day he overtook Drew and his men about midday.

Because the Cherokees had more at stake with the Union troops already occupying portions of northwest Arkansas, they were willing to leave Indian Territory to help drive the Federals from the immediate Cherokee border. The Indians rested near McCulloch's divisional camp at Elm Springs, about thirty miles across the Arkansas border, in the early evening of March 6, with plans to march again at midnight. In the early morning hours of Friday, March 7, 1862, McCulloch's force headed north toward Bentonville. As was typical, the infantry, commanded by Colonel Louis Hebert, took the head of the line, followed by McIntosh and the cavalry, including Pike's Indians. The Confederates marched to Bentonville, turned east, and took the Bentonville Detour around the north side of Pea Vine Ridge to join forces with General Sterling Price and his Missouri troops between Curtis and the Missouri state line.[9] The Indians, led by Drew and Watie, crossed the Little Sugar Creek bridge west of Pea Ridge at dawn, following closely on the heels of McIntosh's Arkansans.

Just before reaching the ridge, McCulloch ordered a detour through the woods on the south side of the road, towards Leetown, where the Federals were entrenched about four-and-half miles away. Pike's Cherokees followed closely behind Colonel William B. Sims and the 6th Texas Cavalry who were bringing up the rear of the Confederate column. Meanwhile, Price and his Missouri troops marched toward Elkhorn Tavern from the eastern edge of Pea Ridge, hoping to attack Curtis around both ends of the rock formation.

About a mile into the woods, Pike discovered a Federal battery consisting of three guns in a clearing about a quarter mile right of the road and protected by a force of Iowa and Missouri cavalry. Pike formed his force into a battle line behind a fence in the edge of the woods, ordering Sims's regiment into position on the right of his line with Welch's squadron of North Texans in the center. Watie and Drew, respectively, formed the Confederate left. The Federal guns were trained on the head of McCulloch's line as they crossed a field near the base of Pea Ridge. When the Federals detected Pike's forces gathering within the tree line to their left, they immediately opened fire with small guns, hoping to protect the artillery. The volley sent the Cherokees into an impassioned charge through the fence and into the clearing toward the guns. Their loud war whoop drove the Federals into a panic, allowing the two Cherokee regiments to drive them easily from the field, capturing the guns.

Union reports of the attack make no mention of the fact that Indians were involved, nor do they mention the "war whoop." Moreover, Federal officers described a running fight between Confederate and Union cavalry forces that resulted in significant loss for Pike's forces.[10] Pike's efforts to reorganize his troops proved futile as the Cherokees celebrated their victory. Soon, however, Watie's men detected a second Federal battery hidden in the opposite tree line across the road. Before Pike could order the captured guns to be turned on the second battery, the Federals fired two shells into the clearing among the Indians, sending Drew's regiment retreating back into the woods from whence they came. The guns kept the Indians pinned among the trees for two-and-a-half hours while McCulloch advanced toward Leetown without his cavalry. Pike found consolation in the fact that the artillery, at least, was not being used against the main force.[11]

While Pike struggled to regain control of his Cherokees, McCulloch's artillery opened fire on the Federal breastworks at Leetown from the base of the Pea Ridge. Leaving Drew's Indians hiding in the woods, Pike, with Watie and the Texans, returned to the road and proceeded in the direction of the artillery fire. Shortly thereafter, Drew's regiment left the safety of the tree line and took a position in the rear of Pike's cavalry. At that moment, Union colonel Nicholas Greusel of the 36th Illinois Infantry arrived on the scene from the direction of Leetown and formed his troops across the road on the edge of a clearing, cutting off Pike's advance. Greusel had learned of the attack on the Federal artillery and marched out in support of members of the 3rd Iowa Cavalry who had rushed past Greusel's men in a wild retreat following the loss of artillery at the hands of the Cherokees. Some of the Iowans reportedly adjured the infantrymen to "Turn back! Turn back! They'll give you hell!"[12] Greusel's force consisted of about 1,600 men from Illinois, Missouri, and Indiana, and positioned themselves behind a rail fence on the southern edge of a farm, supported by a small battery positioned just inside the fence line.[13]

As the Federal force waited for an appearance by the enemy, the men grew increasingly uneasy. When rebel scouts were spotted on the crest of a small mountain, Greusel redirected his artillery and fired. The exploding shells once again sent Drew's Cherokees scurrying for the safety of the woods.[14] Pike soon learned that McCulloch and McIntosh had both been killed, and Hebert was missing and presumed dead.[15] Moreover, Greusel's forces presented a new problem. Pike sent Welch's squadron and Watie's Indians beyond a fence to the left of the road, at the base of a small ridge, and sent orders for Drew's regiment to reassemble. Drew never responded to the order. Instead, after remaining in the woods for a while, he led his men back to the Bentonville Detour and headed back toward Elm Springs. Drew's refusal to obey the order reveals more about the unit's loyalties than previously imagined. As indicated by his final report of the battle, Pike believed that the orders must not have reached Drew, or he would have responded[16]

The significance of Drew's withdrawal has been shrouded by a series of allegations that arose against the Cherokees in the days immediately following the battle. According to Union reports, at least eight Union soldiers were scalped after falling on the field, and others had been stabbed in the throat.[17] According to Union officers, the bedlam of the initial attack against the Federal battery grew worse when the Cherokees celebrated their victory by murdering and mutilating Federal soldiers.[18] Upon learning of the allegations, Van Dorn sent Curtis a letter, expressing outrage and condemning the murders. However, he took the opportunity to accuse Federal soldiers of German descent of murdering Confederates who had surrendered their arms.[19] Pike defended his Indian soldiers further, handing some of the blame to McCulloch, who he believed understood "their mode of fighting," yet opted to use them in battle anyway.[20]

While historians have focused on the allegations, Drew's withdrawal from the field has escaped thorough examination. At the conclusion of the war, when federal commissioners were in Fort Smith, Arkansas, in September 1865, addressing the Indian-Confederate alliances, H. D. Reese of the Cherokee delegation made an incredible admission. Reese, reading from a printed statement, claimed that the Cherokee Nation entered the war looking for the first opportunity to "return to what we claimed to be our true allegiance," he read, "return to the waving of the stars and stripes." He admitted that their first attempt to return, made when most of Drew's regiment defected prior to Cooper's attack at Bird Creek, was not very well conceived and ultimately failed. He added that the second opportunity to return, at Pea Ridge, never fully materialized.[21] He provided no details for either claim.

At least three contemporary sources seem to corroborate the story. One claimed the Cherokees shot at anyone, even if they were Confederates, while another claimed they intentionally planned, prior to the engagement, to shoot only Confederates.[22] Five months later, a Union general in Indian Territory, claimed that about 150 men of Drew's regiment had been at Pea Ridge and had killed white rebel soldiers in a premeditated attack.[23] There is no evidence in the official reports of the engagement that support such claims. Whether true or not, Drew most likely hid out in the woods ignoring Pike's order to advance, hoping the Federals would arrive so he could join them.

Unbeknownst to the Cherokee Nation at the time, the Union victory at Pea Ridge opened the door for the United States to take steps to regain control of Indian Territory and, in turn, restore the loyal tribes to their prewar treaty status. The planned return of Federal troops to the Cherokee Nation would provide Ross with the opportunity to renounce the tribe's alliance with the Confederate States and renew his claim of allegiance to the tribe's treaties with the United States. The only question was whether the federal government would welcome the Cherokees as one of those loyal tribes. Had the tribe done enough to demonstrate its loyalty to their federal treaties prior to the alliance with the Confederacy? Had Ross's followers acted in such a way following the Confederate alliance as to convince the federal government of their reluctance to enter the treasonous relationship in the first place? Ross and the Cherokees could only hope that the federal government was willing to overlook their Confederate alliance and include them among the list of Indians who remained loyal, or at least attempted to.

In November 1861, U.S. Secretary of the Interior Caleb Blood Smith, who replaced Jacob Thompson following his resignation, sent his annual report to President Abraham Lincoln which included a section on the unrest in Indian Territory. Lincoln, who was inaugurated as the sixteenth president two weeks after Jefferson Davis was inaugurated as the president of the new Southern Confederacy, took office at the height of the secession crisis and had little time to discuss a detailed Indian policy. It appeared that he preferred to allow the existing policy to work as it was designed by honoring the nation's treaty responsibilities to the various tribes. Although he would take a hands-on approach to Indian matters when they presented themselves, he sought the advice and counsel of those within his administration who had their fingers on the pulse of the nation's Indian relations. One of those advisors, Secretary Smith, delivered an acerbic indictment that placed the blame for the unrest in Indian Territory squarely on the shoulders of the United States. "The hostile attitude assumed by portions of the tribes referred to, has resulted from . . . the withdrawal from their vicinity of the troops of the United States, whose presence would have afforded a guarantee of protection." And as if that statement was not piercing enough, he offered Lincoln an apparent solution. "It is unfortunate," he continued, "that the War Department has been unable to send to that region such a body of troops as would be adequate to the protection of those tribes, and revive their confidence in the ability as well as the will of the United States *to comply with their treaty stipulations*" (emphasis added). Smith also denounced the War Department's inability, or its unwillingness, to restore peace to Indian Territory. "We have reason to believe," he wrote, this time with more frankness, "that as soon as the United States shall re-establish their authority in the Indian country, and shall send there a sufficient force for the protection of the tribes, they will renounce all connexion [sic] with the rebel government and resume their former relations with the United States."[24]

Enclosed with Smith's scathing report was the report from new commissioner of Indian affairs William Palmer Dole, who had replaced Alfred Greenwood, when Greenwood resigned to go with the South. Dole also sympathized with the plight of the Cherokees. With the withdrawal of the U.S. forces from Indian Territory, "it is not surprising," he wrote, "that many of the Indians have thrown off their allegiance and espoused the cause of the rebellion."[25] Smith and Dole agreed with the sentiment of Reverend Evan Jones, a long-time missionary among the tribe, who called on the government to look graciously toward the Cherokees. "And in consideration of the unfavorable circumstances in which the Cherokees were placed," Jones wrote, "I have no doubt the President will be disposed, on their return, to treat them with a generous lenity and forbearance."[26] On March 13, 1862, following the Union victory at Pea Ridge, Dole once again petitioned Smith to ask for troops to return to Indian Territory and reinstate the treaties.[27]

Incredibly, President Lincoln acceded to the demands of Smith and Dole. On March 19, 1862, less than two weeks after the United States secured control of Missouri at Pea Ridge, Edwin M. Stanton, Lincoln's Secretary of War, issued an order to Major General Henry W. Halleck, who then commanded the Department of the Mississippi.

> GENERAL: It is the desire of the President, on the application of the Secretary of the Interior and the Commissioner of Indian Affairs, that you should detail two regiments to act in the Indian country, with a view to open the way for the friendly Indians who are now refugees in Southern Kansas to return to their homes and to protect them there. Five thousand friendly Indians will also be armed to aid in their own protection, and you will please furnish them with necessary subsistence.[28]

The order from the president authorized the return of Federal forces to Indian Territory to provide the protection promised the tribes in the various treaties. This move on the part of the U.S. government is one of the most important, if not the most important, decisions concerning Indian Territory during the Civil War. With the return of Federal protection, the United States implicitly admitted to abrogating the treaties in April 1861 and assumed responsibility for the Indian-Confederate alliances. The pleadings of Smith and Dole in their official reports the previous November made it quite plain: the United States caused the Indians to turn to the Confederacy by withdrawing their troops from Indian Territory. Both reports called for the government to return the protection and restore the relationships with the Indians. Lincoln's order of March 19 sought to do just that.

The order to return to Indian Territory came at about the same time as the promotion of Samuel D. Sturgis to the rank of brigadier general. Sturgis, a Mexican War veteran and former Indian fighter, took command of Union forces at Wilson's Creek following the death of General Nathaniel Lyon. Now he was given the responsibility of carrying out Lincoln's diplomatic order.[29] He refused. He did not believe in fighting "Southern gentlemen" with "savage" Indians, particularly in the aftermath of the allegations following the Battle of Pea Ridge.[30] Sturgis's refusal was emblematic of a broader resistance to the new objective in Indian Territory, one that would continue to hamper the progress of the mission in the coming months. Instead of disciplining such a veteran officer, the War Department transferred him to Washington to defend the capital. Leaders in Washington were well aware of the allegations of Cherokee brutality at Pea Ridge, yet Lincoln issued his order only eleven days later anyway.[31]

On April 4, 1862, Secretary Stanton, ordered Colonels Robert W. Furnas and John Ritchey to enlist troops among the refugee Indians in southern Kansas.[32] As evidence of the mission's objective, the Indian troops were to be supplied with arms by Southern Superintendent of Indian Affairs William G. Coffin and the federal Indian Department, not the U.S. Army.[33] Four days later, the War Department promoted James G. Blunt, a physician and abolitionist from Maine, to the rank of brigadier general and assigned him to carry out Lincoln's order. However, on May 2, the War Department established the Department of Kansas and placed Blunt in overall command. Blunt quickly turned to Colonel William Weer, a Kansas lawyer, as his replacement in command of the Indian Expedition.[34] The new diplomatic objective of the Department of Kansas brought further change to the command of the Indian Expedition as 29 white officers resigned during the first few weeks.[35]

Meanwhile, Colonels Furnas and Ritchey proceeded to enlist troops from among the refugee Indians to assist with the protection of Indian families once the return to Indian Territory was complete.[36] By May 22, Furnas's 1st Indian Home Guard Regiment, consisting mostly of Creek and Seminole refugees, many of whom had fled Indian Territory with Opothle Yahola, was full, and Ritchey's 2nd Indian Home Guard Regiment, made up of refugee Cherokees, was partially filled.[37] Blunt and Weer had to devise a strategy to enter the Cherokee Nation, eliminate Confederate resistance, and secure Fort Gibson as a base for protecting the Indians. Moreover, the new Indian recruits had to be trained to act as protectors of their homes once the territory was securely in Federal control. Lincoln's order proved difficult, and its implementation proved even more problematic.

Lincoln's order of March 19, 1862, had only one objective: to reinstate U.S. treaty obligations in Indian Territory, primarily the requirement to protect the Indians from internal and external aggressions. The order to return troops to Indian Territory had no military objective. The army was simply the vehicle through which Lincoln's diplomatic strategy was to be delivered. The fact that the president of the United States would even be concerned with the movements of two small regiments on the western frontier should alert historians to the added significance of the order. Moreover, the order implicated the secretary of the interior, the commissioner of Indian affairs, and even included the secretary of war in the discourse. The mission to return to Indian Territory held great significance for the Lincoln administration and had nothing to do with military strategy. The mission would most likely not have happened without Lincoln's desire to reinstate the federal treaties with the Indians.

Blunt's assignment was to organize a military expedition to Indian Territory that would fulfill the diplomatic requirements as laid out by the Lincoln administration. Blunt knew reinstating the treaty relationship with the Native tribes was his priority. He also knew that to carry out the diplomatic mission, he would need to organize and control an army of white and Indian soldiers, supply them adequately, and care for hundreds of refugee Indians along the route. In his preparation and planning, he identified his top three priorities. First, because there was no significant Confederate strength in Indian Territory during the spring of 1862, he had to plan to operate against small forces of resistance, at least initially. However, Blunt underestimated the tenacity with which Watie would resist the movement. Moreover, the likelihood of a troop movement of this caliber drawing Confederate attention to the area was high, so Blunt had to devise a plan to monitor the region for increased Confederate resistance. Second, he had to restore civilian refugee Indians to their homes and protect them as they resumed their everyday lives. To do so required the successful completion of his first objective. Finally, he hoped to establish a military presence at Fort Gibson that was large enough and mobile enough to remain a useful force in Missouri and Arkansas if necessary.[38]

Although the stated purpose of the Indian Expedition was to restore the prewar treaty relationship with all the tribes in Indian Territory, it quickly became obvious that the objective would be satisfied by securing control of the Cherokee Nation. Blunt planned to advance as far as Fort Gibson, and from there liberate any tribes wishing to return to prewar status. On paper, the mission sounded simple. However, Union leaders were unsure what to expect once the force crossed into the Cherokee Nation. Blunt believed that initial resistance would be limited to small guerilla bands of pro-Confederate Indians, but that those could be eradicated with minimal effort.[39] Halleck thought the expedition would find its most difficult obstacle to be the newly enlisted Federal

Indian troops.[40] Federal opinion held that minority troops should be led by white commanders, ensuring maintenance of military discipline and routine military procedures.[41] This provided Union commanders with a greater sense of control over Indian and, later, Black forces. However, Confederate Indian units were led by Indian officers at the regimental level, often creating disunity within ethnically diverse brigades, as Indian commanders usually cared little for white objectives and preferred traditional native techniques of warfare. To this end, Halleck saw the need for strong leadership within the expedition.[42] What he did not expect was trouble from his white commanders.

Weer made his preparations with the belief that the Cherokee people would return en masse to Federal protection as soon as the opportunity presented itself. Moreover, he received intelligence that more than 2,000 Keetoowah warriors were waiting to join the ranks of his troops once he crossed the border.[43] Blunt sent Indian scouts to the Cherokee Nation to visit personally with Ross and ascertain the degree of his commitment to the Confederate alliance. The reports he received indicated Ross's desire to welcome the expedition and the opportunity to return to a relationship with the U.S. government.[44]

Even though intelligence said otherwise, some Union commanders believed the biggest unknown was the disposition of Principal Chief John Ross. Ross's sudden shift from neutrality to the Confederate alliance created doubt in the minds of many in the Union leadership. Halleck was one who doubted Ross's loyalty. He believed that Ross helped influence some of the minor tribes in Indian Territory "to take up arms against the United States," and was sincere in his allegiance to the South.[45] Even after the Confederate alliance, Reverend Evan Jones denounced the accusations that Ross was a traitor. He assured Blunt and Weer that Ross would return to the United States at the first opportunity. Jones's arguments on behalf of the principal chief found a believer in Colonel Weer. "John Ross is undoubtedly with us," he informed Blunt in a letter, "and will come out openly when we reach there."[46] Weer's mission was clear cut: return to Indian Territory, eradicate Watie's resistance, and welcome any tribe ready to return to their prewar treaty relationship with the United States. He believed Ross would lead the way.

On June 25, 1862, Weer left Fort Scott to join the bulk of his force at Baxter Springs, Kansas, near the border of Indian Territory.[47] The Indian Expedition, consisting of about 6,000 men, 1,600 of whom were Indians, was in motion.[48] James A. Phillips, Weer's adjutant, sent a letter to Ross at Park Hill, on the 26th, informing him that the Indian Expedition was "now approaching your country with a strong military force."⁴⁹ The force escorted Indians back to their homes and came to provide the tribes the protection promised them in their treaties. This simple half-page letter provides an important clue as to the mindset of Federal leaders at the time. Lincoln's order demanded that Federal forces return protection to the "friendly" Indians in Indian Territory. Phillips's letter indicates that Union leadership considered Ross to be among those "friendly" Indians, despite the Confederate alliance, and that he had no choice but to sign with Pike. This letter is important for another reason as well. The invitation to Ross and the Cherokee Nation to return to its prewar treaty relationship with the United States is evidence that Lincoln believed the reports of Smith and Dole, and that the federal government implicitly admitted responsibility for the Cherokee-Confederate alliance.

As he approached Baxter Springs, Weer wrote letters to his two brigade commanders, Colonel Frederick Salomon, a German immigrant from Wisconsin, on June 27, and Colonel William R. Judson, a lumberman from New York, on the 28th. The brigades were to depart on consecutive days and scout the area south of the border for Confederate troops, and then rendezvous at a point south of Spring River. Both commanders received the same warning. "I would invite your careful attention to the delicate position your command will occupy in its relation to the Indians. The evident desire of the Government is to restore friendly intercourse with the tribes and restore loyal Indians with us to their homes."⁵⁰ He further urged them to be mindful of how they might treat pro-Confederate Indians. "Our policy toward the rebel portion of them," he warned, "must be a subject of anxious consideration." Clearly, this was much more than a simple military invasion of the Cherokee Nation. The order to carry out the diplomatic wishes of the Lincoln administration would prove to be more difficult than Weer could have imagined.

Shortly after crossing the border, Salomon's force encountered Watie's men. In a series of skirmishes, the Federal soldiers captured a number of Indians and white rebels and drove Watie across the Grand River toward the Arkansas state line.⁵¹ Watie's resistance to the Indian Expedition is difficult to interpret. Did he realize the objective of the mission was to restore relations with his own people when he positioned himself to attack? Did he believe he was resisting an enemy invasion? Was Watie fighting in defense of slavery? Regardless, by positioning himself to resist the advance of the Indian Expedition, and by seeking to prevent the return of Federal forces and the reinstatement of the prewar treaty relationship between his own people and the United States, Watie was acting as an enemy of the Cherokee Nation. Moreover, he attempted to block the return of many refugee families to their homes as they tried to escape the horrors of refugee camps in southern Kansas. History has praised Watie for his heroics and bravery as a Cherokee leader. However, during the war the bulk of the Cherokee Nation held an entirely different opinion of him.

On June 30, 1862, Salomon, camped on Cowskin Prairie, reported that Watie's Indian troops had been reinforced by a sizable detachment of white troops from Arkansas and that they were encamped only eight miles away on Honey Creek. Unwilling to leave his supply trains exposed, he opted to delay an attack until the remainder of his brigade reached his camp.[52]

Hoping to demonstrate Federal strength and determination to his new Indian allies, Weer left Baxter Springs to join Salomon at Cowskin Prairie and attack the Confederate force gathering at Honey Creek. It was here that Weer's expectations began to unwind. On July 2, he wrote to Blunt to apprise him of the situation, relating that Watie's Confederates seemed unwilling to make a stand against the much larger expeditionary force.[53] The Federal plan was to eradicate the limited Confederate presence, clearing the way for the refugee Indians to return safely to their homes. However, Watie's unwillingness to stand and fight prevented Weer from eliminating a major concern for the refugee families. Moreover, as he marched south, many of the citizens who remained in the Cherokee Nation fled south of the Arkansas River, unsure as to the motives and objectives of the invaders. Their flight to the South should not be interpreted as loyalty to or sympathy with the Southern cause. Many if not most of the fleeing Indians, fearing the ravages of a continued war, simply fled to the south to escape the path of a large army advancing from the north. Weer expected the masses of Cherokee citizens to welcome him openly on his arrival. Yet the Indians' unexpected evacuation introduced concerns of potential civil war among the Indian populations, especially if they were so distrusting of each other.[54]

Weer became uneasy as his expectations went unfulfilled, demonstrated by his growing proclivity to refer to the diplomatic mission as "this Indian business." He realized that the War Department had no jurisdiction over Indian matters. If the military expectations of the expedition did not materialize, he would have to resort to Plan B, a plan that did not exist. He expressed his frustration to Blunt, "As the management of this Indian business is more properly the province of the Indian Department, I regret the absence of an officer accredited to represent it." Weer's next sentence offers a foreshadowing of how the Indian Expedition would play out over the next two weeks. He told Blunt, "I hope the general commanding will furnish me instruction on this subject." Weer was unwilling to act decisively if the plans did not materialize. He was afraid to make the wrong decision and create trouble between the War Department and the Indian Department. "I shall in the meantime," he declared, "do nothing but what will be stipulated to be subject to [Blunt's] approval."[55] In other words, Weer had no intention of acting on his own. If the expectations for the expedition went unfulfilled, he would await orders from Blunt before moving. Weer recognized the importance of the diplomatic mission, and the last thing he wanted to do was be responsible for its failure.

Unfortunately for Weer, Blunt appeared to have no immediate answer either. The next day, Blunt sent his reply. "Instructions relative to the treatment of the rebel Indians," he wrote, "and the disposition of those that are loyal, including the refugees now in Kansas, will be forwarded you in a few days." The letter was dated July 3, 1862.[56] His response did not come for another nine days and did not arrive in time to inform Weer's decision.

On July 3, the expeditionary force encountered a band of rebels under the command of Colonel James J. Clarkson, of Missouri, including Watie's men and Drew's regiment, about twenty miles south of Cowskin Prairie on the east side of the Grand River. The rebels were easily defeated, and Clarkson was captured.[57] This one-sided affair was more along the lines of what Weer had expected.

Weer was furthered buoyed by the actions of Drew's regiment following the skirmish. During the melee, the majority of the regiment, about 1,000 strong, reportedly withdrew from the field. Moreover, nearly 400 of the Cherokees applied to Colonel Ritchey for permission to join his Home Guard regiment. Many of the Indians had been looking for the opportunity to join Federal forces, and the easy victory by the Indian Expedition allowed them to finally make the move[58] Weer sent the men to Fort Scott to be formally mustered into Federal service.[59] They were added to Ritchey's 2nd Indian Home Guard unit, giving the colonel a full complement of soldiers. Moreover, Weer was told that as many as 2,000 additional Cherokees would be joining in a few days.[60] The quick victory reaffirmed Weer's confidence in the success of the expedition. On July 6, he announced that "I consider the Cherokee country as virtually conquered." He continued, "Our movements are so rapid and unexpected by the enemy that they are completely bewildered."[61] He reported to Blunt that no enemy force of consequence existed north of the Arkansas River, "They are, however, endeavoring to concentrate south of it."[62]

Weer's renewed confidence prompted an important letter to Ross. "I am here with an armed force of regularly enlisted soldiers," he announced in the letter, "instructed and prepared to enforce the observance of treaty obligations by the Cherokee people." He continued, "I am here to injure no one who is disposed to do what treaties made by his nation bind him to do; but am here to protect all faithful members of the tribe."[63] These were the words Ross had hoped to hear since the United States abandoned Indian Territory in the spring of 1861, some fourteen months earlier. All signs pointed to a quick return for Ross and the Cherokee Nation. Confident that the chief would gladly accept the invitation, Weer requested a formal meeting with Ross at the Federal camp on Wolf Creek to discuss a plan "satisfactory to all parties."[64] Although Weer had advanced deeply into the Cherokee Nation, stretching his supply and communication lines to Fort Leavenworth, the diplomatic objective of the mission seemed finally to be falling into place. It appeared he no longer needed the general's advice.

Ross had to be cautious, however. Even though he had indicated to Blunt's scouts his desire to resume his relationship with the United States, he felt the need to protect himself from Watie's distrust. Had Weer marched into Park Hill and demanded the chief's submission, Ross no doubt would have immediately acquiesced. However, Weer's desire to communicate in writing increased the risk. If Watie somehow got his hands on the letters, Ross's apathy toward the Confederate alliance would be exposed. He had to be calculating in his response. He reminded Weer that the Cherokee Nation had a treaty with the Confederate States, "entered into on the 7th day of October 1861." He continued, "There is no nation of Indians, I venture to say, that has ever been more scrupulous in the faithful observance of their treaty obligations than the Cherokees." He expressed his hope that Weer and the expeditionary force would observe the "strict principles of civilized and honorable warfare." He then declined the invitation to meet at Wolf Creek. "I cannot, under existing circumstances, entertain the proposition for an official interview between us at your camp."[65] It is important to note that Ross did not reject an interview with Weer. He rejected an interview at Weer's camp. Although he did not describe the "existing circumstances" that prevented him from accepting the offer at that time, Ross, no doubt, had Watie and his men in mind when he wrote the letter.

Weer reported the situation to Blunt, who understood Ross's predicament. In a letter to Secretary Stanton two weeks later, Blunt reported, "The verbal reports from Ross, by Indian scouts whom I sent to communicate with him, are much more favorable than his letter to Colonel Weer. He is evidently very cautious in committing himself on paper until he is assured of our ability to hold that country."[66] Ross was understandably hesitant to sign his name to a letter admitting any disloyalty to the Confederacy for two reasons. First, the Cherokee Nation had signed a treaty with the Confederate States, and any such letter would be considered treasonous. Second, if Watie and his men got their hands on that letter, he would have to pay for that treason immediately.

Weer did not know how to respond. He had received no orders or communications from Blunt for nearly a week, and could not move forward without more knowledge of Ross's disposition towards the expedition. Ross included copies of his own correspondence with Pike, McCulloch, and Rector from the spring and summer of 1861 with his response to Weer's letter. Apparently, Ross wanted the Federal leaders to understand how vigilantly he tried to remain neutral before capitulating to Confederate pressure. Still, Weer hoped for orders on how to proceed. He expressed great frustration in a letter to Blunt dated July 12, 1862. "John Ross refused to come see me," he wrote. "I am much embarrassed for want of instructions as to the Indians." While Weer understood the military orders to restore the Indians to their prewar treaty relationship, there were no contingency orders for what to do in case Ross and the Cherokee Nation refused to return.

Because he was a military officer and this was a matter of Indian policy, Weer had no authorization to consider Ross an enemy of the Union Army and was not willing to take such action without orders from his superiors, or without direction from the appropriate authorities of the Indian Department. He bemoaned his situation: "The superintendent [new Southern superintendent, William G. Coffin] should be with me," he complained. In a colorful metaphor of frustration, Weer expressed his uncertainty. "I may be ground between the millstones of the War and Indian Departments ... in short, I would like to turn this Indian business over to its own department."[67] Weer recognized the dilemma. Had the expedition been strictly a military mission, he would have been free to act as an officer of the War Department. However, the mission was more diplomatic and under the watchful eyes of the Bureau of Indian Affairs. Ross's refusal to meet with Weer placed the colonel directly between the two offices, and he knew he would pay a price for his indecision. In the meantime, he awaited orders from Blunt.[68]

While Weer waited, the expedition fell victim to a pair of unexpected enemies: the summer climate in Indian Territory and the lack of supplies from Kansas. The region had suffered from an extended drought, and the excessive heat took its toll on the expeditionary force. One soldier wrote, "Only one spring could be found for the entire army, but even this was all red and really unfit to drink. . . . Many were glad to suck wet sand."[69] Moreover, the disruption of life in the Cherokee Nation prevented the acquisition of supplies through confiscation. Weer had pleaded for the development of an organized supply base at Fort Scott before the force ever left Kansas, yet his demands went unheeded. Blunt had originally sent the supplies for the mission to Humboldt, farther west, causing Weer to redirect his initial movements well away from the border of Indian Territory.[70]

The lack of a suitable depot facility in southeastern Kansas forced Weer to store his initial supplies in wagons, exposing them to possible attack.[71] Confederates, like Watie in the Cherokee Nation and William Clarke Quantrill in Missouri, posed a constant threat to Federal supply trains and outposts in the region. Watie's incessant raids on trains bound for Fort Gibson have been glorified in historical accounts.[72] In 1864, Watie captured a supply train at Cabin Creek that held a contemporary value of about $1.5 million.[73] The supplies were for the garrison at Fort Gibson, composed mostly of Indian soldiers, to feed Cherokee families in the vicinity. While Confederate sympathizers lauded Watie as a hero for the Southern cause, history should view his actions as malicious and merciless toward the Cherokee Nation.

The lack of a supply organization to support the expedition hindered its efforts in Indian Territory. Consequently, Weer ordered his men to seize any mill or subsistence store they encountered on the march.[74] On July 2, he complained to Blunt. "My only drawback is the want of supplies from my rear."[75] Weer not only had to concern himself with the men marching with the expedition, he had to plan for the many refugees and recruits expected to join him as he proceeded deeper into Indian Territory.[76] On July 3, Blunt had ordered Weer to establish a temporary receiving depot where supplies could be sent.[77] Weer did so, near a place called Grand Saline. He then set up his camp on Wolf Creek, roughly halfway between Baxter Springs and Fort Gibson, and awaited further orders.[78] None came.

While Weer was unsure how to respond to Ross's resistance, he was in no way ready to abandon the expedition. The arrival of an additional 1,500 Cherokees seeking to join Union forces gave Weer the ability to form a third Indian regiment under the command of Major William A. Phillips. While awaiting communication from Blunt, he suggested inviting all pro-Confederate Cherokees to lay down their arms and return to their homes under the protection of the Indian Expeditionary Force. He also suggested asking the Cherokee Nation to abolish slavery so that suitable arrangements could be made to care for and control those enslaved by the Cherokees, who were scattered throughout the nation. Fugitive slave laws prevented Federal officers from granting the slaves freedom; instead, the laws required officers to return them to their owners. In addition, Weer asked

Blunt to order the establishment of a mail route between Kansas and Fort Gibson so the expedition could be better connected to headquarters.[79] He also asked for a few howitzers and informed Blunt that he was sending spies into the Creek and Choctaw nations.[80]

Although his need for supplies had grown desperate, Weer forged ahead with the objective of the expedition. He dispatched Captain Harris S. Greeno with a company of white soldiers and about fifty Cherokees to travel to Tahlequah to formally ascertain the disposition of Ross and the Cherokee government. Greeno arrived in Tahlequah about 5 p.m. on July 14 and found it all but abandoned. The next morning, the force proceeded to Park Hill, about three miles to the south, and found the place guarded by about two hundred Cherokees who welcomed them openly. Greeno found Ross at his home surrounded by his closest advisors. The men had been ordered by General Cooper to report to Confederate headquarters at Fort Davis on the south side of the Arkansas River to defend the nation from the approaching Federals, according to their treaty with the Confederacy. The men, however, had no desire to take up arms against the United States. Greeno placed Ross under arrest and then immediately paroled him so that he could legally resist Cooper's orders under the rules of civilized warfare. Ross was hopeful that the expedition could secure possession of the Cherokee Nation and provide his people protection from Watie and the Confederates. However, Greeno left Park Hill on the morning of July 16, and returned to Weer's camp with the two hundred Cherokee guards, leaving Ross and his family unprotected.[81]

On July 18, 1862, the Indian Expedition fell apart. Colonel Salomon, Weer's second in command, arrested Weer and assumed command of the expedition, immediately ordering a march towards the Kansas border to shorten the overstretched line of communication with headquarters. In a letter to Blunt written two days after the arrest, Salomon blamed Weer for the lack of communication, claiming that "it seemed he desired none." He also accused Weer of placing the expedition in danger by not moving from the camp on Wolf Creek for more than ten days. The need for supplies had become a serious concern, and no movement had been made in either direction. When advised by his inferior officers to fall back toward Kansas and restore communications, Weer refused to move, placing the men on half rations instead.[82]

Weer's arrest created confusion. The fourth new Cherokee agent within a year, Edwin H. Carruth of Kansas, who accompanied the returning refugees, wrote a letter to Blunt, claiming that "our whole camp was thrown into confusion by the arrest." Carruth reported that all the white regiments immediately retreated, leaving the three Indian brigades behind.[83] In fact, the retreat was ordered to begin at 2 a.m. on the morning of July 19.[84] The Indian brigades at detached locations did not learn of the arrest for three days.[85] Carruth argued that the retreat of the white forces left the Indians remaining in the Cherokee Nation in grave danger, and considered the arrest nothing short of a mutiny.[86] Albert C. Ellithorpe, an officer with the 1st Indian Home Guard, assumed command of the Indian regiments still in the field and called for a council of the three commanders to be held that evening.[87] The commanders decided to unite their commands and fall back to Pryor Creek, on the west side of the Grand River, where water and forage could be found more readily. The confusion of the arrest caused a number of Indians in the 1st and 2nd Home Guards to desert. The Indian brigade requested an artillery battery and a squadron of white infantry be assigned to their ranks to help better secure the nation.[88]

Blunt was also confused by the arrest. He was unaware that his letters of July 12 and July 14 had not yet been received and was operating under the belief that the expedition, though facing uncertainty, was progressing according to plan. In his letters, Blunt had advised Weer to "endeavor to hold the ground that you have obtained occupancy of," and to use "every vigilance that your communication with Fort Scott is not cut off." He did receive Weer's letter informing him of Ross's resistance, as well as copies of Ross's 1861 correspondence with Confederate officials. Blunt was not concerned.[89] Moreover, on July 20, he declared that the Indian Expedition had succeeded in clearing the Cherokee Nation of Confederate resistance and restoring harmony.[90] Unaware of the disintegration of the expeditionary force, Blunt sent copies of Ross's 1861 correspondence with Confederate officials to the War Department and declared that the diplomatic mission would be a complete success as soon as control of the Cherokee Nation was secured.[91]

Even without white troops, the Indian regiments sought to fulfill the objective of the Indian Expedition. On July 27, Colonel Furnas ordered Major William A. Phillips to move with a force of Indians on Tahlequah to once again determine the temperament of the Cherokee leadership. Phillips encountered Watie's men on Bayou Maynard, about seven miles from Fort Gibson, and attacked, sending them running for cover toward Fort Davis. Phillips reported that his presence may have saved the residents of Park Hill from an attack by Watie's rebels. Phillips, frustrated by the lack of provisions, sent a communique back to Furnas at camp. "As we have important work to do which we can do, please send us down two or three loads of rations for the force from the different regiments," he pleaded. Phillips did not wish to abandon the mission because "I had not time to close my diplomatic business," he complained.[92] He did not divulge the nature of his "business," but the lack of provisions forced him to withdraw to the camp on Wolf Creek.

Apparently, Ross's wavering frustrated Salomon who decided to take a forceful approach. During the withdrawal, Phillips met Colonel William Cloud, who had been dispatched by Salomon from the new camp near the Kansas border to arrest Ross and escort him to Federal lines. Phillips offered him the services of his Indian detachment. Cloud declined the offer but took about 250 or 300 of the Indians with him and sent Phillips on his way.[93]

Cloud proceeded to Park Hill and took Ross into custody. On the morning of August 3, 1862, Cloud issued a statement to the Cherokee people. "The personal safety of your Principal Chief and the safety of the archives of your nation," he wrote, "require that I move him and them within our lines." He continued, "The United States Government is able to protect its friends and punish its enemies." He then invited all the tribes of Indian Territory to "maintain their original nationalities as guaranteed them by their treaties with the U. States Government." Cloud then issued a tacit warning, no doubt aimed directly at Watie and his men. "All personal and real property left behind by the Chief of the Nation or other parties must remain unmolested under the penalties of the severest punishment."[94]

Ross and his family left Park Hill with the Cherokee national archives and much of the nation's treasury and rode north under the protection of the Federal soldiers.[95] On August 7, the procession arrived at Salomon's camp, where Salomon left Cloud in command and personally escorted Ross and his delegation to Fort Scott to visit with Blunt, arriving on August 9, 1862. Blunt, who came to Fort Scott to ascertain the particulars of the Weer arrest, heard firsthand the story of how Ross and the Cherokee Nation resisted Confederate overtures as long as possible before succumbing to the alliance with Pike. Convinced that Ross was sincere in his allegations, Blunt suggested the chief travel to Washington and appeal directly to President Lincoln on behalf of the Cherokee people. Blunt wrote a letter of introduction to Lincoln on Ross's behalf stating, "I have no doubt as to the loyalty of the Ross family and three-fourths of the Cherokee people."[96]

Lincoln had issued the order to return to Indian Territory on the application of Smith and Dole, and now he would have the opportunity to hear the story firsthand from Ross and make an informed decision about how to proceed. His experience with Indian nations was limited due to his preoccupation with the Civil War; but in the summer 1862, he would have to deal with two of the largest Indian-related issues of his administration. While Ross traveled to Washington to visit with Lincoln, Santee Sioux warriors in Minnesota embarked on a war against white settlers in retaliation for constant encroachments on tribal lands and failed promises from the federal government. On Sunday, August 17, 1862, while Ross was en route to Washington, four young Santee men, in a display of manhood and bravado, killed five white settlers in Meeker County, Minnesota, sparking an all-out war.

Under the leadership of Little Crow, the Santee initiated a preemptive war against the settlers of southwestern Minnesota on August 18, killing between 500 and 800 white settlers.[97] The climax of the war occurred between August 19 and 23 when Santee warriors attacked the town of New Ulm, Minnesota. The initial onslaught was repelled by the townspeople who feared another attack would prove disastrous. Four days later, under the leadership of Charles E. Flandrau, an attorney from a nearby town, the citizens once again repelled a massive attack, but not before many people, both white and Indian, lay dead on the Minnesota soil.[98]

The attacks captured the imagination of a nation already at war and provided a timely juxtaposition to the struggles of the Cherokees in Indian Territory. While the Santee Sioux responded to constant abrogation with violence against white citizens of Minnesota, Ross travelled to Washington to seek redress through peaceful diplomacy at the seat of the federal government. Over the next five weeks, U.S. troops under the command of General Henry H. Sibley successfully crushed the Santee attackers on the battlefield. Those he could not kill were brought to trial and the courts of Minnesota convicted 303 of them, sentencing them all to die.[99]

The Santee Sioux response to the repeated abrogation of treaty obligations by the federal government no doubt pressed on Lincoln's mind as Ross arrived at the White House to ask for leniency for the Cherokee Nation. Backed by the testimonies of Commissioner Dole, Secretary Smith, Reverend Jones, and General Blunt, Ross described how faithfully the Cherokee Nation held out for neutrality, hoping for the opportunity to demonstrate its loyalty to the tribe's treaty relationship with the federal government. He described how Confederate leaders intimidated the tribe into an alliance with its Southern neighbors, arguing that the inability to even communicate with U.S. officials left them little option but to accede to the pressure of the rebel emissaries. The meeting, which took place on September 12, 1862, left Ross optimistic about the president's plans for the tribe.[100]

Ross's optimism is evidenced in a written transcript of the meeting, submitted at the president's request. After restating the narrative of Cherokee secession, Ross laid his request before the president. "What the Cherokee People now desire," he wrote, "is ample military Protection, for life and property; and a recognition by the Government of the obligations of existing Treaties and a willingness and determination to carry out the policy *indicated by your Excellency* of enforcing the laws and extending to those who are loyal all the protection in your Power" (emphasis added). What exactly Lincoln had indicated is not known. However, Ross believed that the president had demonstrated a willingness to return to Indian Territory and protect the Cherokees as promised in their existing prewar treaties.

Lincoln, no doubt, requested the written transcript so he could thoroughly investigate Ross's claims. Ross's visit must have weighed heavily on Lincoln's mind because two days after receiving the transcript, he wrote Ross a somewhat apologetic note. "In the multitude of cares claiming my constant attention I have been unable to examine and determine the exact treaty relations between the United States and the Cherokee Nation."[101] To say that Lincoln had more pressing matters would be understating the facts. During September 1862, the president was dealing with the aftermath of the Indian war in Minnesota.[102] Also, he had promoted Halleck to General-in-Chief of the Union Army only two months previously, following the failed Peninsular Campaign in Virginia. Moreover, Robert E. Lee's Army of Northern Virginia was dangerously close to Washington, D.C. at that moment, having engaged Union forces at Antietam, Maryland, the previous day. In fact, the president was still receiving battle reports from the encounter, which took place less than seventy miles north of Washington. Five days later, he issued the preliminary Emancipation Proclamation, which would take effect with the new year.[103] Lincoln's desire to understand the government's relationship—and responsibilities—to the Cherokee Nation would have to wait. Besides, the delay would give the tribe time to further demonstrate loyalty to its own treaty obligations with the United States.

The Cherokees would not have to wait long for the opportunity to show their willingness to fight for the Union cause. On September 30, 1862, the 3rd Indian Home Guard, under the command of Major Phillips, participated in a skirmish at Newtonia, Missouri. Phillips wrote a letter to Ross describing the actions of the Cherokee troops. "The Regiment behaved very gallantly," he wrote, "I dismounted the men and stationed them behind a fence with their rifles, and there for two hours & a half withstood seven charges of the enemy, repulsing them, and only left under a positive order from General Salomon."[104] Ross showed the letter to Commissioner Dole, who asked permission to show it to Lincoln.[105] How the letter affected the president is not clear.

Dole later admitted to Ross that he and the secretary of the interior had been authorized to raise additional regiments from among loyal Indians.[106] Apparently, the loyalty of the Cherokee troops was welcomed by the Lincoln administration. Moreover, on October 10, Lincoln sent a dispatch to General Curtis in Missouri, inquiring as to the ability of the Indian regiments to hold the Cherokee Nation with the help of white troops.[107] Curtis's response was less than encouraging. "I doubt the expediency of occupying ground so remote from supplies," he admitted.[108] However, Curtis understood the message. Four days later, in a letter to General John M. Schofield in command of the Army of the Frontier, Curtis asked that the general send his main force to "operate in the Indian Territory." The reason was clear. "The President also desires Ross re-established in the Cherokee country," he wrote.[109] The following January, the fifth Cherokee agent to serve within eighteen months, Justin Harlan, a judge from Illinois, told some of the Cherokee leadership in Tahlequah that President Lincoln regretted how badly the Cherokees were treated in the past, and had sent him "with special instructions to see that every thing was done for them which can be."[110]

The difficulties supplying the Indian Expedition of 1862 still existed into 1863, however. The distance from Fort Leavenworth to Fort Gibson rendered a supply train impractical, especially with guerilla-like Confederate units patrolling the region. Stand Watie and his men roamed the hills of the Cherokee Nation and would have to be dealt with before supply trains could safely resupply Fort Gibson. In an effort to shorten the supply line, Blunt relocated his headquarters from Fort Leavenworth to Fort Scott, 110 miles closer to the Cherokee border. On November 9, Blunt claimed, "My arrangements are now ample to subsist my command as far south as Fort Smith." He added, "The loyal Indians are in fine spirits as to their future prospects." In Blunt's opinion, "It is all-important to occupy the Indian country as far south as the Arkansas River."[111] Whether Blunt acted on his own, or restated a policy of the Lincoln administration, is not known. However, he admitted that the United States was responsible for the suffering of the Cherokee people, and in a letter to Secretary Smith, Blunt argued that because of that responsibility, the United States must assume the burden of restoring the tribe to its prewar condition.[112]

As the winter of 1862–63 set in, the prospects for immediate relief for the Cherokee people grew slim. Refugee camps in southeastern Kansas were unable to protect the starving families from the bitter cold, and the likelihood of yet another season in mud and squalor only exacerbated their suffering. Those that tried to remain in their homes in Indian Territory suffered immensely as well, due to the attacks by Watie and his men. In early December, Ross's nephew, Daniel, wrote a heartbreaking letter to the chief, "We have lost all at home, nothing left." He blamed Watie's men for forcibly taking property from loyal Cherokee citizens. "Our houses have been pillaged and we are left very destitute," he added. "Our little Johnie is dead. This with other misfortunes tries our Souls—yet we hope it will all be well in the end. I can not say any more now."[113]

In an astounding claim, Southern Superintendent William G. Coffin reported that the Indians under Watie's leadership "now form a large portion of the rebel army in the Indian territory [sic]." He continued, "They have committed nearly all the mischief that has been done in the Cherokee country, and have driven therefrom all the loyal Indians of any prominence."[114] If the Cherokee Nation and its loyal citizens were suffering from starvation and exposure during that miserable winter of 1862–63, it was almost certainly due to the work of Stand Watie and his men. Watie and his band of followers had become little more than enemies of the Cherokee people.

The failure of the Indian Expedition in the summer of 1862 did not mark the end of Lincoln's efforts to reinstate federal treaty relations in the Cherokee Nation. Union military commanders were no longer willing to commit entire white regiments to the liberation of Indian Territory, so the three Indian Home Guard Units were chosen to become the primary enforcers of U.S. Indian policy in the territory. Major William A. Phillips of the 3rd Indian Home Guard was given overall command of the brigade. On January 8, 1863, Major-General John A. Schofield, commander of the Army of the Frontier, met with Phillips and informed him that he was being promoted to colonel and that his brigade was being detached from the 1st Division of the Army of the Frontier and placed in command of the Indian Territory. In a follow-up letter, Schofield wrote, "It is impossible for me to give you very definite instructions for your guidance. Much must be left to your discretion." Phillips's objective was to carry out Lincoln's plan of reinstating the Cherokees to their homes, providing them with the necessary protection. His instructions were to assist the Indians in planting crops as soon as the weather allowed, and to encourage them to help each other with subsistence. He was further instructed to remove to Kansas any families he felt he would be unable to save from starvation.

Just as the Indian Expedition was not a mission of Union military strategy, the Federal Indian Brigade was to occupy its own place in the implementation of U.S. Indian policy. Not only was the brigade separated from the remainder of the Union military west of the Mississippi, but it was also given its own dedicated supply line by the Indian Department. "You will draw your supplies from Fort Scott independently of the rest of the army," Schofield told Phillips, "for which purpose a train has been placed at your disposal."[115] The Department of the Interior had committed its resources to providing food and supplies for the Indians, while the Indian commissioner was to provide all the seeds needed for crops.[116] This was not a military operation. The Lincoln administration had made it clear that the Cherokee people were to be reinstated in the Cherokee Nation and that the United States would provide them the protection promised in the prewar treaties.

On January 13, 1863, Phillips was placed in command of the newly formed District of Western Arkansas and Indian Territory. On the 19th, he wrote a series of letters to General Curtis describing the difficulties he faced with his new assignment. "The Nation is little short of a desert," he lamented. There was no forage and little food for the 2,500 or so Cherokees remaining in the territory, and the harsh weather made the task even more difficult. Severe drought during the summer, followed by snow and below-zero temperatures in the winter, brought more suffering to the destitute people. Phillips planned to occupy the Cherokee Nation in the early spring of 1863. The snow and rain of winter made travel next to impossible earlier than that.[117] Phillips claimed not to have half the food necessary to feed the starving families. He requested that a supply train consisting of two or three hundred wagons be loaded and ready to depart by the end of February in case the weather allowed. His plan was to escort the nearly 7,000 refugee Indians back into the Cherokee Nation and occupy Fort Gibson before the spring equinox so that the people could begin planting crops and resume their lives in their former homes.[118]

Even though Phillips had not yet occupied the Cherokee Nation, his close proximity allowed the tribe to convene the National Council for the first time since finalizing the Confederate alliance. Thomas Pegg, serving as acting principal chief in Ross's absence, issued a call for the Council to assemble at Cowskin Prairie in the extreme northeast corner of Indian Territory, near the protection of Phillips and the Indian Brigade. Pegg, a major in Drew's regiment and a staunch supporter of Ross, issued the call on January 31, 1863, for the Council to convene on February 4. However, the summons had to be distributed carefully among the Cherokee legislators for fear of Watie's reprisal. Consequently, the Council was delayed nearly two weeks, finally convening on February 17.[119]

Lewis Downing, president pro tem of the National Committee, delivered the opening address and called on the legislators to formally abrogate the Confederate treaty, and by doing so "remove all obstacles to the free exercise of the function of our Government."[120] Downing claimed that, unlike the United States, the Confederacy intimidated the Cherokee leaders, limiting the "free and unbiased expression" of the Cherokee people. The United States had allowed the Cherokees the political freedom and autonomy to decide their own laws, including the acceptance and practice of slavery. The Cherokees, who believed the Confederacy would never allow such autonomy, felt constrained by the alliance. After adjourning for the day, the council reconvened on Wednesday, February 18, 1863, and passed a resolution declaring that the Confederate treaty "is hereby abrogated and declared to be abolished and useless."[121] The council did not immediately recognize the need for a new treaty with the United States to reestablish diplomatic relations, and opted instead to declare the sanctity of the prewar treaties on the basis of Cherokee loyalty. The Council did vote, however, to reaffirm Ross as principal chief, even in his absence, and to authorize him to lead a delegation to Washington to inform the Lincoln administration that the Cherokee Nation had returned to its treaty relationship with the United States.[122]

After voting on Friday, February 20, to depose all Cherokee officers who did not join them in redeclaring their loyalty to the United States and to order the purchase and distribution of supplies to the hungry refugees, the council took up the issue of slavery. The recent enactment of Lincoln's Emancipation Proclamation, which took effect only six weeks prior to the council, alerted the Cherokees to the potential for similar action in the Indian nations. Such a measure would represent the encroachment of federal sovereignty over Indian self-rule. Therefore, in a preemptive action, the council exercised its own autonomy and voted to abolish slavery within the Cherokee nation before the Lincoln administration did it for them.[123] The actions of the council at Cowskin Prairie represented the second time in sixteen months that the Cherokee Nation had turned its back on a white government sworn by treaty to protect it. The collapse of the Cherokee-Confederate alliance was complete. The Cherokee government formally expressed its enmity with the Confederate States and would now officially cast its lot with Ross's faith in the Lincoln administration.[124]

Emancipation in the Cherokee Nation did little to change the immediate status of the Cherokees' slaves. Many had previously escaped to Kansas only to find themselves living in the sprawling refugee camps alongside Indian families, while others remained in Indian Territory, surviving as best they could.[125] Some had even been taken south of the Arkansas River by slaveholders hoping to protect their property from the abolitionists in Kansas and the Cherokee Nation. Numerous male slaves had even joined, or had been forced to join, Confederate regiments at the start of the war. However, many of them had also deserted to the Union ranks at the first opportunity.[126] It is likely that the Cherokee regiment under John Drew, which contained both Indians and Blacks, was, perhaps, the only regiment in the Civil War to fight as a unit for both sides at some point during the conflict. It was also one of the earliest units, if not the earliest, to include African American troops among its members.

As spring approached, Phillips and the Indian Brigade finalized plans for the return to Indian Territory. Blunt expressed his satisfaction with Phillips. "I am highly gratified at the result of your efforts," he wrote, "to provide, as far as in your power, for the unfortunate loyal Indian families that have been dependent upon the Government for sustenance." He offered the Colonel some advice as the Indian Brigade prepared to reenter the Cherokee Nation. "The country to the Arkansas River must be occupied at the earliest day practicable," he urged, "which will be as soon as grass is sufficiently raised to sustain animals." Lincoln, who was pleased with the service of the Cherokee troops, authorized two additional regiments to be raised among the Indians still in Indian Territory. Blunt promised to dispatch the appropriate officers to assist Phillips with the enlistment of those forces. Blunt suggested that Phillips unload all supply trains as quickly as possible and return the wagons to Fort Scott before the enemy could attack them. Superintendent Coffin had already provided the refugee Cherokees in Kansas with seeds and farming implements and planned to escort the Indians home as soon as Phillips declared the region secure. Moreover, Blunt suggested the Indians establish close-knit colonies at first, making it easier for Federal troops to protect them than if they were scattered throughout the nation. He told Phillips to rely on his own instincts in directing the operation, promising to do all he could to help him with his monumental task.[127]

By mid-March, Phillips and his Indian Brigade started to move towards Indian Territory. Reports that the Confederates had begun feeding and clothing the Indians south of the Arkansas River concerned the colonel, who feared a shift in loyalty if the United States did not enter the Cherokee Nation soon.

Besides, he told Curtis that "March is the planting month in the Indian Nation, and no crops are secure planted after that time." His plan was to convince the people of Indian Territory of the magnanimity of the United States. He believed that if tribes could feel the security offered by the federal government, the path to Texas would be wide open through a country of friendly Indians.[128] Phillips was prepared to enter the Cherokee Nation with an active force of 3,269 men and six artillery pieces. His forces consisted of the three Indian Home Guard Regiments, the 1st Arkansas Cavalry, four companies of the 6th Kansas Cavalry, and the 3rd Kansas Battery.[129]

As the brigade crossed into the Cherokee Nation from its winter quarters along the Arkansas-Missouri line, Phillips reported excitement among his Indian troops. Arriving at Park Hill, he sent a large portion of the command on to Fort Gibson to secure it. On March 31, the refugee Indians arrived from Kansas, amid a celebration. One white soldier described the scene.

> Some of the Indian soldiers went out several miles to meet their families, but many waited until the train had approached near our camp. I watched them with a good deal of interest. Such manifestations of joy on the meeting of husbands and wives and children, I have never before witnessed. There were, perhaps, nearly a thousand families brought down, and in many instances husbands have been separated from their wives and children for nearly a year. Their joy was, no doubt, increased with the thought of being able to meet one another in their own country and near their own capital.[130]

A white officer of the 1st Indian Home Guard described the enthusiasm. "They are determined to never leave their country again," he wrote, "and woe be to the rebel army that shall attempt to invade their homes."[131] Phillips simply reported to Blunt, that "the Cherokees are greatly rejoiced."[132] The Cherokees immediately began tilling the ground and planting the seeds provided by the Indian Department.[133]

The occupation of Fort Gibson by the Federal Indian Brigade alarmed Confederate commanders who viewed the movement as a precursor to a Union advance on the Red River and North Texas.[134] Two cavalry regiments of North Texans joined Douglas H. Cooper's Choctaw, Chickasaw, and Creek regiments on Butler Creek, two miles from Fort Gibson across the Arkansas River. The troops were to support Watie's destructive raids in the Cherokee Nation. The presence of Phillips's brigade only increased the tenacity with which Watie attacked. His frequent raids on Federal foraging parties became such a nuisance that Phillips limited the maneuvers in order to save his animals. Watie's raids on Cherokee refugee families soon drove many of them into the safety of Fort Gibson, forcing them to abandon their freshly planted crops. The raids increased with such ferocity that Superintendent Coffin suggested removing the refugees and returning them to Kansas.[135]

The regiments of North Texans camped at Butler Creek did very little to harass the Federal forces on their own. Their primary purpose was to position themselves between the Union troops at Fort Gibson and the North Texas border. In the meantime, they were ordered to assist Watie and his men by distracting the Federal troops by pretending they would attack the fort at any moment. Constant demonstrations on the Arkansas River kept Phillips's main force occupied while Watie's men continued to wreak havoc.[136]

In early June 1863, Watie left his camp south of the Arkansas River and rode north towards the new Federal supply depot at Baxter Springs, Kansas. An alert Phillips dispatched a detachment of the 6th Kansas Cavalry to cut him off. After a brief skirmish about eighty miles from the fort, Watie, hampered by high water on the Grand and Illinois rivers, escaped to the southeast with the exhausted Federal detachment on his tail. Cooper quickly sent the 29th Texas Cavalry across the Arkansas south of Fort Gibson to assist Watie's retreat. The Texans briefly engaged the 6th Kansas at Greenleaf Prairie on June 16, while Watie and his men slid to safety across the Arkansas River at Webber's Falls.[137]

On June 26, Blunt acknowledged that the Indian Brigade at Fort Gibson was becoming discouraged by the constant raids and promised to send additional troops to buoy their spirits. "I have sent with the train now en route to Fort Gibson," he wrote to General Schofield, "about 1,600 re-enforcements, including the 1st Kansas Colored Volunteers."[138] The 1st Kansas, raised in 1862 by Colonel James M. Williams, a Kansas Jayhawker, became the first all-Black unit to engage the Confederates in battle and the first to win.[139] He promised additional reinforcements with the next train. Moreover, Blunt planned to march with the second train and join Phillips at Fort Gibson to lead an assault on the gathering Confederates.

As the train entered Indian Territory at the end of June, Watie positioned his men in defense along the south bank of Cabin Creek, while the 29th Texas Cavalry rode up the west side of the Grand River to cover an alternate route.[140] When the train chose the main road towards Cabin Creek, the Texans were unable to cross the swollen Grand River, leaving Watie to defend the advance. However, Watie was unable to hold the line against the larger Union advance, allowing the train to safely reach Fort Gibson. The demoralized Texans fell back across the Arkansas River and regrouped near Honey Springs Depot, about twenty-five miles south of the fort. Blunt took the opportunity to press the attack and led his men out of Kansas across the Arkansas River, catching Cooper's force at Elk Creek, about two miles north of Honey Springs. The Union force overpowered the weary Confederates, driving them towards the Red River. After burning the town of Perryville in the Choctaw Nation, Blunt returned to Fort Gibson, while Cooper set up a defensive line near the Red River, believing the Federals were headed to North Texas.[141]

The withdrawal of the Texans from the Arkansas River Valley angered Watie, who wrote to the governor of the Choctaw and Chickasaw nations asking for help chasing Phillips and the Indian Brigade out of Indian Territory.[142] The Confederates had abandoned Cherokee territory, and Watie took it out on the citizens of his own nation. He had been named "principal chief" by his men when they learned of Ross's arrest and exile the previous August, and escalated his campaign against any non-Confederate Cherokees who remained in the nation.[143] In late October 1863, Watie rode into Tahlequah, killed "a few loyal Indians," and burned the Cherokee Council House in defiance of the Cherokee government. He then turned south toward Park Hill and, disregarding Colonel Cloud's order of August 3, set fire to Rose Cottage, John Ross's home.[144] His constant raiding kept the Indian Brigade confined to the safety of Fort Gibson for the remainder of the war. In 1864, Watie gained widespread fame for capturing two separate Federal supply vessels headed for Fort Gibson. In June, his men captured and burned the steamboat *J. R. Williams* on the Arkansas River between Fort Smith and Fort Gibson. The boat was carrying flour and bacon, which Watie and his men took to their own families. In September, Watie led a second attack on a train at Cabin Creek. The rebels successfully captured the train loaded with supplies for the refugee Indians at Fort Gibson. The train was estimated to be carrying $1.5 million worth of supplies. However, historians have missed the fact that the supplies were not earmarked for the support of Union troops. Instead, they had been sent by the Department of the Interior to relieve the suffering Cherokee people.[145]

By the time the war ended, the Cherokee Nation was devastated.[146] Elijah Sells, the new Southern superintendent, described it as "one vast scene of desolation."[147] The Indian Department estimated that the population of the tribe declined by a third during the war. Even though there were few battles between Union and Confederate forces in Indian Territory, as many as 7,000 Cherokees are believed to have perished.[148] Superintendent Coffin attributed most of the death and destruction to Watie and his men.[149] The destitution among the Cherokee people was greater following the Civil War than it had been following the forced removal along the "Trail of Tears" in the 1830s, when as many as 4,000 out of an estimated 18,000 Cherokees died.[150] Apparently, seldom-maligned Stand Watie brought more suffering to the Cherokee people than did the much-maligned Andrew Jackson.

The end of the Civil War did not bring immediate relief to the devastated Cherokee Nation. For over six weeks following the surrender of Confederate forces in the Trans-Mississippi theater, Watie continued his war on disloyalty in Indian Territory, becoming the last Confederate officer to surrender his troops. In June of 1865, he finally capitulated to Federal forces in the Choctaw Nation and immediately sent representatives to the Cherokee government hoping to "restore harmony in the tribe," but those efforts were quickly rejected. Watie's brutality would not be easily forgotten. Only when the National Council, mandated by a federal treaty, passed an act granting pardon and amnesty to any Cherokee who fought against the United States did Watie return home. However, he refused to sign an oath of allegiance to the Cherokee government and was never pardoned.[151] Despite Watie's belligerence and brutality, it would be Ross who faced the harshest criticism from U.S. officials after the war. Confident that the magnanimity shown by President Lincoln toward Ross and the Cherokee people would result in a formal reinstatement of the prewar treaty relationship, the beleaguered chief prepared to return his people to their prewar position as one of the most prosperous and advanced Indian nations in the United States. However, the bullet that took the life of the president in mid-April caused residual damage to Indian relations, especially with the Cherokee Nation, on a scale never before understood by historians.

CHAPTER 5

THE FORT SMITH COUNCIL AND THE DISMANTLING OF U.S. INDIAN POLICY

Abraham Lincoln stepped out on the balcony to acknowledge the jubilant crowd below. The city had erupted in celebration with the news of Robert E. Lee's surrender to Ulysses S. Grant near Appomattox Courthouse in Virginia in April 1865. Many celebrants had made their way to the White House to rejoice with the president. Lincoln spoke briefly about the difficult road ahead. He reminded the crowd that there was no legitimate Southern government or "authorized organ" with which to treat. Reconstruction would be a contentious and arduous process, he told them, because "no one man has the authority to give up the rebellion for any other man."[1] With that in mind, Lincoln had issued his Proclamation of Amnesty and Reconstruction fifteen months earlier. The Proclamation, known as the "Ten-Percent Plan," opened the door for Southerners to declare loyalty to the United States on an individual basis. When 10 percent of a state's voters took the oath, they could organize a loyal government and return to the Union. Louisiana was the first state to do so.[2]

Indian nations were different. Tribal governments provided an "authorized organ" with which the federal government could treat in the postwar years. Because the Cherokee people had openly declared their loyalty to the United States through the tribe's treaty relationship as early as July 1862, it was unclear whether the Lincoln administration was prepared to accept their claims of loyalty and reestablish the relationship on the same basis as the Ten-Percent Plan. Would Lincoln negotiate a new treaty with the tribe, even before the war ended? Evidence suggests that John Ross believed that Lincoln was willing to restore the tribe to its prewar treaty relationship, especially after the National Council voted to abrogate the Confederate treaty in February 1863 at Cowskin Prairie and many Cherokee men joined the ranks of the Federal Indian Brigade. However, the president would never have the opportunity to do so, for two reasons. First, Stand Watie's resistance to Federal reoccupation efforts prevented physical restoration. Second, three days after Lincoln's impromptu speech from the White House balcony, he was assassinated. The new administration had little interest in treating the Indians with the Lincoln administration's proposed fairness and magnanimity. Andrew Johnson viewed the alliances between the Indians and the Confederates as treason, and was therefore willing to undo the prewar treaties. In the weeks following the assassination, the Johnson administration made decisions that would bring about a new U.S.-Indian relationship in the post–Civil War American West.

Despite Lincoln's assassination, John Ross entered the postwar era convinced that the Cherokees had proven their loyalty to the United States and that the federal government was prepared to treat them accordingly. Ross argued that the Cherokee treaty with the Confederacy was unavoidable and should not be held against them. Secretary of the Interior Caleb B. Smith and Commissioner of Indian Affairs William P. Dole had concurred. President Lincoln acknowledged the fact that the United States had abrogated its treaty obligations to the tribes of Indian Territory and sought to return troops to the territory to resume those obligations and restore the broken relationships with loyal tribes, including Ross and the Cherokees. Yet the two attempts to reoccupy Indian Territory failed for at least two reasons. First, the army was unable or unwilling—or both—to commit the necessary manpower in either attempt. Second, Stand Watie was committed to resisting both reoccupation and restoration of his nation's own government.

Although the physical restoration of the Cherokee Nation was an abject failure, Ross believed political restoration was absolute. His meetings with Lincoln convinced him that the president was willing not only to restore the Cherokees to their lands but also to forgive the Confederate treaty. Moreover, during the winter of 1862–63, the tribe demonstrated its loyalty to its treaties with the United States by its service in the Federal Indian Brigade. As much as 20 percent of the tribe's population joined Federal forces when they entered the Cherokee Nation in the summer of 1862. Ross had at least one additional meeting with Lincoln in summer 1863. He came away even more convinced that the president would restore the tribe to its prewar treaty status. Ross told his executive council that Lincoln had said the Confederate treaty "should never rise up in judgment against the Cherokees, nor stand in the way of perfect justice being done them under their Treaties with the United States."[3] Commissioner Dole agreed. In a postwar affidavit on Ross's behalf, Dole claimed to have been in that 1863 meeting and believed the president to have accepted Ross's explanation for the treaty and "appeared to be satisfied" that those who returned their allegiance to the United States "were excusable for the steps . . . taken."[4]

Much of Ross's confidence stemmed from the knowledge that the decision as to how to respond to the Cherokees belonged solely to the president. On July 5, 1862, Congress passed legislation granting the president sole authority to repudiate any treaty held with an Indian nation "in actual hostility to the United States." Ross spent the last months of 1862 and much of 1863 trying to convince Lincoln that the Cherokees were never in actual hostility to the federal government and were therefore eligible for full restoration under the prewar treaties. Although Lincoln relied on his advisors within the Department of the Interior, especially Commissioner Dole, he maintained a hands-on approach to his administration's Indian policy. In the weeks following the Sioux uprising in Minnesota, Lincoln ordered that no executions be made without his sanction. Following a personal investigation of the evidence, the president reduced the number of Sioux to be executed from 303 to only 38.[5] His apparent sympathy with the Indian condition in the United States indicates a willingness to reverse the trend of U.S. presidents routinely ignoring the civil rights of American Indians. Lincoln reportedly admitted as much to famed Indian advocate John Beeson in 1864: "rest assured that as soon as the pressing matters of this war is settled the Indians shall have my first care and I will not rest untill [sic] Justice is done to their and your Sattisfaction [sic]."[6] Ross believed that the president would finally honor the nation's constitutional responsibilities to the Cherokee Nation by restoring the prewar treaties abrogated by the federal government in 1861. Ross's long-standing faith in U.S. constitutional law appeared to be validated. Lincoln had heard the plight of the Cherokee Nation and intended to respond with justice. Ross's meetings with the president left him convinced that the Cherokee Nation would be restored politically and physically as soon as conditions allowed.

On October 18, 1864, less than a month before the presidential election, the Cherokee National Council, convinced of the president's support, authorized a delegation to Washington to formally reestablish the treaty relationship with the United States while the friendly Lincoln was still in office. New assistant principal chief Lewis Downing wrote to Ross and Evan Jones in Washington informing them of the delegation which was to include Ross, Jones, and three other men, all officers in Drew's regiment, now with the new Indian Home Guard.[7] Downing summarized the written instructions from the Council. First, the Council wanted restoration of the prewar treaty relationship put into writing as a new treaty. Moreover, it wanted the federal government to acknowledge the loyalty of Cherokee troops during the war and to specifically declare the prewar treaty obligations of the United States to be secure. Further, the Council wanted authority to confiscate the property of disloyal Cherokee citizens and to arrest any non-Indian—outside of government agents—caught within the borders of the Cherokee Nation, no doubt aimed at Watie and his men. Finally, and most significantly, the National Council wanted the United States to provide indemnification for financial loss suffered by the Cherokee people due to the war.[8] A stipulation of this magnitude would require the United States to formally admit responsibility for the wartime suffering of the Cherokees. Ross and the Cherokee National Council believed that the Lincoln administration had laid the foundation for restoration by admitting that very responsibility, so a proposed new treaty seemed logical.

Among Ross's personal papers is folder number 1385, which contains three handwritten pages, each bearing an "article" of a would-be treaty. The pages are unsigned and undated, but strongly suggest Ross's belief in a full restoration by the United States. The first article called for Ross to assume control of Cherokee regiments during the war, just as any state governor would control his state's troops. On May 4, 1864, Ross met with Secretary of War Edwin M. Stanton and requested control of Cherokee troops so that a portion of them would not be dispatched away from the post as ordered, leaving the Cherokee people unprotected.[9] The second article sought to establish a commission to investigate damages in the Cherokee Nation caused by the "noncompliance of said stipulations by the United States." The commission was to determine all just claims against the government and report its findings to Congress. The third article stipulated that all persons within the borders of the Cherokee Nation would be subject to Cherokee law unless that law interfered with an "agent of the army of the United States."[10]

The three additional delegates mentioned in Downing's letter, Thomas Pegg, Smith Christie, and George W. Scraper were all captains in the Indian Home Guard stationed at Fort Gibson. However, Union military commanders refused to grant the three a leave of absence during the struggle to secure control of the Cherokee Nation. On January 25, 1865, Ross wrote to Dole, requesting his help in securing leaves for the men so they could join the chief in Washington and formally conduct the business of the tribe.[11] However, the federal government failed to see the necessity of negotiating a new treaty with the Cherokees, most likely because the United States considered the prewar treaties as valid and intact. By late March, Ross hoped to entice the government into negotiations by offering to sell the Neutral Lands, lands in southeastern Kansas designed to be a buffer between the tribe and white settlers, back to the United States.[12] The move did not work, and Ross's efforts to obtain a new treaty with the United States in the closing months of the war were unsuccessful.

The idea of a wartime treaty with the tribes of Indian Territory was not out of the question. On September 3, 1863, Commissioner Dole and Superintendent Coffin agreed to a new treaty with the non-Confederate portion of the Creek Indians in exile in Kansas, many of whom left Indian Territory with Opothle Yahola in late 1861. The U.S. Senate ratified the treaty contingent on additional amendments, the foremost of which proclaimed the Creek national government to have abrogated its treaty with the United States by willfully entering an alliance with the Confederacy and thus forfeiting all rights to its lands and annuities.[13] In contrast, Dole did not immediately believe the Cherokee Nation had forfeited its rights. In his annual report for 1863, he referred to the resolutions passed at Cowskin Prairie by "the only portion of the nation whose rights have not been clearly forfeited by treason."[14] Once again, Dole interceded for leniency on behalf of Ross and the Cherokee Nation.[15] Clearly, Ross had reason to believe in the possibility of a new treaty with the United States.

Even Lincoln's death did not deter Ross's faith in a full restoration. The president's administration appeared to have supported his Indian policies, and Ross had no reason to expect any change following the assassination. Ross claimed to have visited with President Andrew Johnson in the summer following Lincoln's death and received no indication that the new administration had any plans contrary to Lincoln's.[16] Even though U.S. Indian policy had been a topic of heated debate for many years prior to the Civil War, especially its practicality in dealing with the tribes of the Great Plains, there appeared to be no urgency on the part of the Johnson administration to make any changes. However, continued unrest caused many in the government to question the validity of the nation's plan to "civilize" the "savage" Indians of the region. The Johnson administration, however, did not seek to change Indian policy following the Civil War. It merely wanted to change the nation's treaty relationship with the tribes in Indian Territory, particularly the Cherokees.

The debate over U.S. Indian policy in the 1850s and 1860s is best understood through the opinions of the various Indian commissioners of the same period. From the transfer of the Indian Bureau to the Department of the Interior in 1849 to the end of treaty making in 1871, a period of about twenty-two years, U.S. Indian policy made little progress in solving the nation's

"Indian problem," perhaps due to the crippling inconsistency that plagued the bureau's leadership.

Between 1849 and 1871, there were twelve different Indian commissioners, on average a new commissioner every twenty-three months during perhaps the most critical era for the development of the nation's post-Civil War Indian policy. Instead of developing a consistent and functional policy for directing the interactions of the federal government with the nomadic Plains tribes, the various administrations had different ideas about managing the nation's Indian affairs. In short, each successive Indian commissioner held his own opinions as to how to manage U.S.-Indian relations, and with the United States barreling toward Civil War, the nation failed to focus enough attention on its "Indian problem." Instead of building off the one consistent aspect of U.S. Indian policy—the practice of treaty making with Indian nations—the United States opted to abolish it in 1871, leaving the nation with an even less defined, more inconsistent policy.

James W. Denver, President Buchanan's commissioner from 1857 to 1859, admitted the need to reevaluate the nation's policy. "I concur fully with those of my predecessors," he wrote, "who had stated that there have been too great and radical mistakes in our system of Indian policy."[17] Perhaps acting commissioner Charles E. Mix best summarized the problem the following year: "At least three serious and, to the Indians fatal errors, have from the beginning marked our policy towards them."[18] First, the constant removal from one "permanent" reservation to another cultivated a culture of distrust among the Indians. Nathaniel G. Taylor, commissioner during the Andrew Johnson administration from 1867 to 1869, asserted that the United States treated the Indians "as pilgrims, resting a year or two on this reservation, and then removing them to a new one, on the outer verge of civilization, there to linger awhile in sad suspense till the remorseless rapacity of our race requires them to move further back into darkness again."[19]

George W. Manypenny, commissioner during the Franklin Pierce administration from 1853 to 1857, wrote, "Without a fixed, permanent and settled home, in my opinion, all efforts to domesticate and civilize the aboriginal race will hereafter, as they have heretofore, prove of but little benefit or advantage."[20] Manypenny claimed that the Indians would "be trampled under the feet of a rapidly advancing civilization" if permanent homes were not given to them.[21] Alfred B. Greenwood, James Buchanan's second commissioner from 1859 to 1861, concurred. "It is surprising to see the growing disposition on the part of our citizens to wholly disregard our treaty obligations with Indian tribes within our borders," he wrote in 1860, "and it is to be hoped that in future [sic] their rights will be held more sacred or that the government will in every instance promptly see that they are observed and respected."[22] "It is beyond question," wrote Taylor in 1868, "our most solemn duty to protect and care for, to elevate and civilize them. We have taken their heritage, and it is a grand and magnificent heritage. Now is it too much that we carve for them liberal reservations out of their own lands and guarantee them homes forever?"[23]

In Commissioner Mix's view, the second error of U.S. Indian policy was that Indians were given far too much land as part of their reservations. Denver agreed. Greenwood also argued, "It has become the policy to locate a tribe within such limits as would not at first, or, or too suddenly, change the modes and manners of hunter life for purely agricultural."[24] All three commissioners believed that the Indians had to abandon the chase in order to pursue the benefits of subsistence agriculture. If the government continued to give them too much land, there would be no motivation for them to adopt a new way of life.

Third, Mix believed that the practice of trading lands for large annuities was detrimental to overall U.S.-Indian relations. Manypenny claimed that the "money-annuity system" did more to "cripple and thwart" the government's efforts at civilization than it helped.[25] "So long as an Indian remains in expectation of money from the government," he wrote, "it is next to impossible to induce him to take the first step towards civilization."[26] Denver argued that the annuities should be turned over to the chief instead of held in trust, enabling "them to punish the lawless and unruly by withholding it from them, and giving it to the more orderly and meritorious."[27]

Taylor believed that the question of postwar U.S. Indian policy had an obvious answer. "Unless history is a fable," he wrote, "and the observation and the experience of living men a delusion or a lie," the Cherokee Indians "demonstrated that an Indian tribe may become civilized."[28] He claimed that what made the Cherokees such a successful example of acculturation was that they lived in close proximity to white settlers in preremoval Georgia, Alabama, South Carolina, and Tennessee. As whites encroached, the Cherokees were further concentrated in their own homes as the circumscribed boundary of tribal lands grew slowly smaller. This resulted in the eventual abandonment of the chase as more Indian lands were taken from them. Stock raising and agriculture slowly took hold, and then the very tenets of capitalism set in among the tribe, encouraging them to further accept the ideology of African chattel slavery.[29] Historian Theda Perdue and others would argue that the widespread intermarriage of whites and Indians greatly aided acculturation among the Cherokee Indians.[30]

Taylor then made the startling claim that the Cherokees "are not only civilized and self-supporting, but before the fearful disasters of the great rebellion fell upon them, were perhaps the richest people, per capita, in the world."[31] The Cherokees were the prewar example of the successes of U.S. Indian policy, and apparently, they retained that title after the war. "If the Cherokees, Choctaws, Chickasaws, Creeks, and Seminoles, are civilized and advancing in development," Taylor hypothesized, "so will be the Cheyennes, Arapahoes, Apaches, Kiowas, Comanches, Sioux, and all our other tribes if we will only use the means in their cases that have been so wonderfully successful in the first named tribe" (i.e., the Cherokees).[32] However, Taylor ignored another key component of Cherokee acculturation. From the time of the Cherokees' first treaty with European settlers to the establishment of the Cherokee constitution, a period of nearly 150 years elapsed. The acculturation of the Cherokee people was a slow, arduous process. Taylor and the rest of the U.S. Indian bureau, along with the succeeding president Ulysses S. Grant, had no intention of replicating that level of patience.[33] The Cheyennes, Arapahoes, Apaches, Kiowas, Comanches, and Sioux were expected to accept a shortened, more hurried version of acculturation.

Ultimately, members of the Indian bureau argued for three specific changes to Indian policy that they believed would simplify the process of Indian relocation and escalate the process of acculturation among the more nomadic tribes of the Great Plains. First was the need for a uniform policy to eliminate confusion within the Indian bureau. Treaties "have been made from time to time," argued Luke Lea, President Fillmore's commissioner from 1850 to 1853, "to meet the emergency of particular occasions and without reference to system or general principles."[34] During the Civil War, Commissioner Dole of the Lincoln administration explained the reason for much of the lack of uniformity: "The longer experience I have in dealing with the Indians the greater difficulty do I find in laying down general rules applicable to all cases. That which may be successfully applied to one tribe will prove ruinous to another."[35] As early as 1851, a full decade before the start of the Civil War, Lea suggested that there were too many varying opinions from agents on the ground. He went as far as to recommend the nation transition to an Indian commission to negotiate all treaties and set the standard for U.S. Indian policy.[36]

Second, commissioners over the years argued for the establishment of civil government in the majority of Indian lands west of the Mississippi, especially the Great Plains. Lea wrote, "In my judgment the interests of the Indians require that a civil government be immediately organized in the territory" of the Great

Plains.³⁷ He further lamented the fact that there was no government or civilized system of laws anywhere north of the Cherokee Nation. He did, however, praise the "more enlightened tribes" of Indian Territory, more specifically, the Cherokees and Creeks, for attempting to impress upon their less peaceful neighbors the importance of acquiescing to the power of the United States.³⁸ Even so, some argued for the establishment of federal courts in Indian Territory, so the Indians could enjoy an increased sense of security in that their personal rights of property and production would be more secure under the federal government than under a tribal government. Elias Rector, the southern superintendent from 1857 to 1861 during the Buchanan administration, also argued that this would serve to "strengthen their desire for the full benefit of citizenship and a different form of government" altogether.³⁹

The third suggested policy change had to do with the treaty-making process itself. Near the end of the Civil War, Dole was a staunch advocate for retaining the process. He believed the practice was outdated and a better method should be developed, but nonetheless saw it as the best option for the present time. "The policy of negotiating treaties with Indian tribes has recently attracted a large share of public attention," he confessed in 1864, "and it may not, therefore, be considered inappropriate to again allude to the subject."⁴⁰ Military leaders grew weary of using soldiers to enforce treaties negotiated by politically motivated bureaucrats and began calling for the abandonment of the treaty process entirely, calling for full military authority to compel compliance, rather than negotiate for it.⁴¹ Dole disagreed. He claimed that the one true advantage of signing a treaty with an Indian tribe was that the Indians "have been recognized as a separate and distinct people, possessing in a restricted sense the peculiarities and characteristics of distinct nations."⁴² Ross understood that "restricted sense" and the limitations of a suzerain relationship with the United States. However, he also understood the benefits. Ross believed the ability to self-govern, even on a limited basis, was vital to the perpetuation of Cherokee nationality and identity. The treaties with the United States, though restrictive in nature, gave the tribe that ability. Ross fought to protect the Cherokee Nation's treaty relationship with the United States in order to retain the tribe's right to self-government.

Although he believed a better system should eventually be implemented, Dole was a key figure in protecting the treaty-making process during the Civil War years. He asserted that there were those in the government who wished to use the nation's "overwhelming superiority" against the Indians to force compliance with U.S. expectations. However, he believed that the same result could be attained through the treaty-making process and that the tribes could enjoy the sense of nationality and independence provided by a Senate-ratified treaty. This feeling of independence would create a loyalty to the United States that a forced compliance could never do. Dole asserted, "To my mind, the advantages of the latter over the former policy seem so apparent that I can hardly realize that the former is seriously advocated."[43] Although not an outspoken proponent of the treaty-making process, Dennis N. Cooley, Indian commissioner from 1865 to 1866 during the first half of the Johnson administration, advocated for a number of new treaties with various tribes in 1866.[44] Moreover, the Lincoln administration sought to enter new treaties with many of the rebellious tribes even before the war's end. Although the treaty-making process came under fire from various corners of the Indian bureau, the system remained in place throughout the Civil War.

While treaties may have "restricted" the sovereignty of the Indian nations, the United States found that treaties also restricted the Indian policy of the federal government. Wholesale changes could never be made to U.S. Indian policy as long as tribes enjoyed the perpetual "independence" and land ownership granted them by Senate-ratified treaties. How could the United States open up Indian lands for a rapidly expanding white society if there was nowhere to relocate the thousands of Plains Indians already living there? And how could they utilize the land in the territory already set aside for that purpose if it belonged to so few tribes? The bureau had already identified the need to relocate the Plains Indians onto reservations that could be permanently guaranteed to them. Moving them farther away from white society became increasingly difficult as the hunger for even more land brought whites westward into their territories. Commissioners argued that Indian Territory was plenty large enough to hold every Indian west of the Mississippi River and east of the Rocky Mountains and that it was set aside for that very purpose. The federal government, with very little foresight, gave most of the territory's lands to the Five Tribes as an inducement for removal in the 1820s and 1830s. Now, the Indian bureau needed access to that land as homes for other tribes. To overcome this, Luke Lea argued for the elimination of existing treaties. "If a large number of existing treaties were swept away," he asserted, "and others substituted in their stead . . . the day would not be distant when the whole subject of our Indian affairs would assume a far more consistent and systematic form."[45] However, national honor was at stake. Could the United States abrogate another treaty with the Cherokees and the other tribes of Indian Territory without repercussions? Abraham Lincoln recognized the constitutionality of the treaties with the Cherokees and was positioned to restore the tribe to its prewar status, thus denying the federal government access to Cherokee land without the tribe's consent. By admitting to the abrogation of 1861, the Lincoln administration committed the United States to restoring the tribe to that prewar relationship, thus securing the tribe's perpetual ownership of tribal lands. Unfortunately for the Cherokees, and all of the nation's Indians, Lincoln's assassination removed their strongest advocate for retaining the prewar treaties and their definitions of tribal land ownership.

When the Johnson administration summoned the tribes of Indian Territory to a council at Fort Smith, Arkansas, in September 1865 to reestablish peaceful relations between the tribes and the federal government following the Civil War, the presidentially appointed commissioners were given two specific objectives: land and a civil government. Johnson stumbled on the perfect opportunity to begin the process of unifying the nation's Indian policy by establishing civil government in Indian Territory and eradicating the prewar Senate-ratified treaties of the Five Tribes in order to obtain land for other Indians. New secretary of the interior James Harlan, a Republican and former senator from Iowa, wrote to Commissioner Cooley, as Cooley made the journey to Arkansas for the council: "The President is willing to grant them peace, but wants land for other Indians (and) a civil Gov't for the whole territory."[46] Ross slowly made the journey from the East to the Cherokee Nation in support of his people, but felt no need to attend the council. He had spent the past three years interceding for his nation before the federal government and was convinced that the tribe had proven its loyalty. Instead, the executive council sent thirteen delegates, headed by Assistant Principal Chief Lewis Downing, who had been the acting chief in Ross's absence. Ross considered the meetings at Fort Smith with the board of commissioners merely a formality.

The council convened on Friday, September 8, 1865, with Cooley presiding. Cooley was chosen as commissioner by Secretary Harlan upon the resignation of William P. Dole.[47] Lincoln selected Harlan for the post about the time their children started seeing each other romantically. Robert Todd Lincoln and Mary Harlan attended the second inaugural ball as a couple and would marry three years later, in 1867.[48] While Lincoln's approach to the Indians was more hands-on, often refusing to let his subordinates make important decisions without his approval—as had been the case with the Indians convicted in the New Ulm, Minnesota, attack—Johnson opted to focus his attention on reconstructing the Union, allowing his underlings in the Interior Department to address the

Indian situation with less oversight. Harlan and Cooley, Johnson's "underlings," held different opinions about Indian disloyalty than did Smith and Dole of Lincoln's administration, and their unwillingness to accept Cherokee claims of innocence was the most glaring of those. The transition from Dole to Cooley brought hardship to the Cherokee Nation.[49] Although significant, the loss of Dole had little to do with Lincoln's assassination. Lincoln himself appointed Harlan to the head of the Department of the Interior, and Harlan replaced Dole with Cooley.[50] It is unclear, however, whether Dole would have resigned had Lincoln still been president.

Lincoln's assassination silenced a much more important Cherokee advocate than Commissioner Dole; it silenced Lincoln himself. His successor, Andrew Johnson, was tangentially different in his policy towards the Indians. While Lincoln was intent on investigating Indian grievances, Johnson was dismissive of their claims and had little interest in their grievances. Johnson's commissioners were given explicit instructions for what to do and a general leniency for how to do it. Moreover, the new treaty stipulations were to apply to both Confederate and non-Confederate Indians, regardless of their position in the previous administration. The transition from the Lincoln administration to the Johnson administration brought ideological change to Indian policy, and that new policy would confound the non-Confederate Indians at Fort Smith.[51]

Aside from Cooley, the Fort Smith Council consisted of Brigadier General William S. Harney, Thomas Wistar of the Society of Friends, Colonel Ely S. Parker from General Grant's staff, and Southern Superintendent of Indian Affairs Elijah Sells. When Cooley opened the meeting, the only Indians present were those who had claimed to have remained loyal to the United States, including the Cherokee Nation which maintained its innocence. The Confederate Indians gathered at the Armstrong Academy in the Choctaw Nation as a show of solidarity and would not arrive at Fort Smith for another week. Even though the openly rebellious portions of the tribes were not present, Cooley addressed the delegations as if they were.

After calling the council to order, Cooley bluntly informed the loyal delegates that "portions of several tribes and nations have attempted to throw off their allegiance to the United States and have made treaty stipulations with the enemies of the government." He continued, "All such have rightfully forfeited all annuities and interests in the lands in the Indian territory." He did say, however, that the president was willing to hear the extenuating circumstances behind each of the rebellious treaties.[52] In concluding his opening remarks, Cooley addressed "those who remained true, and who have aided [the President] in punishing the rebels ... he is well please [sic] with you, and your rights and interests will be protected by the United States."[53] In response, the delegates, who hoped to avoid any forfeiture, requested a recess until the afternoon to discuss the matter amongst themselves before replying to the council. The request was granted, and the meeting adjourned. Cooley instructed them "to exhibit the authority by which they come to the council." He also instructed them to choose from amongst themselves a small group of no more than five who would be authorized to negotiate and sign treaties on behalf of the tribe.[54] None of the delegations had such authority. None of them knew they would be asked to sign a new treaty. None of them believed they needed to.

Four hours later, the council reconvened with Cooley asking for remarks from the various delegations present. Smith Christie of the Cherokees was first to respond. "We are thankful," he said, "for the kind words expressed this morning for those of the tribes who have been loyal, and for the assurances of continued protection." He informed the commissioners that the Cherokee delegation was not authorized to negotiate treaties. "We beg leave to say," he requested, "that our constitution prescribes the mode of making treaties."[55] The Cherokee delegation arrived at the council unprepared to sign one. They were convinced that they had proven their loyalty and that their prewar treaties had been reconfirmed. Besides, Cherokee law prohibited the signing of a treaty without the approval of their National Council. Following similar claims from other tribes, Cooley agreed to adjourn the council until 10 a.m. the next morning. He encouraged the delegates to be prepared to hear "the wishes and intentions of the government of the United States respecting their future relations with the Indians." He also warned them that additional requests for delay would not be tolerated.[56]

On Saturday, September 9, day two of the council, Cooley wasted no time in getting to the purpose of the commission. He told the delegates that the commissioners were instructed by the president to negotiate new treaties with the tribes of Indians in Indian Territory and Kansas. He then read a list of those nations involved: "The following named nations and tribes have by their own acts, by making treaties with the enemies of the United States ... forfeited all right to annuities, lands and protection by the United States." He began by stating that the Creek Nation entered a treasonous treaty on July 10, 1861, when they formally entered into an alliance with the Confederacy. After announcing the names of eleven other tribes and the dates of their alliance treaties, he ended the list with the one remaining nation: "The Cherokees, October 7, 1861." The

Johnson administration included Ross and the Cherokee Nation on their list of the disloyal, shocking the delegates and angering Ross, who learned for the first time that Lincoln's plan to reestablish the tribe had not been adopted by the new administration.

Under the authority given to him by the law of July 5, 1862, President Johnson did what Abraham Lincoln resisted doing: he declared that John Ross and the Cherokee Nation had abrogated their treaties with the United States by aligning themselves with the Confederacy in 1861. He further declared that they, and the other tribes in Indian Territory, were "left without any treaty whatever, or treaty obligation for protection by the United States."[57] While the Lincoln administration argued that the Cherokee-Confederate alliance happened only because the federal government had abrogated its own treaty responsibilities, Johnson's administration rejected that idea. Johnson claimed that "treason is a crime; and crime must be punished." He announced in the weeks following Lincoln's assassination that "treason must be made infamous and traitors punished."[58] Ironically, Johnson demonstrated great leniency to white Confederate traitors in the South following the war.

Secretary Harlan claimed in his annual report three months after the council that the prewar treaties "had been observed by us with scrupulous good faith, and in the absence of any just ground of complaint, these confederated Indians entered into an alliance with the rebel authorities."[59] He was in no way willing to admit that the United States had abrogated its treaty responsibilities by abandoning Indian Territory in 1861. Cooley was taken aback when H. D. Reese of the Cherokee delegation addressed the council on the second morning of the council and declared that his tribe, under the leadership of John Ross, was "not guilty" of the stated charges.[60] In his annual report, Cooley scornfully claimed that the Cherokees "attempted to charge the causes of their secession upon the United States, as having violated its treaty obligations, in failing to give the tribe protection."[61] Clearly, the transition from the Lincoln to the Johnson administration brought a different perspective to bear on the subject of Indian policy, and the Cherokee Nation found itself uncomfortably in the crosshairs of those seeking to reform that policy.

After listing the guilty nations, Cooley tried to appease the delegates by informing them that the president had no real desire to punish any of them.[62] All he wanted was for each tribe to acknowledge its disloyalty and agree to a new treaty.[63] The commissioners did not want to deal with any recalcitrance. All they wanted was for the delegates to submit themselves to the council in humility and accept the consequences. He then enumerated seven stipulations to be included in those new treaties. The first two called for the tribes to live in peace with themselves, each other, and the United States, and to encourage the tribes of the Plains to adopt a peaceful existence as well. The next two required the tribes to abolish and permanently prohibit slavery within their nations. The fifth and sixth stipulations came directly from Johnson and would prove the most significant. The fifth would require the tribes to cede land to the United States to allow the relocation of Indians from the Plains to Indian Territory. The sixth advocated for the formation of one civil government to rule all the tribes of Indian Territory. The final stipulation limited white intrusion of Indian land only to that which was authorized by the federal government.[64] In short, the Indians were to lose control of their own borders. The only Indians present to hear the new treaty stipulations were those who believed they had remained loyal to the United States. They were dumbfounded to learn that they, too, were to be counted among the guilty of their tribes. Cooley provided each agent with copies of his address and adjourned the council until the following Monday morning, at which time each tribe would be required to answer the charges and agree to the new treaty.

The new treaty attacked Indian autonomy, and the Cherokees were not ready to concede to its demands. Ross arrived from the East and met with the delegation on Sunday to discuss the Cherokee response. The confidence that grew out of the policy of the Lincoln administration was shaken to its core by Cooley's indictment on Saturday morning. Now the tribal leaders had to craft a response to what they believed were inaccurate and unjust charges. Moreover, if the Cherokees were found guilty, the council was prepared to inflict more political damage on the nation than Andrew Jackson had in the 1830s. The loss of land would be a harsh, but bearable, consequence of the treaty. Indians proved willing to relinquish some tribal land in exchange for retaining autonomy. However, the consolidation of tribal governments into one territorial rule and the loss of border control would be an affront to Indian self-rule. In Abraham Lincoln, Ross's faith in the process of constitutional law found a friend. Now the delegation faced the reality that the Johnson administration, like so many before it, was unsympathetic to the Cherokees' plight. The delegation decided to stand firm and demand that the United States recognize its responsibility for the Cherokee-Confederate alliance and act with leniency toward the Cherokee Nation. The immutability of the Cherokee story indicates the level of confidence the delegates had in their principal chief. However, some on the board of commissioners at Fort Smith would take great exception to that immutability, Cooley and Parker in particular.

Most of the Cherokee delegation did not attempt to cross the Arkansas River on Monday morning, September 11, to attend the council, including Ross, who, for some unknown reason, decided to stay away from the proceedings.[65] Two men, however, made the journey; one of them, H. D. Reese, delivered the Cherokee response to the council. He began by reminding the commissioners that the Cherokee National Council would have to be consulted prior to signing any treaty. Ross strongly discouraged the delegates from signing a new agreement with the commissioners because doing so would be admitting guilt.[66] In fact, Reese stood before the council and declared that the Cherokee Nation and its people "earnestly plead 'not guilty'" to all charges of abrogation. Reese then shared the Cherokee secession story, hoping to convince a second presidential administration of the unavoidability of the Cherokee-Confederate alliance. He told how the tribe attempted to return to the Union during the attack on Opothle Yahola at Bird Creek and again at the Battle of Pea Ridge. He outlined how quickly the tribe repudiated its Confederate alliance at the first sign of the Indian Expedition, and how thoroughly the nation had embraced its alliance with the United States since. Reese closed his remarks by stating his belief that the law of July 5, 1862, which authorized the president to declare the tribe in abrogation of its treaty responsibilities and therefore, in forfeiture of its provisions, included a caveat of leniency and forbearance. He argued that if the Cherokee Nation did not meet the qualifications for that caveat, then the United States had not progressed past the brutish and unfeeling legacy of the Medes and Persians.[67]

Following brief remarks by the delegates from the Osage and Wichita nations, the council adjourned until 11 a.m., Wednesday, September 13, no doubt so the commissioners could discuss at length the Cherokee response. On Wednesday morning, the council announced that the Cherokees misinterpreted the intention of the law of July 5, 1862. Cooley attempted to clarify by telling the delegates that, if the tribe simply admitted its disloyalty and signed the new treaty with the United States, the president would happily "waive the forfeiture and reinstate the nation."[68] However, the delegates knew that signing the new treaty meant agreeing to all the new stipulations and relinquishing key components of tribal autonomy. Only six months earlier, the Cherokee Nation had filed a formal protest against the passage of Senate Bill 459, which "provided for the consolidation of the Indian tribes" in Indian Territory, calling the bill "a measure fraught with trouble and wrong and ruin to our people and our institutions."[69] Yet Cooley informed the delegates that "we are surprised to know that any nation or tribe which assumes to be loyal should object to the signing of the treaty, inasmuch as there is nothing in it to which any truly loyal person may take exception."[70] Just as Albert Pike did with his letter of August 1, 1861, the council gave the Cherokee Nation an ultimatum: prove its loyalty by signing the new treaty, or risk the consequences of continued devotion to their faith in Abraham Lincoln and John Ross.

Reese and the other delegates claimed the Cherokee Nation had already repudiated the Confederate treaty by "escaping to a place of safety" at Cowskin Prairie in February 1863.[71] The commissioners, however, did not recognize the act as a full repudiation. They insisted that the treaty could only be repudiated by signing a new one with the United States that required the tribe to accede to the new stipulations. The Cherokee delegation refused to sign the treaty without first consulting with Ross.[72] The commissioners believed that the delegation would readily sign except for Ross's influence and interference. Moreover, his refusal to attend the council meetings sparked outrage among the commissioners, prompting them to issue a harsh edict.

> While John Ross is the principal chief of the Cherokee nation, and the treaty made by him and the nation with those in rebellion against the United States is not repudiated, *and a new treaty made with the United States* . . . you, as a nation, are legally morally, and of right ought to be, as you are, subject to the will and pleasure of the President of the United States touching your interests under any former treaty or treaties with the United States affecting annuities or titles to land in the Indian territory."[73] (italics added)

Until Ross was willing to admit his disloyalty and support the new treaty, the Cherokee Nation would be completely at the mercy of the United States government. Cooley ordered copies of the treaty made and distributed to each agent present. His instructions were simple and clear: "We want it signed by *all* the loyal Indians present; and if signed at all, it must be at the opening of the session to morrow [sic]" (emphasis original).[74]

The next morning, Thursday, September 14, 1865, the Cherokee agent, Justin Harlan, announced to the council that the Cherokee delegation was unable to hold the consultation with Ross due to illness and that the tribe wished to postpone signing the treaty. Harlan realized the growing frustration among the commissioners and encouraged the delegates to sign this provisional treaty and take their chances negotiating a final treaty in Washington later. In the meantime, the delegates from the Creek Nation began to hesitate, leading the commissioners to suspect Ross's influence there as well. The Creeks had previously agreed to sign the treaty, but only under formal protest, causing the council to question the tribe's loyalty.[75] While many of the smaller tribes signed the treaty, Creek agent J. W. Dunn encouraged his delegation to sign and prevent any further repercussions from the commissioners. The Creek delegates signed the treaty shortly before the council was adjourned for the day, but not before expressing their displeasure.[76]

On Friday morning, September 15, agent Harlan announced that the Cherokee delegates were ready to sign the treaty. Before doing so, however, Reese read a prepared statement of protest. "The Cherokee delegation are willing to sign the treaty," he announced, "but in so doing do not acknowledge that they have forfeited their rights and privileges to annuities and lands, for the loyal Cherokees are not guilty."[77] After consultation, the commissioners agreed to allow the delegation to sign under the following protest, "We, the loyal Cherokee delegation, acknowledge the execution of the treaty of October 7, 1861; but we solemnly declare that the execution of the treaty was procured by the coercion of the rebel army." The commissioners reluctantly accepted the protest just to get the Cherokees' signatures on the document. Five Cherokee delegates signed the provisional treaty of 1865.

Ross's faith in constitutional law had always been a guiding principle, but in response to the Fort Smith Council, it became an unwavering mission. His unquestioned leadership among the members of the delegation caused them to remain steadfast in their defiance of the punitive demands of the proposed treaty. Ross's refusal to accede to the wishes of the council angered the commissioners, who took an unprecedented step in U.S.-Indian relations on the afternoon of Friday, September 15, 1865. At 3 p.m., the council reconvened with only one order of business on the agenda. Having heard the earlier attack on his character, Ross decided to attend this session of the council. He was present when Cooley called the council to order and read a proclamation signed by the members of the council deposing Ross as principal chief of the Cherokee Nation.[78]

Ross immediately rose to defend himself. He reminded the council that he had been principal chief of the Cherokee Nation for nearly forty years, having been elected on ten different occasions, most recently while he was in Washington interceding on behalf of his people. He told them that he personally shared his story with many in the Department of the Interior, including the commissioner of Indian affairs, and both President Lincoln and President Johnson, and was "never charged with being an enemy" of the United States by any of them.[79] However, Cooley was not as understanding. Where Cooley and Secretary Harlan differed in their analysis of Cherokee loyalty was with the abandonment of Indian Territory in 1861. While the Lincoln administration readily admitted that the move constituted an abrogation of treaty stipulations on the part of the federal government, Cooley and Harlan refused to do so. Identifying the move as an abrogation would justify the Cherokee response to align with the Confederacy out of self-preservation. On the other hand, refusing to acknowledge the abrogation cast doubt on Ross's motives, allowing the commissioners to view the chief with contempt and to publicly refuse to recognize his authority.

In a published report of the Fort Smith proceedings titled *The Cherokee Question*, Cooley outlined the charges against Ross that led to his deposition.[80] He retraced Ross's prewar correspondence with Confederate officials as they tried to convince the chief of the benefit and necessity of a Southern alliance. Cooley admitted that Ross's earlier correspondence supported his claims by "reiterating his firm purpose to remain neutral."[81] However, when Ross made the decision to align with the Confederacy, he demonstrated his sincerity to Confederate officials, and his subsequent correspondence also convinced Cooley and the other commissioners of the same. Ross's desire for unity, manifested in his efforts to enlist the Shawnees, Quapaws, Osages, and Senecas—as well as his friend, Opothle Yahola—to join the Cherokees in a Confederate alliance, helped convince the commissioners of his sincerity. Cooley included in the report an affidavit signed by Albert Pike on February 17, 1866, in support of Ross's loyalty to the Confederacy. Pike claimed he was fully convinced of Ross's loyalty and downplayed any fears the chief claimed to have had of Watie and his men. "There never was a time," Pike wrote, "when the 'loyal' Cherokees had not the power to destroy the southern ones."[82] Moreover, his refusal to publicly submit to Colonel Weer and the Indian Expedition brought further incrimination upon the chief. Cooley and the other commissioners were convinced that Ross had demonstrated a strong allegiance to the Confederacy.

The presidentially appointed commission used its authority to depose Ross as principal chief of the Cherokee Nation for two reasons. First, the commissioners believed Ross's claims that the Cherokee people were loyal. The efforts of Cherokee soldiers to defect at Bird Creek, and again at Pea Ridge, coupled with the successful mass defections upon the arrival of the Indian Expedition, had convinced them. Second, however, Ross was unable to prove his own loyalty. They accused him of having used "his superior education and ability" to force the nation into an alliance with the Confederacy and of encouraging the neighboring tribes to join them.[83] Moreover, he showed an aloofness during the council meetings at Fort Smith, leading the commissioners to accuse him of standing in the way of a new treaty with the loyal Cherokee people. They also reminded the delegation that he even tried to persuade "that true patriot," Opothle Yahola, to join his Cherokee brothers in rebellion. They noted that Ross raised troops to fight against the United States, and when the Indian Expedition announced its arrival, Ross refused to join it.[84] In their estimation, Ross stood in the way, and was still standing in the way, of true Cherokee loyalty.

In this single decision, the Fort Smith Council clearly demonstrated the significance of Lincoln's assassination. By refusing to follow the precedent set by the Lincoln administration to admit the nation's treaty abrogation in 1861, they could place all the blame for the Cherokee-Confederate alliance on Ross's shoulders. Consequently, the Cherokee Nation found itself listed among the disloyal tribes of Indian Territory, resulting in the abrogation of the tribe's treaties with the United States and a new punitive treaty signed in Washington in June 1866. This new treaty would have lasting effects on the Cherokee Nation into the twenty-first century.

The postwar treaties were grossly inconsistent with the level of loyalty demonstrated by each of the Five Tribes. The Seminoles were first to sign, doing so on March 21, 1866, trading their entire territory for less land farther to the east.[85] The Choctaws and Chickasaws were next, signing on April 28, 1866. They were offered $300,000 for the leased district in western Indian Territory on which to settle their freedmen. If accepted, the freedmen were to be given forty acres of land each. However, the Choctaws and Chickasaws were given the option to accept the offer or not. There was no requirement to give tribal citizenship to any of the freedmen. The next to sign were the Creeks, who did so on June 14, 1866. The treaty cost the nation considerable land holdings. Creek and Seminole freedmen were given no land but were given full tribal citizenship, extending to their descendants. The Creeks were given limited control over tribal citizenship.[86]

The Cherokees were the last to sign on July 19, 1866. Besides losing much of their land, the Cherokees were required to give each freedman full tribal citizenship and representation. In fact, Article 9 of the treaty proved to be among the most significant requirements: "They further agree that all freedmen ... *and their descendants* shall have all the rights of native Cherokees" (emphasis added). This article extended full citizenship and representation to all Cherokee freedmen. Moreover, any and all land privileges were to be extended to all freedmen and their descendants.[87] This is of particular interest in that this article has been debated in the U.S. courts into the twenty-first century as descendants of Cherokee freedmen still seek membership in the tribe.[88] The treaties brought an end to the Civil War era in Indian Territory and introduced a much-misunderstood period of deconstruction, rather than reconstruction, for the indigenous tribes. However, the Cherokees would have to navigate this unprecedented time without their beloved leader. John Ross collapsed in the days following his public confrontation with Cooley and the council. Even though he participated in initial negotiations for the final treaty, he died on August 1, 1866, at the age of seventy-five, less than two weeks after the consummation of the punitive postwar treaty and ten days before its formal proclamation by President Johnson.[89]

Surprisingly, the Choctaws and Chickasaws, who were the first to align with the Confederacy in 1861, with virtually no pro-Federal presence during the war, and who fought solely on the side of the Confederates, received the most lenient of all the postwar treaties. The Cherokees, on the other hand, held out for neutrality for months after the start of the war, had a sizable pro-Federal footprint within the tribe during the war, and abrogated their Confederate treaty in the middle of the war, returning to fight on the side of the United States, yet they received the most punitive treaty. The Choctaws received their lenient treaty simply because they came humbly before the Fort Smith Council, admitted their guilt, and readily signed the new treaty, whereas the Cherokees never admitted guilt, resisted signing for multiple days, and when they did sign, did so under protest. As a result, they received the most punitive treaty of all the Five Tribes. Clearly, the Johnson administration had no intention of investigating guilt or innocence in the postwar Indian treaties. Johnson simply wanted two things: a civil government and land for other tribes. He got both. Lincoln's assassination cost the Cherokee people dearly.

While the Cherokees were negotiating the permanent treaty in Washington, repercussions from Lincoln's assassination continued and would transcend the borders of Indian Territory. Another member of the punitive council that voted to depose Ross rose to prominence in the months following Fort Smith, and the impressions left on him by Ross's aloofness helped define a new Indian policy that would change the way the United States related to the indigenous people of the continent. Ely Samuel Parker was a Seneca Indian and sachem of the Iroquois Confederacy. Prior to the war he befriended Ulysses S. Grant and, as a result, served as Grant's adjutant during much of the war. Parker would later gain fame for having written in his own hand the surrender terms signed by Robert E. Lee. Few, if any, historians recognize the significance of Parker's involvement with the Fort Smith Council, often treating his presence as nothing more than a novelty.[90] But his greatest legacy comes from his involvement in Indian matters in the years following the war, beginning with his participation on the Fort Smith Council.

Parker and Ross represent contrasting examples of the search for indigenous identity in the latter half of the nineteenth century. Parker was three-fourths Indian and raised in a deeply traditional Seneca home, steeped in Native language and culture.[91] Ross, in contrast, was only one-eighth Cherokee and lived a highly assimilated life, embracing the culture and economy of white society. Yet both men held a deep appreciation for their Indian heritage. They both also embraced the advantages given them by a formal education. While the escalation of the Indian Wars in the American West has dominated the historiography of post–Civil War Indian relations, the juxtaposition of indigenous identity represented by Parker and Ross laid the foundation for much of U.S. Indian policy during that turbulent era in American history.[92]

Even though Parker was himself an Indian who supported the idea of tribal identity, Ross's actions went against what Parker believed to be the actions of a true Indian. He watched as Ross thwarted the work of the Fort Smith Council by "exercising his powerful influence to prevent an amicable settlement" between all parties of the "disloyal" Cherokee Nation.[93] Cooley noted that Ross kept "aloof from the council," discouraging the Cherokee delegation from signing the new treaty.[94] The powerful influence Ross displayed both angered and puzzled Parker, who gladly threw his support behind a vote to remove him from office as principal chief.

Parker would later tell an academic audience that, among the many things that separated an Indian from the whites, two things stood out. First, he claimed that "such a thing as a rich North American Indian I do not think was ever known." He asserted that "Indians are always poor." The fact that Ross and many other Indians in Indian Territory owned slaves and lived in wealth and luxury, while the bulk of their populations lived as poor subsistence farmers, gave Parker the idea that Ross was not really an Indian. Second, Parker decried the idea that the Cherokee Nation had a republican form of government, because the tribe had an obvious elite class perpetually in leadership positions. He argued that Indians did not have systematic forms of government but had organizational structures of "the most liberal democratic kind."[95] In short, all Indians were equal. In Parker's eyes, Ross was not an Indian, in that he ruled the Cherokee people like a white man. For Parker, this was not acceptable. He also believed that U.S. Indian policy was to blame.

In a report filed at the request of General Ulysses S. Grant, Parker offered his suggestions for revamping U.S. Indian policy. Submitted on January 27, 1867, the report included four primary proposals. The first suggested that the Bureau of Indian Affairs be transferred from the Department of the Interior and returned to the Department of War, where it had originated. The second proposed that a permanent territorial government be established in Indian Territory as was sought by President Johnson and the Fort Smith Council the previous year. Parker argued that the concentration of Indian tribes under a territorial government would eliminate much of the waste and inefficiency that plagued the Indian bureau. Even though the tribes begrudgingly signed the new treaties outlining the establishment of a territorial government, the institution held no significance for the tribes and was not enforced by federal authorities. Parker's third proposal was for a temporary board of inspectors to oversee the transition of the Indian Bureau to the War Department.[96]

Parker's fourth proposal was the most significant. It suggested the appointment of an Indian commission to handle the negotiations with Indian tribes moving forward. He suggested that the commission work to convince the Indians of the benefits of peace with the United States and of learning an agricultural lifestyle. He also suggested that the commission demonstrate to the Indians the strength and endless numbers of the white population and remind them that all the tribes who resisted the advances of white settlers met with extermination. However, the commission would reassure the Indians of the federal government's desire to protect them and secure their perpetuation as a nation. Parker warned of what he considered the biggest roadblock to the work of such a commission: tribes who were under "the influence and control of interested, unprincipled, and crafty individuals" who sought power at the expense of unsuspecting and faithful Indians. He asserted that the common Indian had an unrealistic desire for liberty and independence, and that those unprincipled men often fed that desire "in order to retain their influence and power."[97]

No doubt, one of those "unprincipled" men Parker had in mind was Ross. He believed that Ross used his "superior education and ability" to induce "many of his people to abjure their allegiance to the United States and to join the states in rebellion."[98] He also argued that Ross set up a false "claim to the office of principal chief, and by his subtle influence is at work poisoning the minds of those who are truly loyal."[99] Parker was angered by the notion that Ross used his position to tell the Cherokee people what they wanted to hear: that they were still an autonomous nation and that the United States promised to protect their right to govern themselves. The fact that Ross blamed the federal government for the Cherokee-Confederate alliance angered Parker and the Fort Smith Council. The only recourse was to remove him as principal chief so that the United States could have open and honest negotiations with the loyal Cherokee people. However, if the council was so anxious to treat with the "loyal" portion of the Cherokee Nation without Ross's influence and if they really believed that Ross was the only reason the Cherokees aligned with the Confederacy, why did they still force the "truly loyal" Cherokees to sign the punitive treaty at Fort Smith? The answer is clear. The Johnson administration was not concerned with guilt or innocence. In fact, the commissioners forced the loyal segments of the tribes to sign the treaty before the pro-Confederate segments even arrived at Fort Smith. They were not looking to determine which Indians were loyal and which were not. Johnson simply wanted Indian lands and a consolidated government in Indian Territory. The only true reason they removed Ross as chief was because he instructed the delegates not to sign the treaty as long as the preamble asserted a "forfeiture of money and lands."[100] Parker, who adopted Johnson's approach to Indian relations at Fort Smith, proposed sweeping changes to the nation's policy. The assassination of Abraham Lincoln brought a new Indian policy to bear on all the tribes of Indian Territory, even those that Lincoln had appeared to forgive.

Parker's proposed changes to U.S. Indian policy were well received in Washington. On the day after the report to Grant was submitted, Senator Henry Wilson from Massachusetts sent Parker a quickly penned note requesting that he "write, draw up, and send me a bill for presentation to Congress, embodying the ideas and propositions embraced in your report."[101] Wilson was part of a group of senators who believed that emancipation and civil rights were given to one race in the South and that it was now "time to take care of the Indians" as well.[102] Wilson supported a more "liberal and generous, humane and civilizing" Indian policy and thought Parker's proposed plan "covers all the ground."[103] Secretary of War Edwin M. Stanton also introduced Parker's proposals into both Senate and House committees on military affairs. Even though Parker's suggestions as a whole were not approved by Congress, the spirit of his ideas took root in the halls of Washington.[104] Less than six months after Parker's initial report, a bill emerged from the Senate Committee on Indian Affairs for the establishment of a commission "to make peace" with the Plains tribes.[105] The bill was presented on the Senate floor by Senator John B. Henderson of Missouri, who bemoaned the high cost of the escalating Indian Wars. "If we can make peace with the Indians," he told his Senate colleagues, "we had better do it."[106]

The bill would empower the commission to concentrate the Plains Indians on one of two reservations: the first to be established north of Nebraska, and the second, south of Kansas and west of Arkansas, "including the present Indian Territory."[107] Johnson's plan to take land from the tribes of Indian Territory as part of his punitive postwar treaty set the stage for this new round of removal in the post–Civil War years.

In his introduction of the bill, Henderson referenced the 1851 Treaty of Fort Laramie, Wyoming, which granted the Sioux ownership of the land they presently occupied, leaving for the United States an east-west route through the North Platte River Valley, the Platte Road, for white citizens chasing gold fever to California. Although the treaty gave the United States the right "to establish roads, military and other posts" within Sioux territory, the understanding was that any necessary infrastructure would be confined to the primary east-west throughway. However, the United States soon demonstrated, once again, its reputation for duplicity by announcing plans to erect three forts along the Bozeman Trail, which diverged from the overland road at Fort Laramie and cut a path northwest through the Powder River Valley and the heart of Sioux territory. This decision interrupted negotiations between federal authorities and the Cheyennes and Arapahoes and their allies, who had grown hostile in the wake of Colonel John Chivington's massacre of peaceful Indians at Sand Creek, Colorado, two years earlier. The leader of the hostile Indians, Red Cloud, promised retaliation if the forts were built. The army went forward with plans to build the forts regardless—Fort Reno, Fort Phil. Kearney, and Fort C. F. Smith—instigating further hostility. When the Indians lured Captain William J. Fetterman and about eighty men out of Fort Phil. Kearney into an ambush on December 21, 1866, the government launched a full-scale investigation to determine responsibility. It was in response to the Fetterman incident that Grant asked Parker to issue his own proposals for revamping U.S. Indian policy. That report, published with the findings on the Fetterman incident, led to Senator Henderson's Peace Commission of 1867.

The duty of the Peace Commission was to "remove, if possible, the causes of war" and to secure the safety of frontier settlements and railroad buildings along the route to the Pacific Ocean. Moreover, the commission was to "suggest or inaugurate some plan for the civilization of the Indians." That plan, according to the commission's report, was to begin with kindness.[108] "Promises have been so often broken by those with whom they usually come in contact," stated the report, "that to obtain their confidence our promises must be scrupulously fulfilled and our professions of friendship divested of all appearance of selfishness

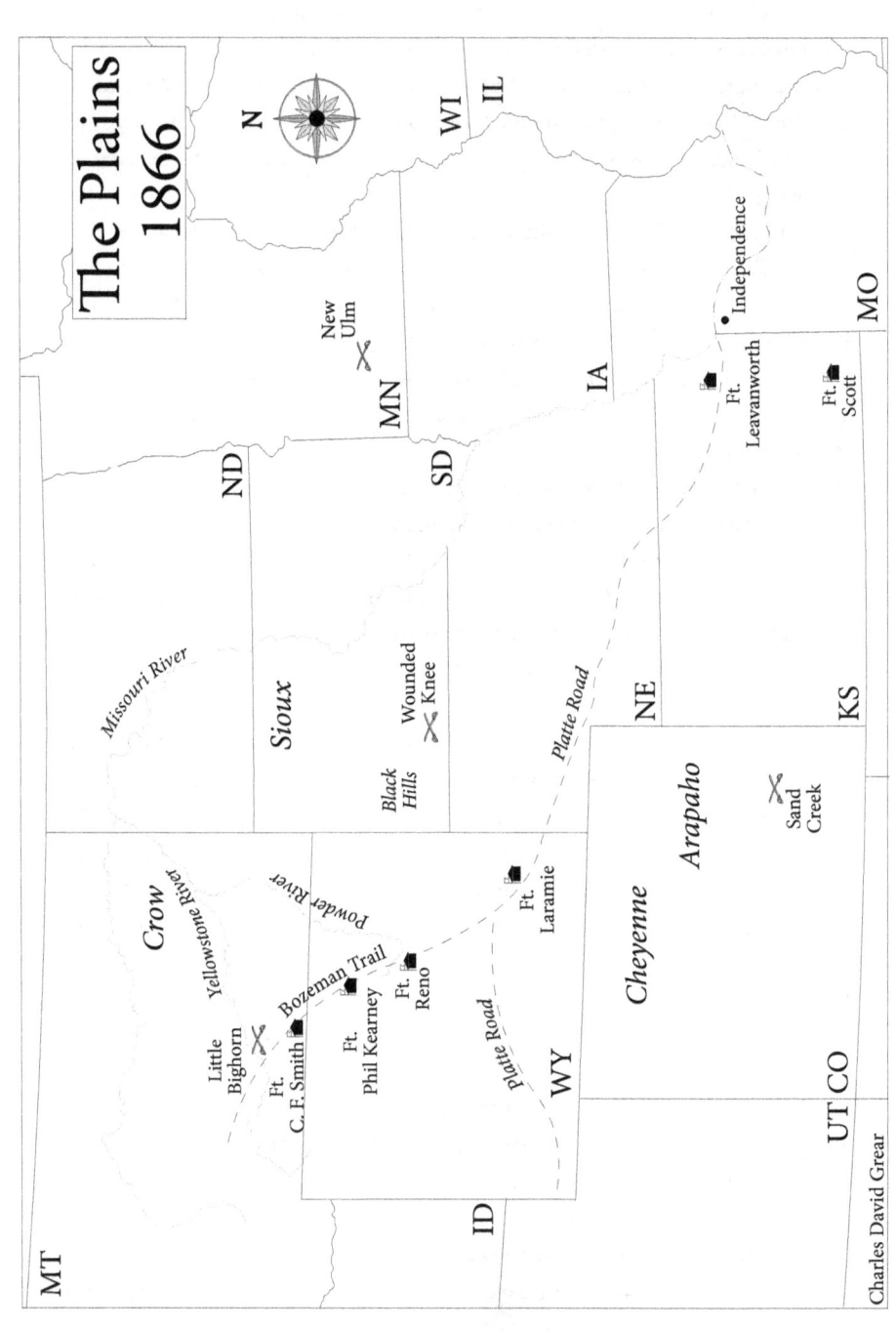

and duplicity."[109] In September 1867, the commission opted to give guns and ammunition to the starving Indians in the vicinity of Fort Laramie, preparing them as best as possible for the approaching winter hunt. This move caused intense debate throughout the nation amid fears that those very weapons would be used against white soldiers and citizens.

After attending a council with the Cheyennes, Arapahoes, Kiowas, Comanches, and Apaches at Medicine Lodge Creek, south of the Arkansas River in October 1867, the commission returned to Fort Laramie to meet with the bulk of the hostile Sioux. They were met by a delegation of Crow warriors; however, Red Cloud, the formidable leader of the hostile Indians, did not attend. Instead, he sent word that the reason for the hostility was to protect their vanishing hunting grounds along the Powder River, endangered by the presence of the three forts along the Bozeman Trail. He promised the commissioners that as soon as the forts were abandoned, the hostility would cease. Within a year, the government decided to close all three of the forts, hoping to appease the recalcitrant chief.[110] General William Tecumseh Sherman warned that abandoning the forts would convince the Indians that the United States had given in and "would invite the whole Sioux nation down to the main Platte Road," reversing any gains the army achieved in the region.[111]

The frantic search for the most effective and efficient method for pacifying the Plains Indians dominated U.S. Indian policy in the 1850s and 1860s. Indian policy of the nineteenth century was built on two major fallacies: that Indians wanted to assimilate and that whites would keep their word. Prior to the Civil War, most treaties signed with indigenous tribes were about land acquisition with little concern for whether or not the Indians became civilized, as long as they remained peaceful and out of the way. However, the Indians soon learned that the white government could not be trusted to keep its treaty promises. After the war, the treaties focused on securing peace, particularly after Indians had grown weary of the white man's constant abrogation and intrusion. Failed efforts to secure peace through acculturation quickly turned into plans to accomplish the same goal using forced compliance. If the United States resorted to military tactics to put down a rebellion among its Southern citizens and restore peace to the nation, it would not think twice about employing the army to bring peace to the American West.

In 1868, General Grant was elected president of the United States and upon taking office, named Ely S. Parker as his commissioner of Indian affairs. Even though the new president was often asked to provide arms to many of the western states to battle the resistant Indians, he promoted the nation's policy as being built on a foundation of peace.[112] Parker's job was to devise a policy for a peaceful solution to the nation's Indian question. Parker's plan was simple: abolish the practice of treaty making with Indians and treat them as wards of the state. Abandoning the treaty-making process was debated throughout the 1850s and 1860s. but in the months and years following the Civil War, the debate escalated. General Pope publicly advocated to end diplomatic negotiations with the recalcitrant tribes of the American West, urging the government to place the matter solely in the hands of the army "to deal with them without treaties and without the use of Indian agents."[113]

Parker's reasons for supporting an end to treaty making were spelled out in his reports to his superiors. First, he argued that tribal governments or organizations were not powerful enough to compel individuals to comply with treaty requirements.[114] On this point, Pope agreed. He believed that the Indians could be subdued only if treated as individuals, not as a communal tribe.[115] Parker's second reason for opposing the continuation of treaties was that the process often prevented its very objective. By signing treaties with the Indians, Parker argued, the United States encouraged tribes to retain vestiges of their tribal identity, which often inhibited assimilation.[116] As long as the Indians sought to retain "their separate creation, nationality, and customs," they would never accept acculturation.[117] Finally, Parker argued that signing treaties with tribal leaders created an elitist class of Indians, like John Ross, that stood in the way of acculturation. These elites would oppose consolidation and assimilation "because now they are something, while under the new order of things," Parker wrote, "they might be nothing."[118] The Fort Smith Council accused Ross of being one of those elites, and Parker no doubt had him in mind when he advocated abolishing the treaty-making process.

Consequently, in 1871, Congress listened to Parker's reasonings and added a clause to its Indian Appropriations Act, formally abolishing the practice of treaty making with Indian nations.[119] In the years following the Civil War, the United States established a new "radical reformist" Indian policy to expedite and compel the acculturation process of the American Indian.[120] President Grant's attempt to pacify the Indians using humanitarianism and philanthropy did little to convince the Indians of the need to assimilate.

Prior to the Civil War, Indian tribes were treated as independent nations, having been granted a certain level of autonomy within a suzerain relationship.

Abraham Lincoln tried to understand the travails of the Indians as they dealt with the expansion of white society. Moreover, his determination to deal with them in accordance with the constitutional parameters of the treaty-making process allowed him to do what his predecessors could or would not do: admit to the nation's treaty abrogation in the spring of 1861. In his final public speech, Lincoln stood on a White House balcony and informed the people below that "no one man has the authority to give up the rebellion for any other man."[121] Of the rebellious governments that swelled the ranks of the Confederate Army with their men, only one, the Cherokee Nation, returned to the United States before the war's end. John Ross may have led the Cherokee Nation into an ill-advised treaty of alliance with the Confederate government in October 1861, but they returned en masse within a year's time.

Even if Ross had stood in the way of Cherokee loyalty at Fort Smith, the individual members of the tribe deserved better than the punitive treaties of 1865 and 1866 because they willingly gave up the rebellion for themselves, as nearly twenty percent of the tribe's entire population joined the Union Army in the summer of 1862, more than satisfying the requirements for Lincoln's "Ten-Percent Plan." However, Lincoln's desire to reinstate the Cherokee Nation, including its principal chief, John Ross, was cut down that night at Ford's Theatre. Had Lincoln not been assassinated, the postwar treaties for the loyal Indians in Indian Territory would have no doubt looked much different. Moreover, the reestablishment of the Cherokee Nation to its prewar treaty status may have helped continue the process of treaty-making in the United States, at least a while longer. The Cherokees served as prewar and postwar examples of how effective U.S. Indian policy could be. At least Lincoln understood. The problem with U.S. Indian policy was not due to an unwillingness on the part of the Indians to become acculturated. The problem, as Lincoln and leaders of his administration saw it, was in the fact that the United States too often failed to honor its treaty obligations to the Indians and then blamed the Indians for how they responded. Lincoln's willingness to honor the nation's obligations and restore the Cherokees to their rightful status was an attempt to right an egregious wrong. With time to implement his policy, the way the United States dealt with the Plains Indians in the years following the war may well have been different than what history rendered. Unfortunately for the indigenous people of the United States, the restoration of the Cherokee Nation and the penitent stance of the chief executive were both buried with the body of the beloved president in a quiet grave in Illinois.

CONCLUSION

In 1997, Jimcy McGirt, a member of the Seminole Nation of Indians, was convicted in district court in Wagoner County, Oklahoma, of three serious sex crimes against a minor and sentenced to five hundred years in prison without the possibility of parole. Two decades later, McGirt's attorneys filed a motion in federal court to have the convictions thrown out and a new trial granted in federal court. McGirt claims that the alleged crimes occurred on the Creek Reservation, outside the jurisdiction of the state of Oklahoma but within the state's borders, reminiscent of Cherokee claims in *Worcester v. Georgia* (1832). The case made it to the U.S. Supreme Court, appearing on the docket during the October 2019 term. Oklahoma attorneys argued that the "Creek Reservation" no longer existed because the United States had dismantled it during the Allotment Era of the 1890s and early twentieth century by parceling out the land to individual members of the tribe at the turn of the twentieth century. The Court disagreed, and in a 5–4 vote, granted McGirt's petition, overturned the convictions, and, after more than a hundred years, reaffirmed Creek Indian sovereignty in the former Indian Territory.[1]

Delivering the opinion of the Court, Justice Neil Gorsuch admitted that the United States has the right to "break its own promises and treaties" with Native Americans whenever it desires, citing the precedent found in *Lone Wolf v. Hitchcock* (1903). The supreme sovereignty of the United States over Indian affairs secures this right. If the federal government abrogates a treaty by refusing to provide protection, monies, or privileges promised in a treaty, no entity can force it to do so. However, Gorsuch acknowledged that a reservation was a tangible object and was not the same as a written promise. Congress still has the sole authority to diminish or disestablish a reservation; however, the only way it can do so is by explicit legislation. Gorsuch opined that "if Congress wishes to withdraw its promise (of a reservation), it must say so."[2] He further added, "Under our Constitution, states have no authority to reduce federal reservations lying within their borders."[3] For the state of Oklahoma, trying to extend its jurisdiction over Indian land, even though it had done so for over a century without resistance, violated the U.S. Constitution. The preliminary treaty signed at Fort Smith in 1865 formally acknowledged the "exclusive jurisdiction" of the United States over the Indian nations that signed the treaty, including the Creeks.

The limits of the Creek Reservation in Oklahoma were first delineated by the removal treaty of 1833 and amended for the final time by the post–Civil War treaty of 1866.[4] Prior to 1871, whenever the United States wished to modify or revamp a treaty with a Native nation, it did so by negotiating a new treaty, either by force or inducement. These new treaties, according to the U.S. Constitution, became the "supreme Law of the Land" upon ratification, and their stipulations superseded those of all previous treaties.[5] But in 1871, Congress, on the recommendation of Ely S. Parker, ended the practice of treaty making with Native nations, thus eliminating its primary method of undoing existing treaties. Moreover, by failing to replace the practice of making treaties with a clearly defined and functional policy, Congress inadvertently christened the postwar treaties of 1866 the *perpetual* "Law of the Land." When Congress believed it was dismantling the Creek Reservation by allotting the land to individual Indians in the late nineteenth century, it failed to "clearly express its intent to do so," the Court ruled in *McGirt*.[6] In short, the paradigm-shifting decision in *McGirt v. Oklahoma* (2020) has its roots in the decision to abolish the practice of treaty making with Native nations in the United States.

The dismantling of U.S. Indian policy in the post–Civil War years began at the Fort Smith Council in 1865, when Andrew Johnson, armed with legislative authority, invalidated the prewar treaties of the Five Tribes in Indian Territory. Johnson gave the commissioners at Fort Smith explicit instructions for the desired terms to be negotiated. Most important, he wanted land on which to relocate the Plains Indians. To seize the needed land, Johnson did not concern himself with whether the tribes were guilty of disloyalty. John Ross and the Cherokees were surprised to learn that they, too, had been included on that list of disloyal tribes. Prior to the Civil War, the United States had envisioned a permanent separation of white and Indian societies. In the early nineteenth century, removal west of the Mississippi seemed a logical solution. However, territorial expansion in the mid-1800s precluded this idea, forcing the nation once again to confront the Indian question.[7] Johnson used an 1862 law, passed during Lincoln's presidency, to declare the Five Tribes' prewar treaties null and void and compel tribal leaders to sign new treaties, relinquishing much of their tribal autonomy and landholdings. Even with the passage of the law, the Cherokees convinced Lincoln of their innocence, citing federal abrogation of the prewar treaties. Lincoln's efforts to reinstate the tribe were eradicated with his assassination, allowing Johnson to undo the prewar treaties and seize the desired tribal lands. These postwar negotiations at Fort Smith in September 1865 led to the complete dismantling of U.S. Indian policy within two decades of the end of the war.

The dismantling of U.S. Indian policy began with the seizure of land in Indian Territory following the Civil War, opening the door for a new round of removal treaties and the relocation of additional tribes into the territory, away from white society. However, these new treaties did not provide as great a separation as did the prewar treaties, nor did they grant the Indians fee simple title to newly obtained lands. Tribes were granted mere possessory rights to the land and what Charles F. Wilkinson calls a "measured separatism."[8] The punitive postwar treaties with the Five Tribes, especially that with the Cherokees, altered the spirit of U.S. Indian policy by removing much of the suzerain autonomy held in the prewar years. Between 1865 and 1868, the nation introduced what Francis Paul Prucha calls a "radical reformist" policy that gave Indians only limited control of tribal lands and forced them into a more hurried plan for acculturation.[9] Unless a tribe discontinued the practice of any semblance of traditional tribalism, "there was little chance that the Indians as individuals could be completely absorbed into mainstream America," that is, assimilated.[10] Many of the tribes that signed treaties during this "reformist" period had no understanding of the expectations thrust upon them.[11] Some of the Indians resisted these new expectations, leading many Americans to question the feasibility of continued treaty making with the more nomadic and recalcitrant Plains tribes. However, the end of the Civil War provided the U.S. Army the opportunity to shift its focus toward the West and the final pacification of the American Indian.[12] The army's increased role as the enforcers of U.S. Indian policy only added to the unrest.

By 1871, the nation had completed the dismantling process by formally abolishing the treaty-making practice with Indian nations. In the immediate postwar years, however, not everyone advocated ending that process. Between 1865 and 1869 there were four different Indian commissioners and one acting commissioner; only one of them, Ely S. Parker, the last in the succession, denounced the practice as counterproductive to the goals of U. S. Indian policy. Even Dennis N. Cooley, who voted to depose John Ross at Fort Smith because he stood in the way of a new treaty with the Cherokee people, supported the practice. In his annual report for 1866, Cooley declared the utility of treaty making by proclaiming that many tribes still desired a treaty relationship with the federal government.[13] If the practice would help induce many Indians to enter a peaceful relationship with the U.S. government, then Cooley was all for it. In his mind, Cooley considered the problem not with the tribes that embraced the treaty relationship but with those who rejected it. He correctly identified the potential for trouble along the Bozeman Trail in the weeks before the Fetterman incident. "A small portion of the Sioux resolutely refuse to treat," he claimed, "and propose to resist, at all hazards, the use of a route to Montana."[14] Cooley believed that, while the treaty-making process worked well for some tribes, it was not the answer for all of them. He argued that the U.S. population included more than 300,000 Indians in 1866, scattered over the continent, representing as many as two hundred different tribes, "varying from the Civilized and educated Cherokees and Choctaws to the miserable lizard-eaters of Arizona," the latter perhaps in reference to some of the Pueblo Indians who reportedly ate the horned toad in times of famine.[15] He advocated for the rights of all of them to be protected "whether under treaty stipulations or roaming at will over [their] wild hunting-grounds."[16] In his first two years as commissioner, Cooley oversaw the negotiations of as many as twenty-eight treaties with tribes west of the Mississippi River, some of them well acculturated and others hardly so.

Nathaniel G. Taylor, who served as commissioner from 1867 to early 1869, believed that even the less civilized Indians had started to see the need for peace. The flood of white settlers into the West and the diminishing buffalo herds, in his opinion, alerted many tribes to the necessity of peaceful relations with the U.S. government. While some bureaucrats criticized the slow pace of acculturation with many tribes, Taylor saw it more optimistically. He believed that any progress was good progress, even if it was numbingly slow, and that acculturation was a process, not a decision. "A civilization of any account with them," he argued, "must be a work of time."[17] The Cherokees were the perfect example. "Agriculture and stock-breeding brought with them the important idea of individual rights or of personal property," he argued, "and the notion of fixed local habitations, of sale and barter, profit and loss." He continued, "Contact with the white settlements all around confirmed and fastened this new class of ideas upon them, and soon resulted in a corresponding change of habits, customs, and manners."[18] He asserted that the process proved a tremendous success and praised the Cherokee Nation as the prime example of how successful the process would be, given the appropriate time. Until acculturation could be realized, faithful observance of all treaty obligations would be required before the United States would see the same successes among the other tribes. "If others have not achieved the same status as the Cherokees," he pronounced, "it can only be the fault of the white government."[19] In other words, if the treaty-making process was not working, it was not the fault of the Indians.

In 1867, acting commissioner of Indian affairs Charles E. Mix, serving in place of Taylor while the latter presided over the Peace Commission, argued for separate treaties with hostile Indians in an effort to remove any "just cause of complaint" on their behalf.[20] He also believed the white population was the root of the problem with many of the Plains tribes, calling them the greatest hindrance "to the consummation of ends so much desired."[21] Their continuous exploitation of the people and the seizure of tribal lands left the Indians with "no certainty as to the permanent possession of the land."[22] He advocated permanent homes for the Indians with no white contact and for the faithful observance of all treaty stipulations on the part of the federal government.[23] Like Cooley, Mix believed that the treaty-making process worked for some tribes. He asserted that the Cherokees, despite the widespread devastation during the war, would soon "attain to more than their former prosperous condition."[24] However, he argued for the need of a new policy when dealing with those Indians less willing to abide by a diplomatic agreement. He also argued that the inhumane treatment at the hands of an intruding white population was unavoidable. As did many if not most Americans of the day, Mix believed in Manifest Destiny, calling the negative influences of the wave of white settlers inevitable.[25] In discussing the objective of the commission sent to investigate the Fetterman incident, he stated its purpose as three-fold: to identify the perpetrators, to distinguish the friendly Indians from the hostile ones, and to separate the two. Even though the acculturation process was slower than the nation had hoped it would be, Mix did not recommend undoing the treaty-making process with all Indians, only those who refused to accept the policy. He asked the Peace Commission to recommend the best policy for dealing with the hostile Indians.[26] Although not on the commission, Ely S. Parker, had plenty to suggest.

Unlike his immediate predecessors, Parker stood against treaty making with any tribe, claiming "great injury has been done by the government in deluding this people into the belief of their being independent sovereignties." He had witnessed Ross's resistance to the wishes of the federal government at the Fort Smith Council in September 1865 and identified the treaty-making process as the culprit. Because Ross believed that the treaties gave the Cherokees a certain autonomy, even within a suzerain relationship, the commissioners at Fort Smith had no authority to override them. He even questioned whether Congress had the right to grant authority to the president to nullify the treaties. In Ross's mind, Lincoln had already restored the prewar treaties, and the only way they could ever be nullified was with a new treaty. With that mindset, Ross vehemently resisted the pleadings of the commissioners at Fort Smith.

Ross and Parker occupy important spaces in the struggle for, and with, indigenous identity in the nineteenth and twentieth centuries. Parker was three-fourths Indian, highly educated, and profoundly conscious of his Seneca heritage. He was an enigmatic representative of indigenous society in that he compartmentalized his Native bloodline and his position in white society. He detested Ross and those he perceived to be like him, because Parker believed they used their Indianness to gain advantage within indigenous society. Ross was only one-eighth Cherokee, and even though his heritage fit society's definition of "Indian blood," and was readily accepted by the vast majority of the Cherokee people, in Parker's mind, Ross was a white man. At Fort Smith, Parker watched Ross stand in the way of the full-blood Cherokees' efforts to negotiate a relationship of peace and friendship with the United States. Parker did not accept the fact that the nation of full-blood Cherokees had elected Ross to be their principal chief at every election since 1828, the same year Parker was born. He claimed Ross had deluded the Cherokees into believing they were autonomous and that he was the only one who could secure that position for them before the U.S. government. Parker, living as a white man, and Ross, claiming to be an Indian, occupy antonymic positions of Indianness.

More important, perhaps, each man thought he knew how best to approach U.S.-Indian relations. Ross's unwavering adherence to the supremacy of constitutional law led him to believe that the federal government had a responsibility to protect the Indians' position within a suzerain relationship. Parker, on the other hand, believed that the Indian was responsible for recognizing his true position within the nation, that of a ward. Ross believed the government should stay out of Indian affairs and allow the Indians to govern themselves. Parker believed that the government had the authority and responsibility to dictate Indian affairs and to govern them with a strong hand. President Lincoln agreed with Ross. However, Presidents Johnson and Grant agreed with Parker.

When Parker became commissioner of Indian affairs in April 1869, he immediately called for abolishing treaty making with all Indians. If any tribe wished to enter a reservation and live in peace, he argued, the arrangements "should not be of a treaty nature."[27] Parker believed the Indians should recognize their inferior position and do as the government instructed them. Within two months of taking office, he distributed a circular to all agents and superintendents that defined the government's new policy for interacting with the Indians. The message was clear: the Indians were to be placed on reservations and acculturated. Any Indian who resisted would be forced by the U.S. Army to comply.[28]

In the post–Civil War years, the army took a more active role in U.S. Indian policy. Robert Utley suggests that much of the wartime violence between Indians and volunteer soldiers occurred because the regular army was distracted fighting a war.[29] Following the surrender at Appomattox, this was no longer the case. Regular soldiers returned to the West in large numbers as the United States could, once again, turn its attention to bringing peace to the Great Plains. Soldiers not only accompanied and protected white government negotiators but also often assisted in the negotiations. The army was so actively involved in U.S.-Indian relations during the postwar years that some historians credit military leaders with having had the authority to *develop* much of the nation's Indian policy.[30] Following the implementation of President Grant's "Peace Policy," which empowered the military to compel compliance, the army assumed an even greater role. Often referred to as the "Rifle and Peace Pipe Policy," Grant's system took on a paradoxical attitude as the military threatened violence to enforce peace.[31] This posture did not achieve the desired results.

The two most infamous failures of U.S.-Indian relations occurred during this period of forced compliance. In 1876, General George Armstrong Custer rode into an ambush at Little Bighorn Creek just as the nation was gearing up to celebrate its one-hundredth birthday. The outrage that swept the nation at the loss of Custer's forces brought a shift to a policy of forced assimilation and an increased attack on Indian autonomy and identity. The period came to a bloody climax in 1890 along another creek in South Dakota. Soldiers at the Pine Ridge Agency massacred a band of Lakota Sioux along Wounded Knee Creek in an effort to stop the practice of an indigenous ceremony known as the Ghost Dance and to compel assimilation.

If the assassination of Abraham Lincoln did not cause the change in Indian policy, it most certainly allowed it to happen. Lincoln's determination to reinstate the prewar treaties with the Cherokee Nation portended a continuation of the existing Indian policy in the immediate postwar years. Moreover, his willingness to acknowledge the nation's abrogation in 1861 demonstrated a tendency to honor the government's treaty obligations to the other tribes as well, a decision Johnson made no effort to duplicate. Lincoln's wartime actions regarding the Cherokee Nation provide sufficient evidence to suggest that his postwar relationship with the tribes in Indian Territory would have differed greatly from that of his successor's, if for no other reason than his simple acknowledgment of the government's abrogation.

The fact that slavery existed in the Cherokee Nation had no apparent impact on Lincoln's decision to reinstate the tribe. His order to return Federal troops to Indian Territory on March 19, 1862, occurred eleven months before the Cherokee National Council, meeting at Cowskin Prairie, formally ended slavery within the tribe. There is no evidence that the topic had been discussed by Ross or the president during their communication. The Emancipation Proclamation, enacted seven weeks prior to the Cowskin council, held authority only in the eleven states in rebellion and not in Indian Territory. For Lincoln, the reinstatement of the Cherokee Nation did not require the abolition of slavery. Moreover, during negotiations for the final postwar treaty in the spring of 1866, General Thomas Ewing, an attorney speaking on behalf of the Cherokee government, put the issue to rest. "The issues which grew out of the slavery question," he argued, "will die out with the cause."[32] Daniel W. Voorhees, an attorney representing Stand Watie and his faction in efforts at reconciliation, agreed. The topic was not broached again during the negotiations. Most of the debate centered on the best way to restore Watie and the pro-Confederate Cherokees to the tribe.

To be sure, the postwar treaty of 1866 did address the peculiar institution and its aftermath, at least as far as the Cherokee Nation was concerned. Article Nine verified the abolition of slavery in the Cherokee Nation and guaranteed to the Cherokee freedmen the same rights as those held by Cherokee citizens. Furthermore, it extended those rights to all the descendants of those former Cherokee slaves, as well. According to the treaty, all these descendants would be elevated to full Cherokee citizenship. The treaty set no temporal limits on the descendants clause, setting the stage for a racial battle that would rage for a century and a half in which Cherokees and their former slaves would contest the limits of identity and recognition. The Treaty of 1866 obliterated preconceived ideas of Indianness in the United States, and by the time of Oklahoma statehood in 1907, Native Americans would be the minority in their own territory.

The redistribution of tribal lands following the Civil War continued into the 1880s as multiple Indian tribes were relocated to Indian Territory. In 1887, the attack on tribal sovereignty continued as the Indian Allotment Act began the process of parceling out tribal land for individual ownership. By 1889, Congress decided to liquidate land in Indian Territory that had been seized following the Civil War but had not yet been assigned to another tribe. This "unassigned land" became the target of the famous Oklahoma land run in which nearly 1.9 million acres of land once belonging to the Creek and Seminole nations was offered on a first-come, first-served basis. So many settlers flooded into the region that by early 1890, Congress established Oklahoma Territory immediately west of Indian Territory (see fig. 3). That year ended with the slaughter at Wounded Knee and the unofficial announcement by the director of the Census Bureau that the American frontier no longer existed; it had been erased by Manifest Destiny.[33] The American heartland had been repainted a new shade of white as Anglo-American settlers flooded the Great Plains, driving the American Indian further down the path toward assimilation.

The creation of Oklahoma Territory and the growing influx of white settlers, businessmen, and profiteers into the region brought an astounding transformation to Indian Territory. While whites comprised 79.4 percent of the population of the new Oklahoma Territory in 1890, surprisingly, whites also outnumbered Indians in Indian Territory more than two-to-one as only 28.5 percent of the population was Native American.[34] Moreover, Blacks constituted 3.8 percent of the population of Oklahoma Territory and 10.3 percent of that of Indian Territory. As the white population of Oklahoma Territory continued to grow, a similar transformation continued to plague the tribes of Indian Territory. By 1900, Indians made up only 13.4 percent of the population of Indian Territory, and by 1907, that number fell to 9.1 percent. Between 1890 and 1907, the Indian population of Indian Territory grew by only 20.8 percent, from 51,279 to 61,925. During that same period, the white population grew by 388.4 percent. Moreover, the number of Blacks living in Indian Territory climbed at roughly the same rate as the white population, from 18,636 in 1890 to 80,649 in 1907. In 1907, Congress combined the two territories into the new state of Oklahoma, further diminishing the presence of Indian people, who made up only 5.3 percent of the new state's population. By 1920, Blacks outnumbered Indians in the state by nearly three to one.

From the founding of the United States to the dawn of the twentieth century, the goal of U.S. Indian policy was the dispossession of indigenous peoples from their communal homelands. The policies for achieving that goal varied over the years, from acculturation to removal to assimilation. At the end of the nineteenth century, the United States completed its primary goal by seizing as much tribal land as it deemed necessary, using military force to compel the compliance of any peoples who resisted and engulfing Native America in a white wave so fierce that many once proud cultures were swept away entirely. The Five Tribes, who had larger populations and stronger governmental organizations, were more difficult

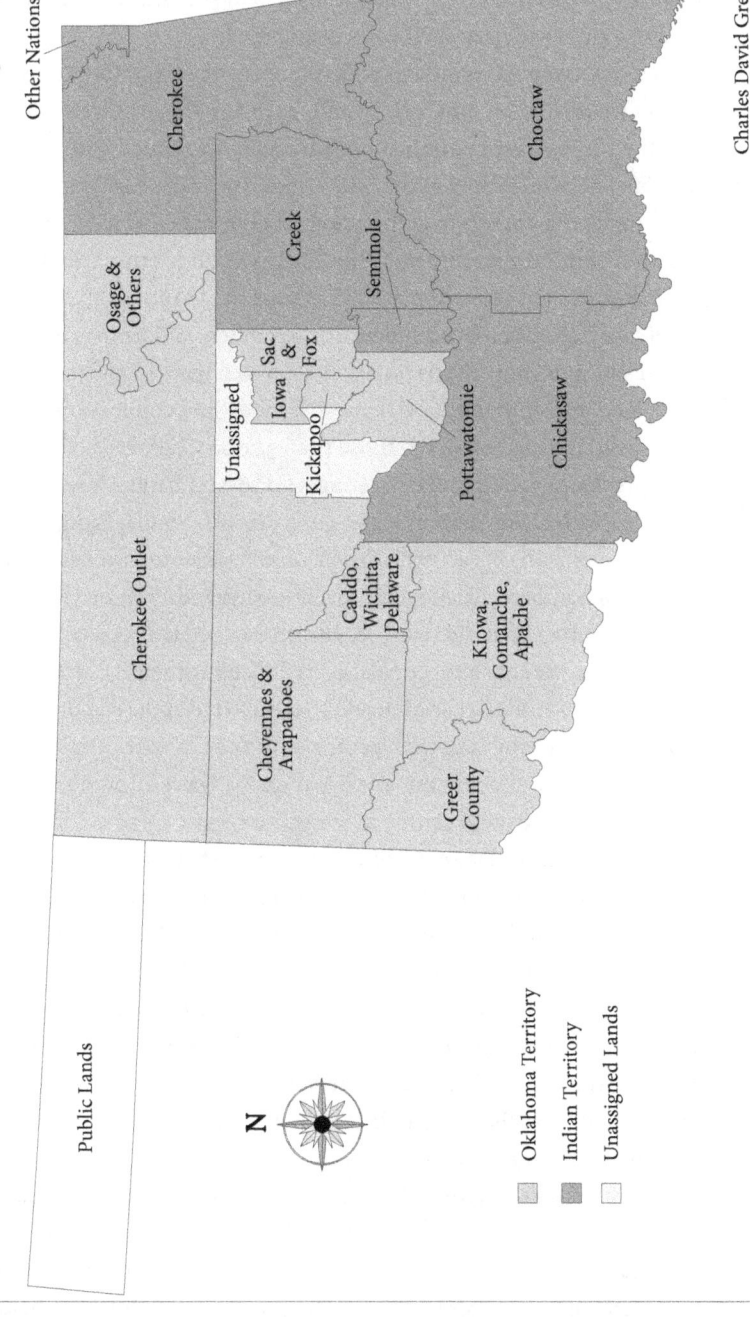

to sweep away. In fact, the Cherokee, Creek, Seminole, Choctaw, and Chickasaw nations had to be dealt with strategically and diplomatically. Therefore, by 1907, the Five Tribes had been politically dismantled.

That dismantling included the division of tribal land into individual allotments. To qualify for a parcel of land, each Cherokee citizen had to register with the Dawes Commission, a presidentially appointed body empowered to negotiate the dismantling of the Five Tribes. The tribes had been asked to begin enrolling their members in preparation for allotment and to be prepared for the cessation of tribal governments. The Cherokees, like other tribes, resisted this procedure, leaving the commissioners themselves to enroll all Indians on either one of two rolls: Cherokee by blood, or freedmen. Citizenship in the Cherokee Nation was guided by the Treaty of 1866, which defined tribal membership by both blood ancestry and slave lineage. By 1906, the commission completed its enrollment, having registered more than 33,000 Cherokees of blood ancestry and more than 4,300 Cherokee freedmen and descendants. Oklahoma statehood coincided with a cessation of tribal governments, ending indigenous self-rule in the former Indian Territory. Other than a three-to-two advantage in total population numbers, Black men had something additional at the time of statehood that Indian men did not: U.S. citizenship and the right to vote.[35]

Analysis of the changing population is difficult without an exhaustive study of the shifting definitions of Indianness that occurred at the end of the nineteenth and beginning of the twentieth centuries in the Cherokee Nation and the rest of Indian Territory. Many Indians listed on the Dawes Commission rolls were also listed on the federal census as white. Moreover, some of the names on the freedmen rolls of the Dawes Commission were listed simply as "black." According to the 1910 census reports, nearly 62 percent of all Cherokees claimed to be of mixed heritage, and more than half of the tribe identified their lineage as being more than half white.[36] It is unclear how many Indians in Indian Territory in the early twentieth century self-identified as white to avoid the racial stigma of being Native American. However, Blacks hardly enjoyed the same racial mobility. Black Americans did not have the same opportunity to redirect their racial heritage simply by checking a different box on an application or a government form. Black Indians in Oklahoma faced racism from two corners: from whites who viewed Blacks as aboriginal and heathenistic, and from Indians who came to view them as a threat to both Indian identity and tribal self-rule.

The 1920s marked the low point for tribal sovereignty in Indian Territory. The 1920 federal census reveals that the Indian population of Oklahoma had declined by 23.4 percent since the previous enumeration, leaving Native Americans as only 2.8 percent of the state's population.[37] The final attack on tribal sovereignty occurred in 1924, when Congress passed the Indian Citizenship Act. Many white Americans believed that making Native Americans U.S. citizens transformed them from "savage" to "civilized."

Perhaps few tribes suffered from the dismantling of indigenous society as much as the Cherokees. In 1930, the federal census identified them as the largest Indian tribe in the United States, with 45,238 members. However, the report said that the Cherokees were "geographically by far the most widely distributed."[38] Cherokee Indians had abandoned Indian Territory in large numbers, and by 1930, Cherokees lived in forty-four of the forty-eight states. Moreover, the census report issued a scathing attack on Cherokee identity by implying that the tribe was less an "Indian" tribe than other groups, because only 17.8 percent of the respondents claimed to be full-blood. The report compared them to the Navajos, who also had more than 40,000 members, yet nearly all full-blood.[39] The Cherokees entered the mid-twentieth century renegotiating the very definitions of their identity. The dismantling of tribal governments and the elevation of Indians to U.S. citizens allowed the United States to close the door on its process of assimilation and, at least in the minds of many, provide better care for the indigenous people of the United States.

Between 1887 and 1934, the United States seized approximately two-thirds of all land belonging to Indian nations, dismantled tribal governments, and denounced tribal membership by transferring Native Americans to U.S. citizenship. For many in the U.S. government, the abolition of tribal sovereignty was not about eradicating indigenous culture and tradition. It was an attempt to elevate Native people up "the steps to civilization."[40] As long as tribal governments remained intact, the perception was that the Indian would remain in uncivilized "savagery."

However, the onset of the Great Depression in the 1930s presented numerous logistical challenges that made providing for Indian families more difficult. In 1934, the federal government allowed for the resuscitation of tribal organizations to more efficiently administer federal programs among Indian people. The Indian Reorganization Act allowed the tribes and their presidentially appointed principal chief, who had served in a ceremonial role since statehood, to implement economic plans to help alleviate much of the suffering among their own people. Although many of the tribes, including the Cherokees, opted not to reorganize immediately, the Act prepared the way for a full resurgence of tribal governance following the Civil Rights Movement of the 1960s.

That resurgence began with the passage of the Principal Chiefs Act in 1970. Congress allowed the tribes of the former Indian Territory to reestablish tribal governments and plan for the election of their own principal chiefs. However, the voting laws governing those elections would have to be approved by the Department of the Interior and, in the case of the Cherokees, to allow for the inclusion of descendants of Cherokee freedpeople as citizens. The Principal Chiefs Act brought on the resurrection of Cherokee tribal government. By 1975, the tribe had adopted a new constitution that followed federal requirements and acknowledged the Indian Civil Rights Act of 1968, which guaranteed the protections of the U.S. Constitution for all Indians. Moreover, it reestablished the office of principal chief to be elected by the people, one legislative body known as the Council of the Cherokee Nation, and a three-member Judicial Appeals Tribunal to resolve disagreements between Cherokee law and the new tribal constitution.

The constitution also set the parameters for tribal membership. Article III required that "all members of the Cherokee Nation must be citizens as proven by reference to the Dawes Commission Rolls."[41] The article did not specifically mention Cherokee freedpeople, though it implied their citizenship because of their inclusion on the Dawes Rolls. It did, however, mention the Shawnees and the Delawares, who had become members of the tribe through separate agreements. Article VI, Section 2, stipulated that only a member of the Cherokee Nation could hold the office of principal chief, and Article V, Section 3, did the same for members of the National Council. The stipulation was interpreted literally, barring freedpeople from holding public office; they could, however, participate in the electoral process and were allowed to vote in national elections. At this point, there had been no formal challenge to the citizenship of freedpeople descendants.

However, the resurrection of tribal government and the new constitution rekindled a passion within the Cherokee Nation. In early 1983, the National Council did something it had not done in 145 years: it asserted itself as a sovereign nation, challenging the validity of a federal treaty. Darell R. Matlock Jr., the chief justice of the Judicial Appeals Tribunal, argued that even though the Cherokee Nation had been dismantled by the U.S. government in the early twentieth century, it had never relinquished its sovereign status; it had only been "almost forced into extinction." Matlock claimed that by redefining tribal membership to fit its own needs, the Cherokees "seized the opportunity... to exert their sovereign status and maintain tribal autonomy."[42] Not since issuing the Resolutions of 1838 prior to the forced removal had the Cherokee Nation taken such a bold legislative stand against the U.S. government. That stand was easily swept aside by the "Trail of Tears." This latest stand, however, would challenge the definitions of Cherokee identity and sovereignty over the next three decades.

The Council enacted legislation in 1983 which undermined the postwar treaty of 1866 by voting to redefine tribal membership as being "derived only through proof of Cherokee blood based on the Final Rolls."[43] The legislation denied freedmen the right to vote in the approaching tribal election. The Cherokee Nation had never really accepted freedmen as citizens of the tribe, even in the years immediately following the ratification of the punitive postwar treaty.[44] Moreover, as late as the first decade of the twenty-first century, the Cherokee Nation still argued against the idea of freedmen citizenship, claiming it had been forced on the tribe by treaty following the conclusion of the Civil War.[45] In 1866, the Cherokees had offered to allow their former slaves free use of tribal lands as long as the land belonged to the Cherokee Nation. However, they stopped short of offering them membership in the tribe.

The Cherokee Citizenship Law of 1983 came under legal scrutiny the following year when eighty-five-year-old Roger Harvey Nero, himself a freedman citizen of the Cherokee Nation and an original Dawes enrollee, filed suit in federal court, claiming he had been denied the right to participate in tribal politics and programs because he was not a blood Cherokee. The case, *Nero v. Cherokee Nation of Oklahoma*, was heard by the U.S. District Court for the Northern District of Oklahoma. Nero's attorneys argued that their client had been recognized as a Cherokee citizen prior to the 1983 law and had voted in the tribal election in 1979.[46] The judge, H. Dale Cook, rejected the suit on the basis of sovereign immunity, which protects sovereign nations from being sued. Nero's attorneys appealed the ruling. On December 22, 1989, the Tenth Circuit Court of Appeals issued its ruling. Citing its own precedent in *Wheeler v. United States Department of the Interior* (1987), the court denied the appeal on the argument that the Cherokee right to self-government precludes the United States from interfering in a tribal election dispute.

Nero's case provides an interesting case study for the shortcomings of the Dawes Rolls and their impact on both indigenous and African American societies in Indian Territory. Although he was only two years old at the time, Nero was listed on the Cherokee Freedmen Roll along with his mother, Sarah, and a three-month-old sister, Jesse. In order to include her children on the rolls, Sarah had to provide a birth affidavit for each. On a form provided by the Interior Department for just this purpose, a midwife named Hanna Lasley affixed her mark before a notary, testifying that Roger Harvey Nero was born on October 26, 1898, to Sarah Nero, an adopted citizen of the Cherokee Nation and to Abe L. Nero, an adopted citizen of the Creek Nation.[47] When Sarah included her mixed-heritage son on the Cherokee Freedman Rolls, she denied him access to the benefits of dual citizenship in the Creek Nation. However, she had little choice. If she wanted him to benefit from allotment, she needed to follow the dictates of the Commission, which required all Indians with dual citizenship to choose one tribe or the other, forcing them to disregard as much as half of their own heritage and identity.

A second shortcoming of the Dawes Rolls is that the membership list compiled by federal agents has rendered previous tribal records obsolete. Any Indian who refused to interact with government commissioners during enrollment forfeited tribal membership for themselves and their descendants, regardless of prior tribal involvement. Numerous Indians, both Cherokee and freedmen, have since applied for membership based on tribal records that predate the Dawes Rolls. However, the Cherokee constitution bars their enrollment because it stipulates membership be directly connected to the Dawes Rolls.[48]

The obstacles to citizenship that confronted Nero were not new. Cherokees began limiting freedpeople's rights almost immediately following the ratification of the punitive treaty of 1866.[49] Prior to the Civil War, divisions within the Cherokee tribe were primarily drawn along lines of blood quantum. Mixed-bloods and full-bloods often disagreed over political and social issues, most notably removal and slavery. However, after the war, blood quantum became less an issue, particularly after the United States helped redefine the limits of Cherokee identity by granting tribal citizenship to the former slaves. Mixed-bloods and full-bloods came together to protect the core of Cherokee identity. If the margins of a racial category create that core, as legal historian Ariela Gross suggests, redefining those margins is what protects it.[50] The Cherokees sought to redefine the racial boundaries between Indian and freedman in the post–Civil War years. However, the dismantling of tribal governments rendered political involvement by Black Cherokees moot for much of the twentieth century. After the resurrection of tribal government in the 1970s, however, the Cherokees were forced to take up the mantle of racial identification once again. Race and identity did not become entangled for the Cherokees until after the punitive postwar treaty of 1866, and for the next 150 years, the Cherokee Nation used its sovereignty to tie that knot securely.[51]

On October 16, 1996, Bernice Riggs, who had direct ancestors on the Freedmen Rolls and possessed a degree of Cherokee blood, submitted an application for membership in the Cherokee Nation. Even though she was a blood Cherokee, her application was rejected because she was Black. Riggs filed suit. The case was argued before the Judicial Appeals Tribunal on June 12, 1998. Three years later, the court rendered its decision. Justice Darell R. Matlock Jr. delivered the court's unanimous opinion. "The Cherokee Nation is a Sovereign Nation," he wrote, "with the absolute right to determine its citizenship."[52] And the Cherokee Nation determined that citizenship no longer belonged to Black Cherokees.[53]

Based on the court's ruling in *Nero*, the Cherokee Nation once again sought to assert its sovereignty and, by doing so, unleashed a tidal wave of litigation in both tribal and federal courts. In May 2003, the Cherokee Nation proposed a constitutional amendment to invalidate a stipulation of the Principal Chiefs Act that required federal approval for any change to a tribe's constitution. Moreover, Cherokee freedmen were barred from voting in the election. Freedmen leaders immediately asked the Bureau of Indian Affairs (BIA) to intervene. However, in July, the Cherokee people approved the new constitution, replacing the one from 1975. This new constitution made no change to the wording of the citizenship requirement as defined by the Citizenship Law of 1983. The BIA refused to approve the new constitution or the earlier amendment, because it removed the bureau's authority. However, it refused to intervene in the election process and approved the election results, stating that any election disputes should be handled within the tribe itself.[54] This passivity, no doubt, angered freedmen leaders, who now turned to federal court for redress.

In 2003, Marilyn Vann, a longtime freedmen activist and president of the Freedmen of the Five Civilized Tribes, filed suit against Interior Secretary Dirk Kempthorne and the Department of the Interior on the grounds that the secretary "breached [his] fiduciary duty to protect the voting rights of the Freedmen" by failing to demand that the Cherokee Nation comply with the Thirteenth Amendment, the Principal Chiefs Act of 1970, and the Treaty of 1866.[55] The suit also named the Cherokee Nation as a defendant in hopes that the court would remove the sovereign immunity barrier and allow the freedmen to bring necessary lawsuits against the Cherokee Nation. Judge Henry H. Kennedy Jr. agreed, throwing out the sovereign immunity protection enjoyed by the tribe since the ruling in *Nero v. Cherokee Nation* in 1989. The court ruled that although the tribe retained the protection, individual leaders of the tribe did not, opening the door for the freedmen to file an amended complaint. The Cherokee Nation appealed the ruling.

Armed with this new ruling, Lucy Allen, another Cherokee freedmen, sued the Cherokee National Council, the registrar, and the registration committee on the grounds that freedmen had not simply been denied their constitutional rights to full tribal citizenship but that those rights had been removed. In *Allen v. The Cherokee Nation Tribal Council* (2006), the Judicial Appeals Tribunal ruled that the language of the Constitution of 1975 allowed freedmen to participate in the electoral process prior to the Citizenship Law of 1983. In a two-to-one vote on March 7, 2006, the court approved Allen's petition, declaring the citizenship law unconstitutional. Justice Stacy L. Leeds agreed that the Cherokee people have ultimate sovereignty over their own citizenship requirements. However, those requirements had been defined by the 1975 constitution. The Cherokee people retain the authority to change the citizenship requirements, but they cannot change the constitution with simple legislation passed by the National Council. As a result, the tribunal also reversed its ruling in *Riggs v. Ummerteskee* (2001), opening the door for Riggs to reapply for citizenship.

The Cherokee National Council wasted little time in responding. Three months after the *Allen* ruling, it approved a constitutional amendment requiring Cherokee blood for tribal membership. However, a resolution to call a special election to amend the constitution for the fall of 2006 failed. Without hesitation, a group of Cherokee citizens began circulating a petition calling for the special election. The petition was successful, and on March 3, 2007, Cherokee voters ratified an amendment adding the words "by blood" to the citizenship requirement of Article III. The amendment formally removed about 2,800 Cherokee freedmen from tribal membership and jeopardized another 3,500 pending applications. Two months later, Cherokee Nation district judge John Cripps issued an injunction temporarily barring implementation of the amendment and restoring the Cherokee freedmen to tribal membership. The injunction allowed Cripps time to rule in a class action suit already before his court. Raymond Nash, another freedmen, had brought the case against the tribe, hoping to have the constitutional amendment overturned.[56]

On June 21, 2007, California congresswoman Diane Watson introduced legislation in the U.S. House of Representatives to effectively sever the government's relations with the Cherokee Nation "until such time as the Cherokee Nation of Oklahoma restores full tribal membership to the Cherokee Freedmen" disenfranchised by the March special election.[57] Cherokee principal chief Chadwick

Smith reiterated the belief that tribal sovereignty allowed the Cherokee people to decide the definitions and parameters of Cherokee citizenship themselves. In 2008, members of the Congressional Black Caucus attempted to block passage of an appropriations bill that would provide housing assistance to Native Americans in the United States until the Cherokee Nation complied with its obligations to Cherokee freedmen under the Treaty of 1866. Newly elected president Barak Obama interceded, however, asking that Congress avoid further involvement while court cases on the matter were pending.

Contained within the text of Representative Watson's resolution is a description of three foundational events in Cherokee history that have frequently been cited in judicial and legislative proceedings to justify freedmen citizenship in the Cherokee Nation. First, the Cherokees owned slaves, and those slaves accompanied the tribe to Indian Territory along the "Trail of Tears" in the 1830s. The third event is the signing of the Treaty of 1866 following the Civil War, which was necessitated by the second event, the Cherokee-Confederate alliance of October 1861.[58] While the Confederate alliance has often been used against the tribe to justify the punitive postwar treaty, neither judicial nor legislative proceedings have mentioned federal culpability for the United States' abandonment of the forts in Indian Territory in April 1861. Had the United States honored its own treaty obligations in 1861, there would most likely not have been a punitive treaty in 1866 forcing the Cherokees to grant citizenship to its former slaves. The Cherokees had no intention of granting it themselves, at least not in 1866. A proposed version of the treaty at the time, proffered by the Cherokee delegation, offered the freedmen only free use of tribal land along with limited rights, as long as the tribe held the land communally.[59]

For the United States to use Cherokee slavery and the Confederate alliance as justification for full freedmen citizenship is further evidence of the punishment meted out to the tribe in the wake of the Fort Smith Council. The Choctaws and Chickasaws held slaves as well, and both entered an alliance with the Confederacy without hesitation at the start of the war. Yet neither tribe was forced to grant full tribal membership to their former slaves, most likely because of their cooperative stance at Fort Smith in September 1865.

On February 3, 2009, the Cherokee Nation filed a lawsuit in U.S. district court, asking for a summary judgement as to whether the Dawes Act (1887) in effect invalidated the citizenship requirement of the Treaty of 1866.[60] A group of freedmen descendants led by Raymond Nash and Marilyn Vann immediately filed a counterclaim against the Cherokee Nation asking the court to uphold the treaty. Three years later, the Department of the Interior filed its own request for a summary judgment, requesting that the court finally and formally declare the Treaty of 1866 to be the standard by which the freedmen citizenship question was to be resolved.

Meanwhile, on January 14, 2011, Cherokee district judge John Cripps issued his ruling on the class action suit brought before him four years earlier. Cripps declared the new amendment unconstitutional and restored the 2,800 Cherokee freedmen to tribal membership. He acknowledged that the United States had not always treated the Cherokee people with honor and dignity. "This does not mean," he wrote, "that the Cherokee Nation should descend into such manner of action and disregard their pledges and agreements."[61] In short, Cripps argued that frequent duplicity on the part of the United States does not justify Cherokee abrogation of the Treaty of 1866. However, he made no mention of the federal abrogation of 1861.

All parties involved–the Cherokee Nation, the freedmen, and the U.S. Department of Interior–awaited the final ruling from the U.S. District Court for the District of Columbia, a ruling that finally came down on August 30, 2017, in favor of the freedmen.[62] District Judge Thomas F. Hagan ruled that the Dawes legislation had no effect on the validity and authority of the Treaty of 1866. He then ruled that the Cherokee right to decide the definitions and limits of citizenship within its own tribe is not more powerful in the twenty-first century than it was in the nineteenth century when the Cherokee Nation limited that right by signing the Treaty of 1866. The treaty, as "supreme Law of the Land," trumps any Cherokee constitution, legislation, or judicial ruling and, therefore, must remain the standard. Hagan held that if the Cherokee Nation decided to "persist in its design to perpetuate a moral injustice, this Court will not be complicit in the perpetuation of a legal injustice."[63]

On August 31, 2017, the day after the court's ruling, Todd Hembree, attorney general for the Cherokee Nation, announced that the tribe would no longer assert its sovereignty in the matter by filing an appeal and would, instead, accept the court's ruling. The following day, September 1, the Cherokee Nation Supreme Court, formerly known as the Judicial Appeals Tribunal, ordered that all freedmen descendants have the same rights and privileges as other Cherokees, including the right to run for tribal office. The Cherokee registrar's office began accepting and processing freedmen applications the same day.

Judge Hagan's refusal to perpetuate a "moral injustice" on the part of the Cherokees by complying with a "legal injustice" in the courtroom rings of irony as the United States continues to perpetuate its own history and legacy of moral injustice toward Native Americans by holding them accountable for treaties that were, perhaps, immorally obtained. However, those treaties—be they moral or immoral—are the only thing that protects the tenuous relationship between the Indians and the U.S. government. Without them, the Native nations of the United States would once again find themselves completely at the mercy of the federal government.

By holding the Cherokee Nation accountable for the Treaty of 1866, the United States once again held the tribe accountable for Principal Chief John Ross's intransigence before the Fort Smith Council in September 1865. The punitive treaty was a response to both Ross's pertinacity and the Cherokee-Confederate alliance of 1861. Ross's insistence that the abandonment of the forts in Indian Territory in 1861, which left the Cherokee Nation with little option but to align with the Confederacy, angered the commissioners at Fort Smith and led to the punitive treaty. In contrast, the Choctaw Nation also held African slaves and immediately signed an alliance with the Confederacy. Yet they acquiesced to the commissioners at Fort Smith and, therefore, avoided much of the punishment given the Cherokees.

The frustrations of dealing with a duplicitous white government took its toll on John Ross during the final days of the Fort Smith Council in 1865. The aging chief spent his last year of life interceding with Andrew Johnson's administration on behalf of his reputation as principal chief of the Cherokee Nation. Accusations of elitism and disloyalty contradicted what Ross believed he had demonstrated in his nearly forty years as leader of the most advanced Indian nation in the United States. While he lay dying at a rented house in Washington, D.C., in the summer of 1866, Ross asked for paper and a pen with which to write. What he scribbled provides insight into the frustration and heartbreak that doubtless describe his interaction with the United States as he led the Cherokee Nation through its two most difficult eras. The notes written on his deathbed betray that frustration and most sincerely reveal the faith in the process of constitutional law that defined his relationship with the United States.

In his deathbed note, Ross quoted four articles from the tribe's two oldest treaties with the United States: the Treaty of Hopewell of 1785 and the Treaty of Holston of 1791. Article Twelve of the Hopewell treaty revealed Ross's faith in the process of constitutional law. It guaranteed the Cherokees the right to send delegates to Washington to lay the tribe's grievances before Congress so that they "may have full Confidence in the justice of the U. States, respecting their interests." Ross must have felt a sickening irony when he thought about the United States' commitment to protect Cherokee rights and interests. Instead, in the months after the Civil War, he had watched as the federal government swept away tribal autonomy. Now, as he lay dying, the U.S. Senate ratified the postwar treaty, and President Andrew Johnson prepared to sign it into law.

The next two articles Ross copied out, numbers two and eight of the Holston treaty, depict the United States' responsibility to protect the Cherokee Nation. Again, Ross had watched the United States fail on multiple occasions to protect the Cherokees from white intruders, first in Georgia and then at the start of the Civil War when Confederates from Texas invaded Indian Territory following the withdrawal of Federal troops.

Finally, he wrote the Seventh article of the Holston treaty, which declared that "the U.S. solemnly guarantees to the Cherokee Nation, all their land." Whether through Andrew Jackson or Andrew Johnson, the United States repeatedly ignored its own treaty obligations in order to seize land legally granted to the Cherokee Nation according to Senate-ratified treaties. Somehow, supreme sovereignty in the United States protects the federal government from the stigma of having committed an immoral injustice.

These four articles reflect the frustration Ross felt during two of the most important eras in Cherokee history. The Removal Era of the 1830s and the Civil War era of the 1860s form heartbreaking bookends to Ross's career as principal chief of the Cherokee Nation, yet he never lost faith in the justice of the treaty system and U.S. constitutional law.

Ross died on August 1, 1866, ten days before Andrew Johnson signed the postwar treaty into law. Ross was seventy-five years old. He died believing the duplicity at Fort Smith was an attack on himself and the Cherokee Nation. He had no idea how much his life would impact U.S. Indian policy in the years immediately following the Civil War and how much that policy would impact his own people into the twenty-first century. His faithful reliance in the process of constitutional law angered Ely S. Parker, who set out to ensure that no other tribe of Indians would have the arrogance to claim autonomy and refuse to cower to the dictates of the U.S. government, be they moral or immoral.

NOTES

Abbreviations

ARSOI	Hathi Trust Digital Library
CHCA	Cherokee Heritage Center Archives
DPLA	Digital Public Library of America online
HC	Helmerich Center for American Research
LOC	Library of Congress
NARA	National Archives and Records Administration
NL	Newberry Library (Chicago, IL)
OHS	Oklahoma Historical Society
OR	*War of the Rebellion: A Compilation of the Official Records of the Union and Confederate Armies*, 128 vols (Washington, DC: Government Printing Office, 1881–1901)
RWRL	Rhesa Walker Read Letters (Williams House Museum, DeKalb, TX)
SARA	Southwest Arkansas Regional Archives
TMRH	Texarkana Museum of Regional History
UG	University of Groningen
UW ARCIA	Annual Reports of the Commissioner of Indian Affairs, University of Wisconsin Libraries online
UW Treaties	Documents Relating to the Negotiation of Ratified and Unratified Treaties with Various Indian Tribes, University of Wisconsin Libraries online
WCU	Western Carolina University, Digital Collections online

Introduction

1. Baird, *A Creek Warrior*, 81–84.
2. Baird, 81–84.
3. Warde, *When the Wolf Came*, 204.
4. Baird, *A Creek Warrior*, 81–84; Franks, *Stand Watie*, 162–63.
5. Confer, *The Cherokee Nation*, 90.
6. Fischer, *The Civil War Era in Indian Territory*, 23.
7. Warde, *When the Wolf Came*, 205.
8. Knight, *Red Fox*, 208.
9. Rhesa Walker Read to Lizzie Read, June 25, 1864, RWRL.
10. Rhesa Walker Read to Lizzie Read, July 15, 1863, RWRL.
11. Rhesa Walker Read to Lizzie Read, November 9, 1863, Rhesa Walker Read Collection, TMRH.
12. William Steele to S. S. Anderson, November 9, 1863, *OR*, Ser. I, Vol. XXII, Part 2, 1065.
13. In 2016, Megan Kate Nelson employed this methodology by rewriting the narratives of the Civil War in New Mexico and Arizona. By examining the era from the perspective of men like Cochise and Mangas Coloradas of the Chiricahua Apaches, Nelson claims that standing in Apache Pass and viewing the war from a new perspective helps "reorient your vision." Nelson, "The Civil War from Apache Pass," 511.
14. Warde, *When the Wolf Came*, 66.
15. See Abel, *The American Indian*, 194–95; Debo, *The Road to Disappearance*, 147; Cutrer, *Theater of a Separate War*, 76; Franks, *Stand Watie*, 120–21; Confer, *The Cherokee Nation*, 61; Warde, *When the Wolf Came*, 56.
16. Leckie, *Angie Debo*, 198–99.
17. Kvasnicka and Viola, *The Commissioners of Indian Affairs*, xv–xvi.
18. Quote cited in Nichols, *Lincoln and the Indians*, 158.
19. "Article Twelve," The Treaty of Hopewell, November 28, 1785, UW Treaties.
20. The number of delegations to Washington has been estimated by the author, taken solely from the letters contained in Moulton, *Papers of Chief John Ross*.
21. Woodward, *The Cherokees*, 113.
22. Prucha, *American Indian Treaties*, 10.
23. Woodward, *The Cherokees*, 128.
24. Perdue, *Slavery*, 68–69.
25. Perdue, 60.
26. Perdue, 50–51.
27. Perdue, 60.
28. Perdue, 57.
29. Vipperman, "The 'Particular Mission' of Wilson Lumpkin," 298.
30. Perdue, *Slavery*, 119.
31. Perdue, 58.
32. Johnston, *Cherokee Women in Crisis*, 3; Miles, *Ties That Bind*, 30.
33. Miles, 30–34.

34. Miles, 30–34.
35. Miles, 30–34.
36. Reese, *Trail Sisters*, 24.
37. Reese, 24.
38. Linda W. Reese, "We Had a lot of Trouble," in Clampitt, *The Civil War*, 133; Saunt, *Black, White, and Indian*, 25.
39. John Ross to the National Council, November 17, 1842, in Moulton, *Papers of Chief John Ross*, 2:154.
40. Moulton, *Papers of Chief John Ross*, 2:738.
41. John Ross to Pierce M. Butler, December 11, 1842, in Moulton, 2:157.
42. Slaves composed only 30.2 percent of the population in Texas, the anomaly among the first seceding states. However, that number might have been considerably higher if state leaders had had their way. They often bemoaned the dearth of available slaves in the state. Governor Hardin Richard Runnels, the only man to defeat Sam Houston in a Texas election, did so because he openly advocated for the reopening of the African slave trade to satisfy the demand. Campbell, *An Empire for Slavery*, 67.
43. Annual Report of the Commissioner of Indian Affairs, November 22, 1856, 125, UW ARCIA; Reese, *Trail Sisters*, 23.
44. The official name is the Bureau of Indian Affairs. However, U.S. government officials have often referred to it by a variety of other names such as the Department of Indian Affairs, the Indian Department, the Office of Indian Affairs, the Indian Office, or the Indian Bureau.
45. Prucha, quoted in Wooster, *The Military*, 5.
46. The bulk of Ross's personal papers are housed at the Helmerich Center for American Research at the Thomas Gilcrease Museum in Tulsa, Oklahoma. Moulton has edited and published most of Ross's correspondence in a two-volume set entitled, Moulton, *Papers of Chief John Ross*. The author's estimates were derived from Moulton's publication.
47. Moulton, *John Ross*, 125.
48. John Ross to Matthew Arbuckle, May 14, 1839, in Moulton, *Papers of Chief John Ross*, 1:710.
49. Moulton, *John Ross*, 153.
50. Numbers taken from the United States Census Bureau records; Texas population totals taken from the Texas State Historical Association website, www.tshaonline.org, accessed July 31, 2020.
51. Population numbers taken from the Kansas State Historical Society website www.kshs.org.
52. Danziger Jr., *Indians and Bureaucrats*, 1–2.
53. McLoughlin, "Cherokee Slaveholders and Baptist Missionaries," 163.
54. McLoughlin, 164.
55. Utley, *The Indian Frontier*, 92.
56. Prucha, *American Indian Treaties*, 16.
57. Prucha, 16.

58. Prucha, 311.
59. Wooster, *The Military*, 3.
60. McPherson, *Tried by War*, 207.
61. Banner, *How the Indians Lost Their Land*, 236–39.
62. Prucha, *American Indian Treaties*, 292.
63. Deloria and DeMallie, *Documents of American Indian Diplomacy*, 233.
64. Genetin-Pilawa, *Crooked Paths*, 87.
65. Prucha, *American Indian Treaties*, 292.
66. Genetin-Pilawa, *Crooked Paths*, 161.

Chapter 1

1. Woodward, *The Cherokees*, 129–30.
2. Woodward, 129–30; Gaines, *The Confederate Cherokees*, 3.
3. Woodward, 129–30, 227; Gaines, 3; Reid, *A Law of Blood*, 58–59.
4. Woodward, *The Cherokees*, 110–12.
5. Article II, "Treaty of Holston," July 2, 1791, UW Treaties.
6. Article VIII, "Treaty of Holston," July 2, 1791, UW Treaties.
7. Article VII, "Treaty of Holston," July 2, 1791, UW Treaties.
8. The Creek treaty was signed before the Cherokee treaty because the Washington administration wanted to secure North Carolina's adoption of the Constitution before signing a treaty with its neighbors, the Cherokees, who had filed formal complaints against intruders from that state, see Prucha, *American Indian Treaties*, 85.
9. This oversight by the United States perhaps came back to haunt them when the Creeks aligned with Britain during the War of 1812.
10. Prucha, *American Indian Treaties*, 2–3.
11. McLoughlin, "Georgia's Role in Instigating Compulsory Indian Removal," 605.
12. Vipperman, "'The Particular Mission,'" 286.
13. Perdue, "The Conflict Within," 468–70.
14. McCluggage, "The Senate and Indian Land Titles, 1800–1825," 419.
15. Vipperman, "'The Particular Mission,'" 301.
16. Woodward, *The Cherokees*, 137.
17. Perdue, "The Conflict Within," 473.
18. "Cherokee Constitution of 1827," Article III, § 1; Article III, § 3; Article III, § 20.
19. "Cherokee Constitution of 1827," Article I, § 34.
20. "Cherokee Constitution of 1839," Article IV, § 18.
21. Kenneth Penn Davis, "Chaos in the Indian Country: The Cherokee Nation, 1828–35," in King, *The Cherokee Indian Nation*, 129; Prucha, "Protest by Petition," 45.
22. "Citizens of Turkey Town to the Cherokee People, February 9, 1829," printed in *Cherokee Phoenix and Indians' Advocate*, March 4, 1829, *Cherokee Phoenix*, WCU.
23. Annual Report of the Commissioner of Indian Affairs, December 1, 1836, UW ARCIA, 7.

24. James Monroe to the House of Representatives, quoted in *Annual Report of the Commissioner of Indian Affairs*, December 1, 1836, UW ARCIA, 7.
25. Davis, "Chaos in the Indian Country," 131.
26. John Ross to David Crockett, January 13, 1831, in Moulton, *Papers of Chief John Ross*, 1:210–12.
27. Vipperman, "The Particular Mission," 303; Foreman, *Indian Removal*, 229–30.
28. Davis, "Chaos in the Indian Country," 129; Ross to John Ridge, et al., December 1, 1831, in Moulton, *Papers of Chief John Ross*, 1:232–33.
29. Williams, "Gambling Away the Inheritance," 524.
30. Williams, 519.
31. Green, "Georgia's Forgotten Industry," 103–4.
32. McCluggage, "The Senate and Indian Land Titles," 420.
33. Perdue, *Slavery*, 62.
34. Foreman, *Indian Removal*, 229–30.
35. Foreman, 229–30.
36. Green, "Georgia's Forgotten Industry," 104; Williams, "Gambling Away the Inheritance," 521.
37. Woodward, *The Cherokees*, 159.
38. Annual Message, October 14, 1829, in Moulton, *Papers of Chief John Ross*, 1:169–72.
39. Citizens of Turkey Town to the Cherokee People, February 9, 1829, printed in *Cherokee Phoenix and Indian Advocate*, March 4, 1829, WCU.
40. John Ridge to John Ross, January 12, 1832, in Moulton, *Papers of Chief John Ross*, 1:235.
41. Moulton, 1:235.
42. Ross to Hugh Montgomery, July 20, 1830, in Moulton, *Papers of Chief John Ross*, 1:193–95.
43. Perdue, *"Mixed Blood" Indians*, 70; Moulton, 1:193–95.
44. Ross to David L. Child, February 11, 1831, in Moulton, *Papers of Chief John Ross*, 1:214.
45. "Article XII," Treaty of Hopewell, 1785, UW Treaties.
46. Ross to Cherokee Delegation, March 30, 1832, in Moulton, *Papers of Chief John Ross*, 1:241.
47. Woodward, *The Cherokees*, 171; John Ridge to John Ross, April 3, 1832, in Moulton, *Papers of Chief John Ross*, 1:241.
48. Ehle, *Trail of Tears*, 255.
49. John Ridge to Stand Watie, April 6, 1832, in Dale and Litton, *Cherokee Cavaliers*, 8.
50. John Ridge to John Ross, April 3, 1832, in Moulton, *Papers of Chief John Ross*, 1:241.
51. Moulton, 1:241.
52. Moulton, 1:241.
53. John Ridge to Stand Watie, April 6, 1832, in Dale and Litton, *Cherokee Cavaliers*, 8.
54. John Ridge to Stand Watie, April 6, 1832.
55. John Ridge to Stand Watie, April 6, 1832.
56. Woodward, *The Cherokees*, 170.

57. Wardell, *A Political History of the Cherokee Nation*, 18.
58. John Ridge to John Ross, April 3, 1832, in Moulton, *Papers of Chief John Ross*, 1:241.
59. Foreman, *Indian Removal*, 246.
60. Ehle, *Trail of Tears*, 256.
61. Williams, "Gambling Away the Inheritance," 522; Ehle, *Trail of Tears*, 256.
62. Ehle, *Trail of Tears*, 258–59.
63. Perdue, *Cherokee Editor* 25–6.
64. John Ridge to John Ross, February 2, 1833, in Moulton, *Papers of Chief John Ross*, 1:260.
65. John Ridge to John Ross, February 2, 1833.
66. John Ridge to John Ross, February 2, 1833.
67. Vipperman, "The Particular Mission," 311.
68. John Ross to Friedrich Ludwig von Roenne, March 5, 1835, in Moulton, *Papers of Chief John Ross*, 1:330.
69. John Ridge to Wilson Lumpkin, May 18, 1835, in Perdue, *Cherokee Editor*, 183.
70. John Ridge to Major Ridge, et al., March 10, 1835, Dale and Litton, *Cherokee Cavaliers*, 12–14.
71. Moulton, *John Ross*, 60.
72. John Ross to Lewis Cass, March 9, 1835, in Moulton, *Papers of Chief John Ross*, 1:332.
73. Moulton, *John Ross*, 54; Perdue, "The Conflict Within," 483.
74. Twenty-seven of the fifty sitting members of the U.S. Senate were avowed Jacksonians. Jackson also knew that Congress had approved the Indian Removal Act in 1830, and was no doubt weary of dealing with the Cherokee problem.
75. La Vere, *Contrary Neighbors*, 15; Moulton, *John Ross*, 54.
76. Dale and Litton, *Cherokee Cavaliers*, 12–14; Vipperman, "The Particular Mission," 311.
77. Woodward, *The Cherokees*, 183.
78. Ehle, *Trail of Tears*, 280.
79. John Ross to John Schermerhorn, July 7, 1835, in Moulton, *Papers of Chief John Ross*, 1:339.
80. The vote was 2,225 in favor of a lump sum payment to the national treasury to 114 votes for individual distribution; Woodward, *The Cherokees*, 183.
81. Woodward, *The Cherokees*, 182; Vipperman, "The Particular Mission," 307.
82. Moulton, *John Ross*, 72.
83. Confer, *The Cherokee Nation*, 20.
84. See Knight, *Red Fox*, 26; Rampp and Rampp, *The Civil War in the Indian Territory*, vii; Barbara Cloud, "Introduction," in Slover, *Minister to the Cherokees*, xxiii; Fischer, *The Civil War Era in Indian Territory*, 48; Confer, *The Cherokee Nation*, 20–22; Perdue, "The Conflict Within," 483.
85. Moulton, *John Ross*, 76.
86. Perdue, *Slavery*, 67.

87. John Ridge to Wilson Lumpkin, September 22, 1835, Cherokee Removal and the Trail of Tears Collection, DPLA.
88. John Ridge to Major Ridge, et al., March 10, 1835, Dale and Litton, *Cherokee Cavaliers*, 13.
89. Vipperman, "The Particular Mission," 313; Confer, *The Cherokee Nation*, 20; Foreman, *Indian Removal*, 269.
90. LeRoy H. Fischer argues that the treaty became law despite the signatures of unauthorized persons; Fischer, *The Civil War Era*, 47.
91. John Ross to the Senate, March 8, 1836, in Moulton, *Papers of Chief John Ross*, 1:412.
92. Foreman, "The Murder of Elias Boudinot," 19.
93. William M. Davis to Lewis Cass, March 5, 1836, *House Documents*, 24th Cong., 1st sess., No. 286, pp. 148–54, LOC.
94. Foreman, *Indian Removal*, 269; Woodward, *The Cherokees*, 190; Moulton, *John Ross*, 76.
95. Moulton, 76; Ehle, *Trail of Tears*, 300; Vipperman, "The Particular Mission," 307; McLoughlin, *Champions of the Cherokees*, 136.
96. Jonathan Hooper to M. W. Bateman, February 5, 1836; C. M. Hitchcock to M. W. Bateman, February 5, 1836; James C. Price to M. W. Bateman, February 4, 1836, all in *House Documents*, 24th Cong., 1st sess., No. 286, pp. 164–65, LOC.
97. Wimberly, *Cherokees in Controversy*, 67–68.
98. Foreman, "The Murder of Elias Boudinot," 19.
99. Perdue, *Slavery*, 67; McLoughlin, *Champions of the Cherokees*, 136; Confer, *The Cherokee Nation*, 20; Foreman, *Indian Removal*, 269.
100. Moulton, *John Ross*, 77.
101. Perdue, *Slavery*, 67.
102. Perdue, 19–20.
103. Moulton, *John Ross*, 76.
104. Vipperman, "The Bungled Treaty of New Echota," 540.
105. Dale and Gaston, *Cherokee Cavaliers*, 4.
106. Warde, *When the Wolf Came*, 19.
107. Foreman, "The Murder of Elias Boudinot," 23.
108. Foreman, 23.
109. Foreman, 23.
110. Dale and Gaston, *Cherokee Cavaliers*, 4.
111. Foreman, "The Murder of Elias Boudinot," 22.
112. Elias Boudinot to John Ross, November 25, 1835, in Moulton, *Papers of Chief John Ross*, 1:376.
113. La Vere, *Contrary Neighbors*, 24–25.
114. John Ross to the Chiefs of the Shawnees, Senecas, and Quapaws, September 10, 1861, in Moulton, *Papers of Chief John Ross*, 2:487.
115. William P. Adair and James M. Bell to Stand Watie, August 29, 1861, in Dale, "Some Letters of General Stand Watie," 36–38.

Chapter 2

1. Annual Report of the Commissioner of Indian Affairs, November 25, 1839, UW ARCIA.
2. Annual Report of the Commissioner of Indian Affairs, November 25, 1839, UW ARCIA.
3. Annual Report of the Commissioner of Indian Affairs, December 1, 1836, UW ARCIA.
4. *Johnson v. McIntosh*, 21 US 543 (1832).
5. Wilkins and Stark, *American Indian Politics*, 72.
6. Sundquist, "Worcester v. Georgia," 250.
7. Hoxie, *A Final Promise*, 155.
8. Prucha, *American Indian Treaties*, 7.
9. Prucha, 7.
10. Prucha, 2–3.
11. Prucha, 157.
12. "Address to the Cherokees," August 21, 1861, in Moulton, *Papers of Chief John Ross*, 2:481.
13. Prucha, *American Indian Treaties*, 2–3.
14. Prucha, 157.
15. La Vere, *Contrary Neighbors*, 25–27.
16. Annual Report of the Commissioner of Indian Affairs, December 1, 1836, UW ARCIA.
17. John Ross to Matthew Arbuckle, May 14, 1839, in Moulton, *Papers of Chief John Ross*, 1:710.
18. John Ross to Matthew Arbuckle, November 4, 1839, Moulton, 1:710.
19. John Ross to Montfort Stokes, April 5, 1839, Moulton, 1:702.
20. Moulton, 1:702.
21. Annual Report of the Commissioner of Indian Affairs, November 27, 1851, UW ARCIA.
22. Prucha, *Indian Policy*, 153–54.
23. Annual Report of the Commissioner of Indian Affairs, November 26, 1853, UW ARCIA.
24. John Ross to John Thorn, et al., November 22, 1854, in Moulton, *Papers of Chief John Ross*, 2:390.
25. Etcheson, *Bleeding Kansas*, 66–67.
26. Etcheson, 101.
27. Etcheson, 109–10.
28. Fellman, Gordon, and Sutherland, *This Terrible War*, 1.
29. McCaslin, *Tainted Breeze*, 22–23.
30. Rhesa Walker Read to Lizzie Read, February 10, 1863. RWRL.
31. John Ross to The National Council, November 19, 1857, in Moulton, *Papers of Chief John Ross*, 2:411.

32. John Ross to William P. Ross, June 1860, Moulton, 2:448.
33. John Ross to William P. Ross, June 1860, Moulton, 2:448.
34. John Ross to Alfred B. Greenwood, April 2, 1860, Moulton, 2:437.
35. Moulton, 2:448; Perdue, *Slavery*, 127.
36. John Ross to William P. Ross, et al., February 12, 1861, in Moulton, *Papers of Chief John Ross*, 2:462.
37. "Annual Message," October 4, 1860, Moulton, 2:450.
38. John Ross to David Hubbard, June 17, 1861, Moulton, 2:473.
39. Jacob Derrysaw to John Ross, February 4, 1861, Moulton, 2:459; John Ross to Cyrus Harris, February 9, 1861, in Moulton, 2:459.
40. John Ross to Cyrus Harris, February 9, 1861, Moulton, 2:460.
41. Article II, Treaty of Holston, November 11, 1791, UW Treaties.
42. John Ross to Cyrus Harris, February 9, 1861, in Moulton, *Papers of Chief John Ross*, 2:460.
43. Texas voters approved secession on February 23, 1861. The Arkansas voters called for a secession convention to be held on March 4, while the Missouri convention would meet on February 28.
44. John Ross to William P. Ross, et al., February 12, 1861, in Moulton, *Papers of Chief John Ross*, 2:462.
45. The letter was delivered to Ross by Colonel J. J. Gaines, aide-de-camp to Arkansas Governor Henry Rector. Gaines was accompanied by a letter of introduction from Elias Rector, the Confederate Superintendent of Indians Affairs for Indian Territory, Elias Rector to John Ross, February 14, 1861, *OR*, Ser. I, Vol. I, 683.
46. Henry Rector to John Ross, January 29, 1861, *OR*, Ser. I, Vol. I, 683.
47. John Ross to Henry Rector, February 22, 1861, *OR*, Ser. I. Vol I, 687.
48. William P. Ross et al. to John Ross, March 15, 1861, in Moulton, *Papers of Chief John Ross*, 2:467.
49. "Proclamation," May 17, 1861, in Moulton, 2:470.
50. E. D. Townsend to William H. Emory, April 17, 1861, *OR*, Ser. I, Vol. I, 648.
51. See Cunningham, *General Stand Watie*, 44; Rampp and Rampp, *The Civil War*, 3–5; Knight, *Red Fox*, 59; La Vere, *Contrary Neighbors*, 169; Fischer, *The Civil War Era*, 20–21; Gaines, *The Confederate Cherokees*, 9; McLoughlin, *Champions of the Cherokees*, 388; Confer, *The Cherokee Nation*, 46; Nichols, *Lincoln and the Indians*, 26–28; Cutrer, *Theater of a Separate War*, 72–73; McBride, *Opothleyaholo*, 147–48; Warde, *When the Wolf Came*, 51–59.
52. E. D. Townsend to William W. Averell, April 17, 1861, *OR*, Ser. I, Vol. LIII, 493.
53. Peskin, *Winfield Scott*, 108; Eisenhower, *Agent of Destiny*, 185–87.
54. Smith, *Old Fuss and Feathers*, 368; Peskin, *Winfield Scott*, 247.
55. Special Order #102, June 12, 1861, *OR*, Ser. I, Vol. LIII, 496; E. D. William W. Averell to L. Thomas, May 31, 1861, *OR*, Ser. I, Vol. LIII, 494.
56. E. D. William W. Averell to L. Thomas, May 31, 1861, *OR*, Ser. I, Vol. LIII, 493.
57. Hafen and Young, *Fort Laramie*, 303.
58. Eisenhower, *Agent of Destiny*, 348–49.

59. Annual Report of the Commissioner of Indian Affairs, November 27, 1861, 34. UW ARCIA.
60. William W. Averell to L. Thomas, May 31, 1861, *OR*, Ser. I, Vol. LIII, 496.
61. John Ross to John Drew, May 9, 1861, in Moulton, *Papers of Chief John Ross*, 2:468.
62. Mark Bean, et al., to John Ross, May 9, 1861, *OR*, Ser. I. Vol. XIII, 494.
63. L. P. Walker to Douglas H. Cooper, May 13, 1861, *OR*, Ser. I, Vol. III, 574.
64. J. R. Kannady to John Ross, May 15, 1861, Ross Papers, HC.
65. Proclamation, May 17, 1861, in Moulton, *Papers of Chief John Ross*, 2:469–70.
66. Moulton, 2:469.
67. Moulton, 2:469.
68. Moulton, 2:469.
69. John Ross to J. R. Kannady, May 17, 1861, Moulton, 2:468.
70. "Proclamation," May 17, 1861, Moulton, 2:469.
71. Moulton, 2:469.
72. Dale, "Some Letters of General Stand Watie," 34–36.
73. Confer, *The Cherokee Nation*, 55.
74. At the Battle of Honey Springs in July 1863, the largest battle in Indian Territory, Watie's regiment joined the Confederate line against James Blunt's Union attack. Watie himself was not present. He was present, however, at the Battle of Pea Ridge, Arkansas, in March 1862.
75. Jonathan C. Burnett to Thomas Ewing Jr., November 28, 1863, *OR*, Ser. I, Vol. XXII, Part 2, 722–23.
76. M. LaRue Harrison to James Totten, December 1, 1863, *OR*, Ser. I, Vol. XXII, Part 2, 722–23.
77. Albert Pike to the Commissioner of Indian Affairs, February 17, 1866, printed in footnote number 228 in Abel, *The Indian as Slaveholder*, 134–40.
78. William Steele to S. S. Anderson, November 9, 1863, *OR*, Ser. I, Vol. XXII, 2:1065.
79. No definitive study of the compiled service records of the Cherokee regiments has been done to date. Poor record keeping, infrequent muster recordings, and high mobility levels render an accurate analysis difficult if not impossible. However, a quick examination of Watie's Cherokee Mounted Volunteer regiment by the author reveals multiple names that were easily cross-referenced on the 1860 federal census in Arkansas, as well as twenty-nine names found on the roles of the Union Army's Federal Indian Brigade of 1863. Historians have identified widespread desertions within the Cherokee ranks, so this comes as no surprise.
80. David Hubbard to John Ross, June 12, 1861, *OR*, Ser. I, Vol. XIII, 498.
81. David Hubbard to John Ross, June 12, 1861, *OR*, Ser. I, Vol. XIII, 498.
82. Benjamin McCulloch to John Ross, June 12, 1861, *OR*, Ser. I, Vol. III, 591–92.
83. Albert Pike to Robert Tombs, May 20, 1861, *OR*, Ser. I, Vol. III, 580–81.
84. Albert Pike to John Ross, August 1, 1861, Ross Papers, HC.
85. "Minutes of the Cherokee Executive Council," July 2, 181, in Moulton, *Papers of Chief John Ross*, 2:476–77.

86. John Ross to Albert Pike, July 1, 1861, Moulton, 2:476.
87. Moulton, *John Ross*, 168.
88. Moulton, 169.
89. Albert Pike to John Ross, August 1, 1861, Ross Papers, HC.
90. John Ross to Benjamin McCulloch, June 17, 1861, *OR*, Ser. I, Vol. XIII, 495.
91. John Ross to Benjamin McCulloch, June 17, 1861, *OR*, Ser. I, Vol. XIII, 495.
92. Confer, *The Cherokee Nation*, 49.
93. Warde, *When the Wolf Came*, 66.

Chapter 3

1. The Executive Council adjourned its meeting on August 1, 1861, Moulton, *Papers of Chief John Ross*, 2:479.
2. John Ross to Joseph Vann, July 28, 1861, Moulton, 2:478.
3. John Ross to Joseph Vann, July 28, 1861.
4. Albert Pike to John Ross, August 1, 1861, Ross Papers, HC.
5. Motey Kennard to John Ross, October 1, 1861, in Moulton, *Papers of Chief John Ross*, 2:489.
6. Patrick, *Campaign for Wilson's Creek*, 96–99.
7. Piston and Hatcher, *Wilson's Creek*, 92, 160.
8. Albert Pike to John Ross, August 1, 1861, Papers of John Ross, HC.
9. Albert Pike to John Ross, August 1, 1861.
10. See Woodward, *The Cherokees*, 265; Rampp and Rampp, *The Civil War*, 5; Franks, *Stand Watie*, 119; McLoughlin, *After the Trail of Tears*, 184; and Confer, *The Cherokee Nation*, 49–50.
11. "Minutes of the Cherokee Executive Council," August 1, 161, in Moulton, *Papers of Chief John Ross*, 2:479.
12. The Confederate forces then in Indian Territory had not yet invaded the Cherokee Nation. The three forts, abandoned by the United States and occupied by the Confederates, were located in the Chickasaw Nation and the Wichita Agency in southwest Indian Territory.
13. "Address to the Cherokees," August 21, 1861, in Moulton, *Papers of Chief John Ross*, 2:479–81.
14. John Ross to the Chiefs and Headmen of the Creek Nation, August 24, 1861, Moulton, 2:482.
15. McLoughlin, *After the Trail of Tears*, 184.
16. McLoughlin, 184.
17. Leeds, *The United Keetoowah Band of Cherokee*, 5.
18. Leeds, 5.
19. Leeds, 5–6.
20. Confer, *The Cherokee Nation*, 33.
21. Confer, 33.
22. John Ross to George W. Clark, in Moulton, *Papers of Chief John Ross*, 2:482.

23. John Ross to The Chiefs and Headmen of the Creek Nation, August 24, 1861, Moulton, 2:482.
24. John Ross to The Chiefs and Headmen of the Creek Nation, August 24, 1861.
25. William P. Adair and James M. Bell to Stand Watie, August 29, 1861, in Dale, "Some Letters of General Stand Watie," 30–59.
26. Franks, *Stand Watie*, 114.
27. William P. Adair and James M. Bell to Stand Watie, August 29, 1861, Dale, "Some Letters of General Stand Watie," 36–38.
28. William P. Adair and James M. Bell to Stand Watie, August 29, 1861.
29. William P. Adair and James M. Bell to Stand Watie, August 29, 1861.
30. Knight, *Red Fox*, 66; Franks, *Stand Watie*, 118.
31. Douglas H. Cooper to Charles DeMorse, reprinted in *Clarksville (TX) Standard*, September 24, 1863.
32. John Ross to Joseph Vann, September 10, 1861, in Moulton, *Papers of Chief John Ross*, 2:484–85; John Ross to Albert Pike, September 25, 1861, Moulton, 2:488.
33. John Ross to James Brown, September 10, 1861, Moulton, 2:484; John Ross to Joseph Vann, September 10, 1861, Moulton, 2:484–85.
34. John Ross to the Chiefs of the Osage Nation, September 19, 1861, Moulton, 2:485–86.
35. John Ross to the Chiefs of the Osage Nation, September 19, 1861.
36. John Ross to the Chiefs of the Shawnees, Senecas, and Quapaws, Moulton, 2:486–87.
37. John Ross to Opothle Yahola and Other Chiefs and Headmen of the Creek Nation, September 19, 1861, Moulton, 2:487–88.
38. John W. Stapler to John Ross, September 25, 1861, Moulton, 2:488–89.
39. John W. Stapler to John Ross, September 25, 1861.
40. Conley, *The Cherokee Nation*, 175.
41. John Ross to Motey Kennard and Echo Harjo, October 20, 1861, in Moulton, *Papers of Chief John Ross*, 2:497–99.
42. Lowe, *A Texas Cavalry Officer's Civil War*, 19; McBride, *Opothleyoholo*, 8.
43. John Ross to Motey Kennard and Echo Harjo, October 20, 1861, in Moulton, *Papers of Chief John Ross*, 2:497–99.
44. Motey Kennard to John Ross, October 1, 1861, Moulton, 2:489.
45. Motey Kennard to John Ross, October 1, 1861.
46. Motey Kennard to John Ross, October 3, 1861, Moulton 2:489.
47. John Ross to Motey Kennard, October 4, 1861, Moulton, 2:490.
48. Deloria and DeMallie, *Documents of American Indian Diplomacy*, 2:1511.
49. Deloria and DeMallie, 1:666–80.
50. John Ross to Motey Kennard, October 8, 1861, in Moulton, *Papers of Chief John Ross*, 2:490–91.
51. John Ross to Opothle Yahola, October 8, 1861, Moulton, 2:491–92.
52. John Ross to Opothle Yahola, October 11, 1861, Moulton, 2:495–96.
53. John Ross to Opothle Yahola, October 11, 1861.
54. Debo, *Road to Disappearance*, 149–50; McBride, *Opothleyaholo*, 150.

55. Motey Kennard and Echo Harjo to John Ross, October 18, 1861, in Moulton, *Papers of Chief John Ross*, 2:496–97.
56. John Ross to Motey Kennard and Echo Harjo, October 20, 1861, Moulton, 2:497–99.
57. John Ross to Motey Kennard and Echo Harjo, October 20, 1861, 497.
58. John Ross to Motey Kennard and Echo Harjo, October 20, 1861, 497.
59. John Ross to John Drew and William P. Ross, October 20, 1861, Moulton, 2:499–500.
60. John Ross to John Drew and William P. Ross, October 20, 1861.
61. Motey Kennard and Echo Harjo, et al, to Douglas H. Cooper, October 31, 1861, Papers of the Creek Nation, OHS.
62. Douglas H. Cooper to Motey Kennard and Echo Harjo, et al., October 31, 1861, Papers of the Creek Nation, OHS.
63. Annie H. Abel (1915), Angie Debo (1925), Kenny A. Franks (1979), W. Craig Gaines (1989), Lela J. McBride (2000), Clarissa Confer (2007), Mary Jane Warde (2013), and Thomas W. Cutrer (2017) all cite only Creek and Confederate sources in their narratives of Opothle Yahola's flight to Kansas and treat the events as the first battles of the Civil War in Indian Territory.
64. Report of Douglas H. Cooper, January 20, 1862, *OR*, Ser. I, Vol. VIII, 5.
65. Motey Kennard and Echo Harjo to John Ross, October 18, 1861, in Moulton, *Papers of Chief John Ross*, 496–97.
66. The 4th Texas Cavalry was commanded by Colonel William B. Sims and would later become the 9th Texas Cavalry; Lowe, *A Texas Cavalry Officer's Civil War*, 21.
67. Lowe, 21.
68. John Ross to William P. Ross, November 16, 1861, in Moulton, *Papers of Chief John Ross*, 2:502–3.
69. John Ross to William P. Ross, November 16, 1861, 503–4.
70. John Ross to William P. Ross, November 16, 1861, 504.
71. Douglas H. Cooper to Judah P. Benjamin, January 20, 1862, *OR*, Ser. I, Vol. XIII, 5; Quayle's detachment of the 4th Texas Cavalry is from William B. Sims's regiment that later became the 9th Texas Cavalry; Lowe, *A Texas Cavalry Officer's Civil War*, 21.
72. John Ross to William P. Ross, November 16, 1861, in Moulton, *Papers of Chief John Ross*, 2:503–4.
73. McBride, *Opothleyaholo*, 165.
74. Lowe, *A Texas Cavalry Officer's Civil War*, 23–24.
75. Gaines mentions the message but implies that it is simply an ongoing desire for peace within Indian Territory, Gaines, *Confederate Cherokees*, 38.
76. Lowe, *A Texas Cavalry Officer's Civil War*, 19; Confer, *The Cherokee Nation*, 59; Cutrer, *Theater of a Separate War*, 77; Baird, *A Creek Warrior for the Confederacy*, 59.
77. Gaines, *The Confederate Cherokees*, 38.
78. The original message has not been found; however, a handwritten note among Ross's papers, references Opothle Yahola's message, see "Notes," in Moulton, *Papers of Chief John Ross*, 2:506.
79. John Ross to James McDaniel, Porum, and Cabbin Smith, November 20, 1861, Moulton, 2:504–5.

80. McBride, *Opothleyaholo*, 165–66; see the map in Lowe, *A Texas Cavalry Officer's Civil War*, 20.
81. Report of Douglas H. Cooper, January 20, 1862, *OR*, Ser. I, Vol. VIII, 7.
82. Cutrer, *Theater of a Separate War*, 77.
83. McBride, *Opothleyaholo*, 166; Warde, *When the Wolf Came*, 78.
84. Cottrell, *Civil War in the Indian Territory*, 25–27.
85. Douglas H. Cooper to Judah P. Benjamin, January 29, 1862, *OR*, Ser. I, Vol. VIII, 5–14.
86. Douglas H. Cooper to Judah P. Benjamin, January 29, 1862.
87. Douglas H. Cooper to Judah P. Benjamin, January 29, 1862.
88. Warde, *When the Wolf Came*, 75.
89. Warde, 77.
90. McBride, *Opothleyaholo*, 168–69.
91. John Drew to John Ross, December 16, 1861, in Moulton, *Papers of Chief John Ross*, 2:507.
92. Lela McBride asserts that the deserters were victims of psychological warfare employed by Opothle Yahola, who constantly threatened to attack in order to keep Confederates off guard, McBride, *Opothleyaholo*, 168; Abel and Warde argue that the Cherokees simply did not want to fight against other Indians. This is an unlikely scenario because they would then be fighting Indians on the Confederate side, Warde, *When the Wolf Came*, 75, Confer, *The Cherokee Nation*, 62–64; Gaines suggests that the desertions had been planned in advance by anti-Ross men. When Pegg sought to deliver Cooper's message to Opothle Yahola, the men deserted because they despised the fact Ross had led them into the Confederacy. This is also unlikely because many of the deserters were pro-Ross men, including James Vann, a loyal Ross supporter. Gaines, *Confederate Cherokees*, 47.
93. John Drew to John Ross, December 16, 1861, in Moulton, *Papers of Chief John Ross*, 2:507.
94. John Drew to John Ross, December 16, 1861.
95. Gaines, *Confederate Cherokees*, 56–57.
96. Douglas H. Cooper to Judah P. Benjamin, January 29, 1862, *OR*, Ser. I, Vol. VIII, 5–14.
97. James McIntosh to S. Cooper, January 1, 1862, *OR*, Ser. I, Vol. VIII, 22–26; James McIntosh to S. Cooper, January 10, 1862, *OR*, Ser. I, Vol. VIII, 31.
98. James McIntosh to S. Cooper, January 1, 1862; James McIntosh to S. Cooper, January 10, 1862.
99. See *Confederate Cherokees*, 59; Confer, *The Cherokee Nation*, 66; and Cutrer, *Theater of a Separate War*, 80.
100. Hatley, *Reluctant Rebels*, 12.
101. Report of Colonel James McIntosh, January 1, 1862, *OR*, Ser. I, Vol. VIII, 24.
102. Stand Watie to James McIntosh, December 28, 1861, *OR*, Ser. I, Vol. VIII, 32.
103. Stand Watie to James McIntosh, December 28, 1861.

Chapter 4

1. Britton, *Memoirs*, 204.
2. Britton, 204.
3. Stand Watie to John Drew, December 4, 1861, Papers of John Drew, HC.
4. John Ross to Douglas H. Cooper, January 7, 1862, in Moulton, *Papers of Chief John Ross*, 2:508.
5. John Ross to Douglas H. Cooper, January 7, 1862.
6. John Ross to Albert Pike, February 25, 1862, Moulton, 2:509–10; Confer, *The Cherokee Nation*, 68.
7. John Ross to Benjamin McCulloch, June 17, 1861, in Moulton, *Papers of Chief John Ross*, 2:474–475.
8. D. H. Maury to Colonels Drew, McIntosh, and Stand Watie, March 3, 1862, *OR*, Ser. I, Vol. VIII, 764–65.
9. Albert Pike to D. H. Maury, March 14, 1862, *OR*, Ser. I, Vol. VIII, 286–92; Earl Van Dorn to Braxton Bragg, March 27, 1862, *OR*, Ser. I, Vol. VIII, 283–86.
10. Report of Colonel Cyrus Bussey, Third Iowa Cavalry, March 14, 1862, *OR*, Ser. I, Vol. VIII, 233–34.
11. Albert Pike to D. H. Maury, March 14, 1862, *OR*, Ser. I, Vol. VIII, 286–92.
12. Shea and Hess, *Pea Ridge*, 103.
13. Shea and Hess, 104.
14. Shea and Hess, 107.
15. Hebert was thought to be dead in initial Confederate reports; however, he had only been captured. Earl Van Dorn to Albert Sidney Johnston, March 10, 1862, *OR*, Ser. I, Vol. VIII, 281.
16. Earl Van Dorn to Albert Sidney Johnston, March 10, 1862, 290.
17. Samuel R. Curtis to J. C. Kelton, March 13, 1862, *OR*, Ser. I, Vol. VIII, 195; Report of Colonel Cyrus Bussey, Third Iowa Cavalry, March 14, 1862, *OR*, Ser. I, Vol. VIII, 237.
18. Shea and Hess, *Pea Ridge*, 102.
19. Dabney H. Maury to Samuel R. Curtis, March 14, 1862, *OR*, Ser. I, Vol. VIII, 237.
20. Albert Pike to Headquarters, May 4, 1862, *OR*, Ser. I, Vol. XIII, 819.
21. Annual Report of the Commissioner of Indian Affairs, October 31, 1865, 323, UW ARCIA.
22. Shea and Hess, *Pea Ridge: Civil War*, 143; Cunningham, *General Stand Watie's Confederate Indians*, 62.
23. James G. Blunt to Edwin M. Stanton, July 21, 1862, *OR*, Ser. I, Vol. XIII, 486.
24. Annual Report of the Secretary of the Interior, U.S. Department of the Interior, November 30, 1861, 447, ARSOI.
25. Annual Report of the Commissioner of Indian Affairs, November 27, 1861, 10, UW ARCIA.
26. Annual Report of the Commissioner of Indian Affairs, November 27, 1861.
27. Annual Report of the Commissioner of Indian Affairs, November 26, 1862, 147–49, UW ARCIA.

28. L. Thomas to Henry W. Halleck, March 19, 1862, *OR*, Ser. I, Ch. XIII, 626.
29. Castel, *Civil War Kansas*, 81–82; Henry W. Halleck to S. D. Sturgis, April 6, 1862, *OR*, Ser. I, Vol. VIII, 665.
30. Blunt, "General Blunt's Account," 222–23.
31. M. Jane Johansson argues that the atrocities at Pea Ridge caused a delay in the organization of the Indian Expedition. Johansson, ed., *Albert C. Ellithorpe*, 15.
32. L. Thomas to Henry W. Halleck, April 4, 1862, *OR*, Ser. I, Vol. VIII, 664.
33. Thomas Moonlight to William G. Coffin, June 9, 1862, Record Group 393, Book 137, Page 131, National Archives and Records Administration, Washington, D.C.
34. Castel, *Civil War Kansas*, 82; Blunt, "General Blunt's Account," 218.
35. Thomas Moonlight to L. Thomas, June 6, 1862, Record Group 393, U.S. Army Continental Commands, Part 1, no. 2079, box 137, page 119, National Archives and Records Administration.
36. For a detailed description of the politics behind the commission, see Collins, *General James G. Blunt*.
37. Rein, "The U.S. Army, Indian Agency, and the Path to Assimilation," 7.
38. Blunt, "General Blunt's Account," 223.
39. Blunt, 223; Collins, *General James G. Blunt*, 61.
40. H. W. Halleck to S. D. Sturgis, April 6, 1862, *OR*, Ser. I, Vol. VIII, 665.
41. Rein, "The U.S. Army," 7.
42. H. W. Halleck to S. D. Sturgis, April 6, 1862, *OR*, Ser. I, Vol. VIII, 665.
43. William Weer to Thomas Moonlight, June 13, 1862, *OR*, Ser. I, Vol. XIII, 430–31.
44. James G. Blunt to Edwin M. Stanton, July 21, 1862, *OR*, Ser. I, Vol. XIII, 486.
45. H. W. Halleck to S. D. Sturgis, *OR*, Ser. I, Vol. VIII, 665.
46. William Weer to Thomas Moonlight, June 13, 1862, *OR*, Ser. I, Vol. XIII, 430–31.
47. Johansson, *Albert C. Ellithorpe*, 21–22.
48. Confer, *The Cherokee Nation*, 76.
49. James A. Phillips to John Ross, June 26, 1862, *OR*, Ser. I, Vol. XIII, 451.
50. James A. Phillips to Frederick Salomon, June 27, 1862, *OR*, Ser. I, Vol. XIII, 452; James A. Phillips to William R. Judson, June 28, 1862, *OR*, Ser. I, Vol. XIII, 453.
51. Franks, *Stand Watie*, 129; Frederick Salomon to William Weer, June 30, 1862, Record Group 393, U.S. Army Continental Commands, Part 2, no. 3149, letter 19, NARA.
52. Frederick Salomon to William Weer, June 30, 1862, NARA.
53. William Weer to Thomas Moonlight, July 2, 1862, *OR*, Ser. I, Vol. XIII, 459–61.
54. William Weer to Thomas Moonlight, July 2, 1862.
55. William Weer to Thomas Moonlight, July 2, 1862.
56. James G. Blunt to William Weer, July 3, 1862, *OR*, Ser. I, Vol. XIII, 461.
57. William Weer to Thomas Moonlight, July 4, 1862, *OR*, Ser. I, Vol. XIII, 463.
58. William Weer to Thomas Moonlight, July 6, 1862, *OR*, Ser. I, Vol. XIII, 137–38.
59. John Ritchey to James G. Blunt, July 5, 1862, *OR*, Ser. I, Vol. XIII, 463–64.
60. John Ritchey to James G. Blunt, July 5, 1862.
61. William Weer to Thomas Moonlight, July 6, 1862, *OR*, Ser. I, Vol. XIII, 464–65.

62. William Weer to Thomas Moonlight, July 12, 1862, *OR*, Ser. I, Vol. XIII, 487–88.
63. William Weer to John Ross, July 7, 1862, *OR*, Ser. I, Vol. XIII, 486.
64. William Weer to John Ross, July 7, 1862.
65. John Ross to William Weer, July 7, 1862, *OR*, Ser. I, Vol. XIII, 486–87.
66. James G. Blunt to Edwin M. Stanton, July 21, 1862, *OR*, Ser. I, Vol. XIII, 486.
67. William Weer to Thomas J. Moonlight, July 12, 1862, *OR*, Ser. I, Vol. XIII, 487–88.
68. Weer's "millstone statement" has been omitted from the historiography of the Indian Expedition. See Cunningham, *General Stand Watie*, 70–71; Moulton, *John Ross*, 174; Collins, *General James G. Blunt*, 61–63; McCaslin, "Bitter Legacy," 25; Johansson, *Albert C. Ellithorpe*, 24; and Confer, *The Cherokee Nation*, 79. Although Franks, Knight, Gaines, and McLoughlin make mention of the letter, none of them mention the "millstone statement"; Gaines includes quotations from the same letter, Franks, *Stand Watie*, 129; Knight, *Red Fox*, 116; Gaines, *The Confederate Cherokees*, 105–6; McLoughlin, *Champions of the Cherokees*, 403.
69. Christ, "This Day We Marched Again," 33–34.
70. William Weer to Thomas J. Moonlight, June 13, 1862, *OR*, Ser. I, Vol. XIII, 430–31.
71. William Weer to Thomas J. Moonlight, June 13, 1862.
72. Franks, *Stand Watie*, 139–140; Knight, *Red Fox*, 156; Cunningham, *General Stand Watie's Confederate Indians*, 99–100.
73. Brad Agnew, "Our Doom as a Nation is Sealed: The Five Nations in the Civil War," in Clampitt, *The Civil War and Reconstruction in Indian Territory*, 77.
74. James A. Phillips to Frederick Salomon, June 27, 1862, *OR*, Ser. I. Vol. XIII, 452; James A. Phillips to William R. Judson, June 28, 1862, *OR*, Ser. I, Vol. XIII, 453.
75. William Weer to Thomas J. Moonlight, July 2, 1862, *OR*, Ser. I, Vol. XIII, 459–61.
76. William Weer to Thomas J. Moonlight, June 13, 1862, *OR*, Ser. I, Vol. XIII, 430–31.
77. James G. Blunt to William Weer, July 3, 1862, *OR*, Ser. I, Vol. XIII, 461.
78. William Weer to Thomas Moonlight, July 6, 1862, *OR*, Ser. I, Vol. XIII, 464–65.
79. William Weer to Thomas Moonlight, July 12, 1862, *OR*, Ser. I, Vol. XIII, 487–88.
80. William Weer to Thomas Moonlight, July 12, 1862.
81. H. S. Greeno to William Weer, July 17, 1862, *OR*, Ser. I, Vol. XIII, 161–162; H. S. Greeno to William Weer, July 15, 1862, *OR*, Ser. I, Vol. XIII, 473.
82. Frederick Salomon to James G. Blunt, July 20, 1862, *OR*, Ser. I, Vol. XIII, 484–85.
83. E. H. Carruth to James G. Blunt, July 19, 1862, *OR*, Ser. I, Vol. XIII, 476.
84. General Orders No. 1, July 18, 1862, *OR*, Ser. I, Vol. XIII, 476–477.
85. R. W. Furnas to James G. Blunt, July 25, 1862, *OR*, Ser. I, Vol. XIII, 511–12.
86. E. H. Carruth to James G. Blunt, July 19, 1862, *OR*, Ser. I, Vol. XIII, 476.
87. General Orders No. 1, A. C. Ellithorpe, July 19, 1862, *OR*, Ser. I, Vol. XIII, 476.
88. R. W. Furnas to James G. Blunt, July 25, 1862, *OR*, Ser. I, Vol. XIII, 511–12.
89. James G. Blunt to William Weer, July 19, 1862, *OR*, Ser. I, Vol. XIII, 476.
90. James G. Blunt to Edwin M. Stanton, July 20, 1862, *OR*, Ser. I, Vol. XIII, 482–83.
91. James G. Blunt to Edwin M. Stanton, July 21, 1862, *OR*, Ser. I, Vol. XIII, 486.
92. William A. Phillips to Colonel Furnas, July 27, 1862, *OR*, Ser. I, Vol. XIII, 182.
93. William A. Phillips to R. W. Furnas, August 6, 1862, *OR*, Ser. I, Vol. XIII, 183–84.

94. W.F. Cloud to the Members of the Cherokee Nation, August 3, 1862, Papers of Abraham Lincoln, LOC.
95. Frederick Salomon to James G. Blunt, August 9, 1862, *OR*, Ser. I, Vol. XIII, 551–52; Moulton, *John Ross*, 175.
96. James G. Blunt to Abraham Lincoln, August 13, 1862, *OR*, Ser. I, Vol. XIII, 565–66.
97. Phillips and Rieke, *Fire in the North*, 3–5.
98. Phillips and Rieke, 29–34; 75–80.
99. Utley, *The Indian Frontier*, 79–80.
100. John Ross to Abraham Lincoln, September 16, 1862, in Moulton, *Papers of Chief John Ross*, 2:516–18.
101. Abraham Lincoln to John Ross, September 25, 1862, Papers of Abraham Lincoln, LOC.
102. Abraham Lincoln, "State of the Union," December 1, 1862, UG, www.let.rug.nl/usa/presidents/.
103. McPherson, *Battle Cry of Freedom*, 545; Long, *Civil War Day by Day*, 267.
104. John Ross to Edwin M. Stanton, November 8, 1862, *OR*, Ser. I, Vol. XXII, 520–21.
105. John Ross to William A. Phillips, January 4, 1863, *OR*, Ser. I, Vol. XXII, 525.
106. John Ross to William A. Phillips, January 4, 1863.
107. Abraham Lincoln to Samuel R. Curtis, October 10, 1862, *OR*, Ser. I, Vol. XIII, 723.
108. Samuel R. Curtis to Abraham Lincoln, October 10, 1862, *OR*, Ser. I, Vol. XIII, 723.
109. Samuel R. Curtis to John M. Schofield, October 14, 1862, *OR*, Ser. I, Vol. XIII, 736.
110. Huckleberry Downing and Tahlahlah to John Ross, January 12, 1863, in Moulton, *Papers of Chief John Ross*, 2:530.
111. James G. Blunt to John M. Schofield, November 9, 1862, *OR*, Ser. I, Vol. XIII, 785.
112. James G. Blunt to Caleb B. Smith, November 21, 1862, referenced in Moulton, *Papers of Chief John Ross*, 522.
113. Daniel H. Ross to John Ross, December 2, 1862, Moulton, 523–24.
114. Annual Report of the Commissioner of Indian Affairs, October 31, 1863, 175, UW ARCIA.
115. John M. Schofield to William A. Phillips, January 11, 1863, *OR*, Ser. I, Vol. XXII, 33.
116. William A. Phillips to James G. Blunt, April 2, 1863, *OR*, Ser. I, Vol. XXII, 190–91; James G. Blunt to William A. Phillips, February 22, 1863, *OR*, Ser. I, Vol. XXII, 121–22.
117. William A. Phillips to Samuel R. Curtis, January 19, 1863, *OR*, Ser. I, Vol. XXII, 55–56.
118. William A. Phillips to Samuel R, Curtis, January 19, 1863, 60–61.
119. "Opening Address at Cowskin Prairie," Cherokee National Papers, CHN8, Vol. 241, pp. 1–3, OHS.
120. "Opening Address at Cowskin Prairie."
121. "Act to Abrogate the Cherokee-Confederate Alliance," Cherokee National Papers, CHN8, Vol. 251, pp. 3–5, OHS.
122. John Ross to William P. Dole, April 2, 1863, in Moulton, *Papers of Chief John Ross*, 2:534–35.
123. John Ross to William P. Dole, April 2, 1863.

124. Annual Report of the Commissioner of Indian Affairs, October 31, 1863, UW ARCIA; Cherokee National Papers, OHS.
125. Baker and Baker, *The WPA Oklahoma Slave Narratives*, 275.
126. Baker and Baker, 195.
127. James G. Blunt to William A. Phillips, March 9, 1863, *OR*, Ser. I, Vol. XXII, 147–48.
128. William A. Phillips to Samuel R. Curtis, March 20, 1863, *OR*, Ser. I, Vol. XXII, 165–66.
129. William A. Phillips to Samuel R. Curtis, March 20, 1863, 131.
130. Britton, *Memoirs*, 204.
131. Johansson, *Albert C. Ellithorpe*, 159.
132. William A. Phillips to James G. Blunt, April 2, 1863, *OR*, Ser. I, Vol. XXII, 190–91.
133. James G. Blunt to Samuel R. Curtis, April 17, 1863, *OR*, Ser. I, Vol. XXII, 223–24.
134. William Steele to A. M. Alexander, March 30, 1863, *OR*, Ser. I, Vol. XXII, 804–5.
135. Annual Report of the Commissioner of Indian Affairs, October 31, 1863, 176, UW ARCIA.
136. Rhesa Walker Read to LIzzie Read, May 28, 1863, RWRL.
137. Grady and Felmly, *Suffering to Silence*, 67–69.
138. James G. Blunt to John M. Schofield, June 26, 1863, *OR*, Ser. I, Vol. XXII, 337–38.
139. For a detailed look at the First Kansas Colored Infantry and its commander, see Lull, *Civil War General and Indian Fighter*.
140. William Steele to Brigadier General Cabell, June 25, 1863, *OR*, Ser. I, Vol. XXII, Pt. 2, 885.
141. Confer, *The Cherokee Nation*, 77–89; William Steele to W.B. Blair, August 7, 1863, *OR*, Ser. I, Vol. XXII, Pt. 2, 956.
142. Stand Watie to His Excellency the Governor of the Choctaw and Chickasaw Nations, August 9, 1863, *OR*, Ser. I, Vol. XXII, 961–62.
143. Franks, *Stand Watie*, 129–31.
144. Franks, 148.
145. Rhesa Walker Read to Lizzie Read, June 25, 1864, RWRL.
146. Adkins-Rochette, *Bourland in North Texas*, 333.
147. Knight, *Red Fox*, 278.
148. Confer, *The Cherokee Nation*, 145.
149. Annual Report of the Commissioner of Indian Affairs, October 31, 1863, 175, UW ARCIA.
150. Adkins-Rochette, *Bourland in North Texas*, 333; Warde, *When the Wolf Came*, 19.
151. Franks, *Stand Watie*, 182–83.

Chapter 5

1. Lincoln's Final Speech, April 11, 1865, Presidential Speeches, UG.
2. McPherson, *Tried by War*, 207–8.
3. Smith Christie et al., to His Excellency Andrew Johnson, January 31, 1866, Folder 1298, John Ross Papers, HC.

4. William P. Dole to John Ross, January 26, 1866, Folder 1298, John Ross Papers, HC.
5. Berg, *38 Nooses*, 219–20.
6. Nichols, *Lincoln and the Indians*, 158.
7. Lewis Downing to John Ross and Evan Jones, n.d., in Moulton, *Papers of Chief John Ross*, 2:612.
8. Lewis Downing to John Ross and Evan Jones, n.d.
9. Members of the Second and Third Indian Home Guards were ordered to Arkansas in spring 1864 in support of General Frederick Steele and his Union forces as they advanced toward Shreveport, Louisiana, during the failed Red River Campaign of April 1864; John Ross to Edwin M. Stanton, May 25, 1864, in Moulton, *Papers of Chief John Ross*, 2:578; Rhesa Walker Read to Lizzie Read, April 17, 1864, RWRL.
10. The "Three Articles" are in Folder 1385, John Ross Papers, HC.
11. John Ross to William P. Dole, January 25, 1865, in Moulton, *Papers of Chief John Ross*, 2:618.
12. John Ross to William P. Dole, March 25, 1865, in Moulton, 2:640.
13. "Documents Relating to the Negotiations of an Unratified Treaty of September 3, 1863, with the Creek Indians," University of Wisconsin Libraries, accessed February 12, 2020, http://images.library.wisc.edu/History/EFacs/IndianTreatiesMicro/Unrat1863n034/reference/history.unrat1863n034.i0001.pdf.
14. Annual Report of the Commissioner of Indian Affairs, October 31,1863, 23, UW ARCIA.
15. Annual Report of the Commissioner of Indian Affairs, October 31,1863, 23.
16. "Dialogue Between John Ross and Dennis N. Cooley," September 15, 1865, in Moulton, *Papers of Chief John Ross*, 2:676–78.
17. Annual Report of the Commissioner of Indian Affairs, November 30, 1857, 11, UW ARCIA.
18. Annual Report of the Commissioner of Indian Affairs, November 6, 1858, 6, UW ARCIA.
19. Annual Report of the Commissioner of Indian Affairs, November 23, 1868, 18, UW ARCIA.
20. Annual Report of the Commissioner of Indian Affairs, November 26, 1855, 17, UW ARCIA.
21. Annual Report of the Commissioner of Indian Affairs, November 22, 1856, 23, UW ARCIA.
22. Annual Report of the Commissioner of Indian Affairs, November 30, 1860, 17, UW ARCIA.
23. Annual Report of the Commissioner of Indian Affairs, November 23, 1868, 19, UW ARCIA.
24. Annual Report of the Commissioner of Indian Affairs, November 30, 1857, 4, UW ARCIA; Annual Report of the Commissioner of Indian Affairs, November 30, 1860, 25, UW ARCIA.
25. Annual Report of the Commissioner of Indian Affairs, November 26, 1853, 20, UW ARCIA.

26. Annual Report of the Commissioner of Indian Affairs, November 26, 1853, 21.
27. Annual Report of the Commissioner of Indian Affairs, November 30, 1857, 7, UW ARCIA.
28. Annual Report of the Commissioner of Indian Affairs, November 23, 1868, 18, UW ARCIA.
29. Annual Report of the Commissioner of Indian Affairs, November 23, 1868, 18.
30. Perdue, *Slavery*, 60; see also Saunt, *Black, White, and Indian*, and Baird, *A Creek Warrior*.
31. There is no evidence that Taylor knew about the large oil reserves in the Cherokee Nation at the time. Most likely, he based his estimation solely on their widespread capital wealth. Annual Report of the Commissioner of Indian Affairs, November 23, 1868, 18, UW ARCIA.
32. Annual Report of the Commissioner of Indian Affairs, November 23, 1868, 18.
33. Kvasnicka and Viola, *The Commissioners of Indian Affairs*, 100; Chernow, *Grant*, 658.
34. Annual Report of the Commissioner of Indian Affairs, November 27, 1851, 11, UW ARCIA.
35. Annual Report of the Commissioner of Indian Affairs, November 15, 1864, 41, UW ARCIA.
36. Annual Report of the Commissioner of Indian Affairs, November 26, 1853, 20, UW ARCIA.
37. Annual Report of the Commissioner of Indian Affairs, November 26, 1853, 20, 11.
38. Annual Report of the Commissioner of Indian Affairs, November 26, 1853, 20, 13.
39. Annual Report of the Commissioner of Indian Affairs, November 30, 1857, 197, UW ARCIA.
40. Annual Report of the Commissioner of Indian Affairs, November 15, 1864, 5, UW ARCIA.
41. Prucha, *American Indian Treaties*, 273.
42. Prucha, 3.
43. Prucha, 5–6.
44. Annual Report of the Commissioner of Indian Affairs, October 22, 1866, UW ARCIA.
45. Annual Report of the Commissioner of Indian Affairs, November 27, 1851, 12, UW ARCIA.
46. James Harlan to D. N. Cooley, August 4, 1865, *Documents Relating to the Negotiations of an Unratified Treaty on September 13, 1865*, UW Treaties.
47. Gary L. Roberts, "Dennis Nelson Cooley," in Kvasnicka and Viola, *The Commissioners of Indian Affairs*, 99.
48. Helm, *Mary, Wife of Lincoln*, 274–75.
49. Gary Moulton, "Chief John Ross and William P. Dole: A Case Study of Lincoln's Indian Policy," in Fischer, *The Civil War Era in Indian Territory*, 93.
50. Kvasnicka and Viola, *The Commissioners of Indian Affairs*, 99.
51. Warde, *When the Wolf Came*, 257.

52. Annual Report of the Commissioner of Indian Affairs, October 31, 1865, 314, UW ARCIA.
53. Annual Report of the Commissioner of Indian Affairs, October 31, 1865, 314.
54. Annual Report of the Commissioner of Indian Affairs, October 31, 1865, 315.
55. Annual Report of the Commissioner of Indian Affairs, October 31, 1865, 315.
56. Annual Report of the Commissioner of Indian Affairs, October 31, 1865, 317.
57. Annual Report of the Commissioner of Indian Affairs, October 31, 1865, 318.
58. Trefousse, *Andrew Johnson*, 197–98.
59. Annual Report of the Commissioner of Indian Affairs, October 31, 1865, 322, UW ARCIA.
60. Annual Report of the Secretary of the Interior, December 4, 1865, 7, ARSOI.
61. Annual Report of the Secretary of the Interior, December 4, 1865, 35.
62. Annual Report of the Secretary of the Interior, December 4, 1865, 318.
63. Annual Report of the Secretary of the Interior, December 4, 1865, 327.
64. Annual Report of the Secretary of the Interior, December 4, 1865, 318.
65. Annual Report of the Secretary of the Interior, December 4, 1865, 318.
66. Dialogue Between Ross and Dennis N. Cooley, September 15, 1865, in Moulton, *Papers of Chief John Ross*, 2:646–48.
67. Annual Report of the Commissioner of Indian Affairs, October 31, 1865, 323, UW ARCIA.
68. Annual Report of the Commissioner of Indian Affairs, October 31, 1865, 325–26.
69. H. R. Misc. Doc. No. 56, 38th Cong., 2nd Sess. (1865), LOC.
70. Annual Report of the Commissioner of Indian Affairs, October 31, 1865, 333, UW ARCIA.
71. Annual Report of the Commissioner of Indian Affairs, October 31, 1865, 323, UW ARCIA.
72. Annual Report of the Commissioner of Indian Affairs, October 31, 1865, 331.
73. Annual Report of the Commissioner of Indian Affairs, October 31, 1865, 327.
74. Annual Report of the Commissioner of Indian Affairs, October 31, 1865, 331–32.
75. Annual Report of the Commissioner of Indian Affairs, October 31, 1865, 331–32.
76. Annual Report of the Commissioner of Indian Affairs, October 31, 1865, 331–32.
77. Annual Report of the Commissioner of Indian Affairs, October 31, 1865, 336.
78. Annual Report of the Commissioner of Indian Affairs, October 31, 1865, 336.
79. Dialogue Between Ross and Dennis N. Cooley, September 15, 1865, in Moulton, *Papers of Chief John Ross*, 2:646–48.
80. *The Cherokee Question. Report of the Commissioner of Indian Affairs to the President of the United States, June 15, 1866. Supplementary to the Report of the Commissioners Appointed by the President to Treat with the Indians South of Kansas, and Which Assembled at Fort Smith, Ark., in September 1865* (Washington: Government Printing Office, 1866), Ely Samuel Parker Papers, NL.
81. *The Cherokee Question*, 28.
82. *The Cherokee Question*, 28.

83. *The Cherokee Question*, 28.
84. Annual Report of the Commissioner of Indian Affairs, October 31, 1865, 325–26, UW ARCIA.
85. Prucha, *American Indian Treaties*, 267.
86. Marion Ray McCullar, "The Choctaw-Chickasaw Reconstruction Treaty of 1866," in Fischer, *The Civil War Era in Indian Territory*, 138.
87. "Treaty with the Cherokee, 1866," July 19, 1866, RG 75, Documents Related to Ratified and Unratified Treaties with the Various Indian Tribes, NARA.
88. See Cherokee Nation v. Nash, 267 F. Supp. 3d 86 (D.D.C. 2017) and Vann v. Kempthorne, 534 F.3d 741 (D.C. Cir. 2008).
89. Prucha, *American Indian Treaties*, 268.
90. For example, Confer and Frank Cunningham mention Parker as being a member of the Fort Smith Council, without elaborating on his role. Knight and Bean do not even mention him in regard to the council. Confer, *The Cherokee Nation*; 148; Cunningham, *General Stand Watie's Confederate Indians*, 204; Knight, *Red Fox*, 277–80; Bean, "Who Defines a Nation?" 119–20.
91. Armstrong, *Warrior in Two Camps*, 10.
92. St. Germain, *Indian Treaty-Making Policy*, 27.
93. "Lecture," n.d., Ely Samuel Parker Papers, Ayers MS 674, NL.
94. Annual Report of the Commissioner of Indian Affairs, October 31, 1865, 35, UW ARCIA.
95. "Lecture," n.d., Ely Samuel Parker Papers, Ayers MS 674, NL.
96. E. S. Parker to U. S. Grant, January 24, 1867, *Reports of the Secretaries of War and Interior in Answer to Resolutions of the Senate and House of Representatives in Relation to the Massacre at Fort Phil. Kearney, on December 21, 1866* (Washington: Government Printing Office, 1867), 47–56, Ely Samuel Parker Papers, NL.
97. E. S. Parker to U. S. Grant, January 24, 1867, 53.
98. Annual Report of the Commissioner of Indian Affairs, October 31, 1865, 304, UW ARCIA.
99. Annual Report of the Commissioner of Indian Affairs, October 31, 1865, 304.
100. *The Cherokee Question*, 4.
101. H. Wilson to Colonel E. S. Parker, January 28, 1867, Ayer MS 109, Ely Samuel Parker Papers, NL.
102. Myers, *Henry Wilson*, 130.
103. H. Wilson to Colonel E. S. Parker, January 28, 1867, Ayer MS 1009, Ely Samuel Parker Papers, NL.
104. Armstrong, *Warrior in Two Camps*, 120–21.
105. *Congressional Globe*, 40th Cong., 1st sess., 1867, 668, LOC.
106. *Congressional Globe*, 40th Cong., 1st sess., 1867, 667.
107. *Congressional Globe*, 40th Cong., 1st sess., 1867, 667.
108. Report to the President by the Indian Peace Commission, January 7, 1868. RG 75 NARA.

109. Report to the President by the Indian Peace Commission, January 7, 1868.
110. Annual Report of the Commissioner of Indian Affairs, November 23, 1868, 4, UW ARCIA.
111. Utley, *The Indian Frontier*, 109–10.
112. Chernow, *Grant*, 658.
113. Prucha, *American Indian Treaties*, 273.
114. Annual Report of the Commissioner of Indian Affairs, December 23, 1869, 6, UW ARCIA.
115. Prucha, *American Indian Treaties*, 273.
116. Prucha, 287.
117. Annual Report of the Commissioner of Indian Affairs, December 23, 1869, 6, UW ARCIA.
118. E. S. Parker to U. S. Grant, January 24, 1867, *Reports of the Secretaries of War and Interior*, 52–53, Ely Samuel Parker Papers, NL.
119. Bean, "Who Defines a Nation?" 120.
120. Prucha, *American Indian Treaties*, 279.
121. Lincoln's Final Speech, April 11, 1865, UG.

Conclusion

1. McGirt v. Oklahoma, 140 S.Ct. 2452 (2020).
2. McGirt, 2482.
3. McGirt, 2462.
4. McGirt, 2459–62.
5. Art. VI, sec. 2, Constitution of the United States.
6. McGirt, 2462.
7. Hoxie, *A Final Promise*, 2.
8. Wilkinson, *American Indians, Time, and the Law*, 14.
9. Prucha, *American Indian Treaties*, 279.
10. Prucha, 334.
11. Prucha, 282–83.
12. Wooster, *The Military*, 112.
13. Annual Report of the Commissioner of Indian Affairs, October 22, 1866, 41, UW ARCIA.
14. Annual Report of the Commissioner of Indian Affairs, October 22, 1866, 41.
15. Annual Report of the Commissioner of Indian Affairs, October 22, 1866, 1–2.
16. Annual Report of the Commissioner of Indian Affairs, October 22, 1866, 2.
17. Annual Report of the Commissioner of Indian Affairs, November 23, 1868, 1, UW ARCIA.
18. Annual Report of the Commissioner of Indian Affairs, November 23, 1868, 17.
19. Annual Report of the Commissioner of Indian Affairs, November 23, 1868, 18.
20. Annual Report of the Commissioner of Indian Affairs, November 15, 1867, 4, UW ARCIA.

21. Annual Report of the Commissioner of Indian Affairs, November 15, 1867, 1.
22. Annual Report of the Commissioner of Indian Affairs, November 15, 1867, 1
23. Annual Report of the Commissioner of Indian Affairs, November 15, 1867, 2.
24. Annual Report of the Commissioner of Indian Affairs, November 15, 1867, 22.
25. Annual Report of the Commissioner of Indian Affairs, November 15, 1867, 27.
26. Annual Report of the Commissioner of Indian Affairs, November 15, 1867, 2–3.
27. Annual Report of the Commissioner of Indian Affairs, December 23, 1869, 6, UW ARCIA.
28. Annual Report of the Commissioner of Indian Affairs, December 23, 1869, 5.
29. Utley, *The Indian Frontier*, 98.
30. Wooster, *The Military*, 3.
31. Utley, *The Indian Frontier*, 101.
32. "March 30 Interview," Documents Relating to the Negotiation of the Treaty of July 19, 1866, with the Cherokee Indians, RG 75, Documents Related to Ratified and Unratified Treaties with the Various Tribes, NARA.
33. Faragher, *Rereading Frederick Jackson Turner*, 31.
34. Indian Territory and Oklahoma Territory are not to be confused as they were two separate entities from 1890 until they were combined in 1907 to form the new state of Oklahoma.
35. According to the U.S. Census Bureau, there were 112,160 Blacks in the new state of Oklahoma and only 75,012 Indians.
36. 1930 United States Census, "Indian Population of the United States and Alaska," 43.
37. 1930 United States Census, "Indian Population of the United States and Alaska," 43.
38. 1930 United States Census, "Indian Population of the United States and Alaska," 43.
39. 1930 United States Census, "Indian Population of the United States and Alaska," 43.
40. Dippie, *The Vanishing American*, 192.
41. Cherokee Constitution of 1975, Article III, § 1.
42. "Opinion of the Court," Lucy Allen v. Cherokee Nation Tribal Council, Lela Ummerteskee, Registrar, and Registration Committee (2006), JAT-04–09, 33.
43. Article III, 11 C.N.C.A. § 12.
44. Strum, "Blood Politics," 233.
45. "Opinion of the Court," Lucy Allen v. Cherokee Nation Tribal Council, Lela Ummerteskee, Registrar, and Registration Committee (2006), JAT-04–09, 18.
46. Sturm, "Blood Politics," 239.
47. Cherokee Freemen, Card 500, in "Search the Dawes Rolls, 1898–1914," OHS, https://www.okhistory.org/research/dawesresults.php?cardnum=500&tribe=Cherokee&type=Freedmen, accessed December 28, 2021.
48. Sturm, "Blood Politics," 236–37.
49. Sturm, "Blood Politics," 233.
50. Quoted in Schreier, "Indian or Freedman?," 462.
51. Schreier, "Indian or Freedman?" 468.
52. "Opinion of the Court," Riggs v. Ummerteskee, December 7, 2001, No. JAT 97-03, Cherokee Nation Judicial Appeals Tribunal.

53. Schreier describes a similar mindset that developed in the Choctaw Nation, Schreier, "Indian or Freedman?" 476.
54. Riggs v. Ummerteskee, JAT 97-03.
55. Vann v. Kempthorne, 467 F.Supp. 2d 56 (D.D.C. 2006).
56. Nash, et al. v. Cherokee Nation Registrar, Cherokee District Court, January 14, 2011.
57. H.R. 2824, June 21, 2007, 110th Congress, 1st Session.
58. H.R. 2824, June 21, 2007, 110th Congress, 1st Session.
59. Ratified Treaty No. 358, Documents Relating to the Negotiation of the Treaty of July 19, 1866, with the Cherokee Indians, RG 75, Documents Related to Ratified and Unratified Treaties with the Various Tribes, NARA.
60. Cherokee Nation v. Nash, 267 F.Supp. 3d 86, 94 n.11 (D.D.C. 2017).
61. Nash, et al. v. Cherokee Nation Registrar, Cherokee District Court, January 14, 2011.
62. Cherokee Nation v. Nash, 267 F.Supp. 3d 86 (D.D.C. 2017).
63. Cherokee Nation v. Nash, 267 F.Supp. 3d 86.

BIBLIOGRAPHY

Manuscript Collections

Library of Congress (Washington, D.C.)

Grant, Ulysses S., Papers
Jackson, Andrew, Papers
Johnson, Andrew, Papers
Lincoln, Abraham, Papers
Madison, James, Papers
Van Buren, Martin, Papers

National Archives and Records Administration (Washington, D.C.)

Record Group 75. Records of the Bureau of Indian Affairs
Confederate Records
    Accounts and Other Records, 1861–1862
    Correspondence of the Arkansas Superintendency, 1861–1862
    Correspondence of the Wichita Agency, 1861–1862
Federal Records
    Letters Received by the Office of Indian Affairs, 1824–1880
    Letters Sent by the Office of Indian Affairs, 1824–1881
    Register of Letters Received that were Registered Out of Date, 1836–1864
    Registers of Letters Received, 1824–1880
Letters Sent by the Indian Division of the Office of the Secretary of the Interior, 1849–1903
Letters Received by the Indian Division of the Office of the Secretary of the Interior, 1849–1880
    Miscellaneous Records
    Minutes of Board Meetings, 1869–1915
    Minutes of Board Meetings, 1869–1933
    Special Case No. 188, The Ghost Dance, 1890–1898
    Documents Relating to the Negotiations of Ratified and Unratified Treaties with Various Indian Tribes, 1861–1869
Record Group 153. Records of the Office of the Judge Advocate General Army, Court Martial Case Files, 1809–1894
    NN 2369—Colonel William Weer

Record Group 393. Records of the United States Army Continental Commands
    Department of the Missouri, Adjutant General's Office, Letters Sent, June–September 1862
    Letters Sent, January 1862–March 1862
    Letters Sent, April 1862–May 1862
    Letters Sent, June 1862–August 1862
    Letters Sent, August 1862–September 1862
    Monthly Reports by Commissioned Officers, 1862–1865
    Press Copies of Letters and Telegrams Sent, May 1862–May 1863

American Philosophical Society Library (Philadelphia, Pennsylvania)

Parker, Ely Samuel, Papers

Cherokee Heritage Center Archives (Tahlequah, Oklahoma)

Cherokee National Papers
Ross, John, Papers

Helmerich Center for American Research, Thomas Gilcrease Library and Archive (Tulsa, Oklahoma)

Cherokee Papers
Ross, John, Papers
Watie, Stand, Papers

Newberry Library (Chicago, Illinois)

Parker, Ely Samuel, Papers

Oklahoma Historical Society (Oklahoma City, Oklahoma)

Cherokee National Papers
Creek National Papers
Ross, John, Papers

Southwest Arkansas Regional Archives (Washington, Arkansas)

Map Collection

Texarkana Museum of Regional History (Texarkana, Texas)

Read Family Papers

University of Rochester Libraries (Rochester, New York)

Parker, Ely Samuel, Papers

Williams House Museum (DeKalb, Texas)

Read, Rhesa Walker, Letters

Online Collections

Cornell University (Oyez)

U.S. Supreme Court Cases

Digital Public Library of America

Cherokee Removal and the Trail of Tears collection

Hathi Trust Digital Library

Annual Reports of the Department of the Interior, 1850–1963

Kansas State Historical Society
Texas State Historical Association
University of Groningen

Inaugural Addresses
Presidential Addresses
State of the Union Addresses

University of Wisconsin Libraries

Annual Reports of the Commissioners of Indian Affairs, 1826–1932
Documents Relating to the Negotiation of Ratified and Unratified Treaties with Various Indian Tribes
Foreign Relations of the United States

Western Carolina University Library

Digital Collections

Yale Law School

The Avalon Project, Documents in Law, History, and Diplomacy

Government Documents

Civil War Compiled Service Records
U.S. Census Records
U.S. Congress, *Congressional Globe*, 23rd–32nd Congress (1833–1853).
U.S. Congress, *Congressional Globe*, 39th–42nd Congress (1866–1873).
U.S. War Department, *The War of the Rebellion, A Compilation of the Official Records of the Union and Confederate Armies*. 128 vols. Washington, D.C., U.S. Government Printing Office, 1880–1901.

Books

Abel, Annie Heloise. *The American Indian as Slaveholder and Secessionist*. Cleveland, OH: Arthur H. Clark Co., 1915. Reprinted, Lincoln: University of Nebraska Press, 1992.
——. *The American Indian under Reconstruction*. Cleveland, OH: Arthur H. Clark Co., 1925.
Adkins-Rochette, Patricia. *Bourland in North Texas and Indian Territory during the Civil War: Fort Cobb, Fort Arbuckle, and the Wichita Mountains*. Broken Arrow, OK: Bourlandcivilwar.com, 2004.
Agnew, Brad. "Our Doom as a Nation Is Sealed: The Five Nations in the Civil War." In *The Civil War and Reconstruction in Indian Territory*, edited by Bradley R. Clampitt, 64–87. Lincoln: University of Nebraska Press, 2015.
Anderson, Mabel Washbourne. *The Life of General Stand Watie: The Only Indian Brigadier General of the Confederate Army and the Last General to Surrender*. Jay, OK: Delaware County Historical Society, 2010.
Armstrong, William H. *Warrior in Two Camps: Ely S. Parker, Union General and Seneca Chief*. Syracuse, NY: Syracuse University Press, 1978.
Bailey, Anne J. *Between the Enemy and Texas*. Fort Worth: Texas Christian University Press, 1989.
Bailey, Joseph M. *Confederate Guerilla: The Civil War Memoir of Joseph M. Bailey*. Edited by T. Lindsay Baker. Fayetteville: University of Arkansas Press, 2007.
Baird, W. David, ed. *A Creek Warrior for the Confederacy: The Autobiography of Chief G. W. Grayson*. Norman: University of Oklahoma Press, 1988.
Banner, Stuart. *How the Indians Lost Their Land: Law and Power on the Frontier*. Cambridge, MA: Harvard University Press, 2005.
Bean, Christopher B. "Who Defines a Nation? Reconstruction in Indian Territory." In *The Civil War and Reconstruction in Indian Territory*, edited by Bradley R. Clampitt, 110–31. Lincoln: University of Nebraska Press, 2015.
Bearss, Edwin C. *The Battle of Wilson's Creek*. Bozeman, MT: Artcraft Printers, 1975.
Berg, Scott W. *38 Nooses: Lincoln, Little Crow, and the Beginning of the Frontier's End*. New York: Pantheon, 2012.
Brady, Cyrus Townsend. *The Sioux Indian Wars: From the Powder River to the Little Big Horn*. New York: Indian Head Books, 1992.

Brigham, Johnson. *James Harlan.* Iowa City: State Historical Society of Iowa, 1913.
Britton, Wiley. *The Civil War on the Border.* 2 vols. New York: G. P. Putnam's Sons, 1899.
———. *The Union Indian Brigade in the Civil War.* Kansas City, MO: Franklin Hudson, 1922.
———. *Memoirs of the Rebellion on the Border, 1863.* Chicago: Cushing, Thomas, and Co., 1882. Reprinted, Lincoln: University of Nebraska Press, 1993.
Brooksher, William Riley. *Bloody Hill: The Civil War Battle of Wilson's Creek.* Washington, DC: Brassey, 1995.
Brown, Thomas J., ed. *Reconstructions: New Perspectives on the Postbellum United States.* New York: Oxford University Press, 2006.
Brown, Walter Lee. *A Life of Albert Pike.* Fayetteville: University of Arkansas Press, 1997.
Buchanan, John. *Jackson's Way: Andrew Jackson and People of the Western Waters.* Edison, NJ: Castle Books. 2005.
Campbell, Randolph B. *An Empire for Slavery: The Peculiar Institution in Texas.* Baton Rouge: Louisiana State University Press, 1989.
Castel, Albert. *Civil War Kansas: Reaping the Whirlwind.* Ithaca, NY: Cornell University Press, 1958. Reprinted, Lawrence: University Press of Kansas, 1997.
———. *William Clarke Quantrill.* New York: F. Fell, 1962. Reprinted, Norman: University of Oklahoma Press, 1992.
Casto, David E. *Arkansas Late in the Civil War: The 8th Missouri Volunteer Cavalry, April 1864–July 1865.* Charleston, SC: History Press, 2013.
Chernow, Ron. *Grant.* New York: Penguin Books, 2017.
Christ, Mark, ed. *Getting Used to Being Shot At: The Spence Family Civil War Letters.* Fayetteville: University of Arkansas Press, 2002.
———. *Civil War Arkansas, 1863: The Battle for a State.* Norman: University of Oklahoma Press, 2010.
———, ed. *"This Day We Marched Again:" A Union Soldier's Account of War in Arkansas and the Trans-Mississippi.* Little Rock: Butler Center Press, 2014.
Clampitt, Bradley R., ed. *The Civil War and Reconstruction in Indian Territory.* Lincoln: University of Nebraska Press, 2015.
Collins, Robert. *General James G. Blunt: Tarnished Glory.* Gretna, LA: Pelican, 2005.
Colton, Ray C. *The Civil War in the Western Territories: Arizona, Colorado, New Mexico, and Utah.* Norman: University of Oklahoma Press, 1959.
Confer, Clarissa W. *The Cherokee Nation in the Civil War.* Norman: University of Oklahoma Press, 2007.
Conley, Robert J. *The Cherokee Nation: A History.* Albuquerque: University of New Mexico Press, 2005.
Connole, Joseph. *The Civil War and the Subversion of American Indian Sovereignty.* Jefferson, NC: McFarland, 2017.
Cottrell, Steve. *Civil War in the Indian Territory.* Gretna, LA: Pelican, 1995.
Cunningham, Frank. *General Stand Watie's Confederate Indians.* San Antonio: Naylor, 1959. Reprinted Norman: University of Oklahoma Press, 1998.

Cutrer, Thomas W. *Theater of a Separate War: The Civil War West of the Mississippi River, 1861–1865*. Chapel Hill: University of North Carolina Press, 2017.

Dale, Edward Everett, and Gaston Litton. *Cherokee Cavaliers: Forty Years of Cherokee History as Told in the Correspondence of the Ridge-Watie-Boudinot Family*. Norman: University of Oklahoma Press, 1939. Reprinted Norman: University of Oklahoma Press, 1995.

Danziger, Edmund Jefferson, Jr. *Indians and Bureaucrats: Administering the Reservation Policy during the Civil War*. Urbana: University of Illinois Press, 1974.

Davis, Kenneth Penn. "Chaos in the Indian Country: The Cherokee Nation, 1828–35, in *The Cherokee Indian Nation: A Troubled History*, edited by Duane H. King. Knoxville: University of Tennessee Press, 1979.

DeBlack, Thomas A. *With Fire and Sword: Arkansas, 1861–1874*. Fayetteville: University of Arkansas Press, 2003.

Debo, Angie. *The Road to Disappearance: A History of the Creek Indians*. Norman: University of Oklahoma Press, 1941.

Deloria, Vine, Jr. *Custer Died for Your Sins: An Indian Manifesto*. New York: MacMillan, 1969.

Deloria, Vine, Jr., and Raymond J. DeMallie. *Documents of American Indian Diplomacy: Treaties, Agreements, and Conventions, 1775–1979*. 2 vols. Norman: University of Oklahoma Press, 1999.

Dippie, Brian W. *The Vanishing American: White Attitudes and Indian Policy*. Lawrence: University Press of Kansas, 1982.

Dougan, Michael B. *Confederate Arkansas: The People and Policies of a Frontier State in Wartime*. Tuscaloosa: University of Alabama Press, 1976.

Downs, Gregory P. *After Appomattox: Military Occupation and the Ends of War*. Cambridge, MA: Harvard University Press, 2015.

Duncan, Robert Lipscomb. *Reluctant General: The Life and Times of Albert Pike*. New York: E. P. Dutton, 1961.

Ehle, John. *Trail of Tears: The Rise and Fall of the Cherokee Nation*. New York: Anchor, 1988.

Eisenhower, John S. D. *Agent of Destiny: The Life and Times of General Winfield Scott*. New York: The Free Press, 1997.

Ellis, Richard N. *General Pope and U.S. Indian Policy*. Albuquerque: University of New Mexico Press, 1970.

Etcheson, Nicole. *Bleeding Kansas: Contested Liberty in the Civil War Era*. Lawrence: University Press of Kansas, 2004.

Evans, Clement A., ed. *Confederate Military History*. 12 vols. Atlanta: Confederate Publishing Company, 1899.

Faragher, John Mack. *Rereading Frederick Jackson Turner*. New York: Henry Holt, 1994.

Fellman, Michael, Lesley J. Gordon, and Daniel E. Sutherland. *This Terrible War: The Civil War and Its Aftermath*. New York: Longman, 2003.

Fischer, LeRoy H. *The Civil War Era in Indian Territory*. Los Angeles: Lorrin L. Morrison, 1974.

Fischer, LeRoy H. and Lary C. Rampp. *Quantrill's Civil War Operations in Indian Territory*. Oklahoma City: Oklahoma Historical Society, 1968.

Fischer, LeRoy H. and Jerry Gill. *Confederate Indian Forces Outside of Indian Territory.* Oklahoma City: Oklahoma Historical Society, 1969.

Flemly, Bradford K. and John C. Grady. *Suffering to Silence: 29th Texas Cavalry, CSA, Regimental History.* Quanah, TX: Nortex Press, 1975.

Foote, Shelby. *Five Forks to Appomattox: Victory and Defeat.* New York: Random House. 1974.

Foreman, Grant. *Indian Removal: The Emigration of the Five Civilized Tribes of Indians.* Norman: University of Oklahoma Press, 1932.

Fowles, Brian Dexter. *A Guard in Peace and War: The History of the Kansas National Guard, 1854–1987.* Manhattan, KS: Sunflower University Press, 1982.

Franks, Kenny A. *Stand Watie and the Agony of the Cherokee Nation.* Memphis: Memphis State University Press, 1979.

Gaines, W. Craig. *The Confederate Cherokees: John Drew's Regiment of Mounted Rifles.* Baton Rouge: Louisiana State University Press, 1989.

Genetin-Pilawa, C. Joseph. *Crooked Paths to Allotment: The Fight over Federal Indian Policy after the Civil War.* Chapel Hill: University of North Carolina Press, 2012.

Gigantino, James J. II. *Slavery and Secession in Arkansas: A Documentary History.* Fayetteville: University of Arkansas Press, 2015.

Glatthaar, Joseph T. *Forged in Battle: The Civil War Alliance of Black Soldiers and White Officers.* New York: The Free Press, 1990.

Grady, John C. and Bradford K. Felmly. *Suffering to Silence: 29th Texas Cavalry, CSA Regimental History.* Quanah, TX: Nortex, 1975.

Greenberg, Amy S. *A Wicked War: Polk, Clay, Lincoln, and the 1846 U.S. Invasion of Mexico.* New York: Alfred A. Knopf, 2012.

Hafen, LeRoy R. and Francis Marion Young. *Fort Laramie and the Pageant of the West, 1834–1890.* Glendale, CA: A. H. Clark, 1938. Reprinted Lincoln: University of Nebraska Press, 1984.

Hale, Douglas. *The Third Texas Cavalry in the Civil War.* Norman: University of Oklahoma Press, 1993.

Hatley, Allen G. *Reluctant Rebels: The Eleventh Texas Cavalry Regiment.* Hillsboro, TX: Hill College Press, 2006.

Hauptman, Laurence M. *The Iroquois in the Civil War: From Battlefield to Reservation.* Syracuse: Syracuse University Press, 1993.

Helm, Katherine. *Mary, Wife of Lincoln.* Springfield, IL: The Lincoln Family Home, 2007.

Hewitt, Lawrence Lee and Arthur W. Bergeron Jr. eds. *Confederate Generals in the Western Theater*, 2 vols. Knoxville: University of Tennessee Press, 2010.

Holcombe, Return I. *An Account of the Battle Wilson's Creek.* Springfield, MO: Dow and Adams, 1883. Reprinted Springfield, MO: Midwest Publishing, 1961.

Hoxie, Frederick E. *A Final Promise: The Campaign to Assimilate the Indians, 1880–1920.* Lincoln: University of Nebraska Press, 1984.

Ishii, Izumi. *Bad Fruits of the Civilized Tree: Alcohol and the Sovereignty of the Cherokee Nation.* Lincoln: University of Nebraska Press, 2008.

Johansson, M. Jane, ed. *Albert C. Ellithorpe: The First Indian Home Guards and the Civil War on the Trans-Mississippi Frontier.* Baton Rouge: Louisiana State University Press, 2016.

Johnson, Timothy D. *Winfield Scott: The Quest for Military Glory.* Lawrence: University Press of Kansas, 1998.

Johnston, Carolyn Ross. *Cherokee Women in Crisis: Trail of Tears, Civil War, and Allotment, 1838–1907.* Tuscaloosa: University of Alabama Press, 2003.

Josephy, Alvin M. Jr. *The Civil War in the American West.* New York: Alfred A. Knopf, 1991.

Keehn, David C. *Knights of the Golden Circle: Secret Empire, Southern Secession, Civil War.* Baton Rouge: Louisiana State University Press, 2013.

King, Duane H., ed. *The Cherokee Indian Nation: A Troubled History.* Knoxville: University of Tennessee Press, 1979.

Knight, James R. *The Battle of Pea Ridge: The Civil War Fight for the Ozarks.* Charleston, SC: History Press, 2012.

Knight, Wilfred. *Red Fox: Stand Watie and the Confederate Indian Nations during the Civil War Years in Indian Territory.* Glendale, CA: Arthur H. Clark, Co., 1988.

Kvasnicka, Robert M. and Herman J. Viola, eds. *The Commissioners of Indian Affairs, 1824–1977.* Lincoln: University of Nebraska Press, 1979.

Lale, Max, and Hobart Key, eds. *The Civil War Letters of David R. Garrett: Detailing the Adventures of the 6th Texas Cavalry 1861–1865.* Marshall, TX: Port Caddo Press, n.d.

La Vere, David. *Contrary Neighbors: Southern Plains and Removed Indians in Indian Territory.* Norman: University of Oklahoma Press, 2000.

———. *The Texas Indians.* College Station: Texas A&M University Press, 2004.

Leckie, Shirley A. *Angie Debo: Pioneering Historian.* Norman: University of Oklahoma Press, 2000.

Lee, Wayne E. *Barbarians and Brothers: Anglo-American Warfare, 1500–1865.* New York: Oxford University Press, 2011.

Leeds, Georgia Rae. *The United Keetoowah Band of Cherokee Indians in Oklahoma.* New York: Peter Lang, 1996.

Littlefield, Daniel F., Jr. *Africans and Creeks: From the Colonial Period to the Civil War.* Westport, CT: Greenwood Press, 1979.

Long, E. B. *Civil War Day by Day: An Almanac 1861–1865.* Garden City, NJ: Doubleday, 1971.

Lowe, Richard, ed. *A Texas Cavalry Officer's Civil War: The Diary and Letters of James C. Bates.* Baton Rouge: Louisiana State University Press, 1999.

———. *Walker's Texas Division, C.S.A.: Greyhounds of the Trans-Mississippi.* Baton Rouge: Louisiana State University Press, 2004.

Lull, Robert W. *Civil War General and Indian Fighter James M. Williams: Leader of the First Kansas Colored Volunteer Infantry and the 8th U.S. Cavalry.* Denton: University of North Texas Press, 2013.

Mackey, Robert R. *The Uncivil War: Irregular Warfare in the Upper South, 1861–1865.* Norman: Oklahoma University Press, 2004.

May, Katja. *African Americans and Native Americans in the Creek and Cherokee Nations, 1830s to 1920s: Collision and Collusion.* New York: Garland, 1996.

McBride, Lela J. *Opothleyaholo and the Loyal Muskogee: Their Flight to Kansas in the Civil War*. Jefferson, NC: McFarland, 2000.

McCaslin, Richard B. *Tainted Breeze: The Great Hanging at Gainesville, Texas 1862*. Baton Rouge: Louisiana State University Press, 1994.

———. "Bitter Legacy: The Battle Front." In *The Civil War and Reconstruction in Indian Territory*, edited by Bradley R. Clampitt, 19–37. Lincoln: University of Nebraska Press, 2015.

McCullar Marion Ray. "The Choctaw-Chickasaw Reconstruction Treaty of 1866." In *The Civil War Era in Indian Territory*, edited by LeRoy H. Fischer, 131–39. Los Angeles: Lorrin L. Morrission, 1974.

McKitrick, Eric L. *Andrew Johnson and Reconstruction*. Chicago: University of Chicago Press, 1960.

McLoughlin, William G. *Cherokee Renascence in the New Republic*. Princeton, NJ: Princeton University Press, 1986.

———. *Champions of the Cherokees: Evan and John B. Jones*. Princeton, NJ: Princeton University Press, 1990.

———. *After the Trail of Tears: The Cherokees' Struggle for Sovereignty, 1839–1880*. Chapel Hill: University of North Carolina Press, 1993.

———. *The Cherokees and Christianity, 1794–1870*. Edited by Walter H. Conser Jr. Athens: University of Georgia Press, 1994.

McPherson, James M. *Battle Cry of Freedom: The Civil War Era*. New York: Oxford University Press, 1988. Reprinted, New York: Ballantine Books, 1989.

———. *Tried By War: Abraham Lincoln as Commander in Chief*. New York: Penguin, 2008.

Means, Howard. *The Avenger Takes His Place: Andrew Johnson and the 45 Days That Changed the Nation*. Orlando, FL: Harcourt, 2006.

Miles, Tyla. *Ties That Bind: The Story of an Afro-Cherokee Family in Slavery and Freedom*. Berkeley: University of California Press, 2005.

Minges, Patrick N. *Slavery in the Cherokee Nation: The Keetoowah Society and the Defining of a People 1855–1867*. New York: Routledge, 2003.

Monaghan, Jay. *Civil War on the Western Border 1854–1865*. Boston: Little, Brown, 1955. Reprinted, Lincoln: University of Nebraska Press, 1984.

Moulton, Gary E. "Chief John Ross and William P. Dole: A Case Study of Lincoln's Indian Policy." In *The Civil War Era in Indian Territory*, edited by LeRoy H. Fischer, 84–93. Los Angeles: Lorrin L. Morrison, 1974.

———. *John Ross: Cherokee Chief*. Athens: University of Georgia Press, 1978.

———, ed. *The Papers of Chief John Ross*. 2 vols. Norman: University of Oklahoma Press, 1985.

Myers, John L. *Henry Wilson and the Era of Reconstruction*. Lanham, MD: University Press of America, 2009.

Nash, Gary B. *Red, White, and Black: The Peoples of Early America*. Englewood Cliffs, NJ: Prentice-Hall, 1974.

Nash, Howard P. *Andrew Johnson: Congress and Reconstruction*. Cranbury, NJ: Fairleigh Dickinson University Press, 1972.

Naylor, Celia E. *African Cherokees in Indian Territory: From Chattel to Citizens*. Chapel Hill: University of North Carolina Press, 2008.

Nichols, David A. *Lincoln and the Indians: Civil War Policy and Politics*. Columbia: University of Missouri Press, 1978.

Niven, James. *John C. Calhoun and the Price of Union: A Biography*. Baton Rouge: Louisiana State University Press, 1988.

Ormsby, Waterman L. *The Butterfield Overland Mail: Only Through Passenger on the First Westbound Stage*. San Marino, CA: Huntington Library Press, 1960.

Ostler, Jeffrey. *The Plains Sioux and U.S. Colonialism from Lewis and Clark to Wounded Knee*. Cambridge: Cambridge University Press, 2004.

Patrick, Jeffrey L. *The Campaign for Wilson's Creek: The Fight for Missouri Begins*. Buffalo Gap, TX: McWhiney Foundation Press, 2011.

Perdue, Theda. *Slavery and the Evolution of Cherokee Society, 1540–1866*. Knoxville: University of Tennessee Press, 1979.

———, ed. *Cherokee Editor: The Writings of Elias Boudinot*. Athens: University of Georgia Press, 1996.

———. *"Mixed Blood" Indians: Racial Construction in the Early South*. Athens: University of Georgia Press, 2003.

———. "Cherokee Planters: The Development of Plantation Slavery Before Removal." In *The Cherokee Indian Nation: A Troubled History*, edited by Duane H. King. Knoxville: University of Tennessee Press, 1979.

Peskin, Allan. *Winfield Scott and the Profession of Arms*. Kent, OH: Kent State University Press, 2003.

Phillips, Thomas D. and Reuben D. Rieke. *Fire in the North: The Minnesota Uprising and the Sioux War in Dakota Territory*. Ashland, OR: Hellgate Press, 2018.

Piston, William Garrett and Richard W. Hatcher, III. *Wilson's Creek: The Second Battle of the Civil War and the Men Who Fought It*. Chapel Hill: University of North Carolina Press, 2000.

Pitcock, Cynthia DeHaven, and Bill H. Gurley. *I Acted from Principle: The Civil War Diary of Dr. William M. McPheeters, Confederate Surgeon in the Trans-Mississippi*. Fayetteville: University of Arkansas Press, 2002.

Prucha, Francis Paul. *American Indian Policy in the Formative Years: The Indian Trade and Intercourse Acts*. Cambridge, MA: Harvard University Press, 1962.

———. *American Indian Treaties: The History of a Political Anomaly*. Berkeley: University of California Press, 1994.

———. *Indian Policy in the United States: Historical Essays*. Lincoln: University of Nebraska Press, 1981.

Rampp, Lary C., and Donald L. Rampp. *The Civil War in the Indian Territory*. Austin, TX: Presidial Press, 1975.

Reese, Linda Williams. *Trail Sisters: Freedwomen in Indian Territory, 1850–1890*. Lubbock: Texas Tech University Press, 2013.

Reid, John Phillip. *A Law of Blood: The Primitive Law of the Cherokee Nation*. New York: New York University Press, 1970. Reprinted, DeKalb: Northern Illinois University Press, 2006.

Richardson, Elmo R., and Alan W. Farley. *John Palmer Usher: Lincoln's Secretary of the Interior*. Lawrence: University Press of Kansas, 1960.

Richardson, Heather Cox. *West from Appomattox: The Reconstruction of America after the Civil War*. New Haven, CT: Yale University Press, 2007.

Roberts, Gary. "Dennis Nelson Cooley." In *The Commissioners of Indian Affairs, 1824–1977*, edited by Robert M. Kvasnicka and Herman J. Viola, 99–108. Lincoln: University of Nebraska Press, 1979.

Robertson, James I., Jr. *Soldiers Blue and Gray*. Columbia: University of South Carolina Press, 1988.

Robertson, Lindsay G. *Conquest by Law: How the Discovery of American Dispossessed Indigenous Peoples of Their Lands*. Oxford: Oxford University Press, 2005.

Saunt, Claudio. *Black, White, and Indian: Race and the Unmaking of an American Family*. New York: Oxford University Press, 2005.

Scharff, Virginia, ed. *Empire and Liberty: The Civil War and the West*. Oakland: University of California Press, 2015.

Sefton, James E. *Andrew Johnson and the Uses of Constitutional Power*. Boston: Little, Brown, 1980.

Shea, William L. *War in the West: Pea Ridge and Prairie Grove*. Abilene, TX: McWhiney Foundation Press, 1998.

Shea, William L., and Earl J. Hess. *Pea Ridge: Civil War Campaign in the West*. Chapel Hill: University of North Carolina Press, 1992.

Slover, James Anderson. *Minister to the Cherokees: A Civil War Autobiography*. Edited by Barbara Cloud. Lincoln: University of Nebraska Press, 2001.

Smith, Arthur D. Howden. *Old Fuss and Feathers: The Life and Exploits of Lt. General Winfield Scott*. New York: Greystone Press, 1937.

Spencer, John D. *The American Civil War in the Indian Territory*. New York: Osprey, 2006.

St. Germain, Jill. *Indian Treaty-Making Policy in the United States and Canada, 1867–1877*. Lincoln: University of Nebraska Press, 2001.

Steele, Phillip W., and Steve Cottrell. *Civil War in the Ozarks*. Gretna, LA: Pelican, 2003.

Stevenson, Joan Nabseth. *Deliverance from the Little Bighorn: Doctor Henry Porter and Custer's Seventh Cavalry*. Norman: University of Oklahoma Press, 2012.

Stith, Matthew M. *Extreme Civil War: Guerilla Warfare, Environment, and Race on the Trans-Mississippi Frontier*. Baton Rouge: Louisiana State University Press, 2016.

Sturm, Circe. *Becoming Indian: The Struggle over Cherokee Identity in the Twenty-First Century*. Santa Fe: School of Advanced Research Press, 2010.

Sullivan, Roy. *Scattered Graves: The Civil War Campaigns of Confederate Brigadier General and Cherokee Chief Stand Watie*. Bloomington, IN: AuthorHouse, 2006.

Taylor, Ethel Crisp. *Indian Territory, 1861–1865: The Forts, the Battles, the Soldiers*. Westminster, MD: Heritage, 2010.

Trefousse, Hans. *Andrew Johnson: A Biography*. New York: W. W. Norton, 1989.

Utley, Robert M. *The Indian Frontier 1846–1890*. Albuquerque: University of New Mexico Press, 1984.

Van de Logt, Mark. *War Party in Blue: Pawnee Scouts in the U.S. Army*. Norman: University of Oklahoma Press. 2010.

Warde, Mary Jane. *When the Wolf Came: The Civil War and the Indian Territory*. Fayetteville: University of Arkansas Press, 2013.

Wardell, Morris. *A Political History of the Cherokee Nation*. Norman: University of Oklahoma Press, 1938.

Warner, Ezra J. *Generals in Gray: Lives of the Confederate Commanders*. Baton Rouge: Louisiana State University Press, 1959.

———. *Generals in Blue: Lives of the Union Commanders*. Baton Rouge: Louisiana State University Press, 1964.

Weitz, Mark A. *More Damning than Slaughter: Desertion in the Confederate Army*. Lincoln: University of Nebraska Press, 2005.

Whipple, Henry Benjamin. *Lights and Shadows of a Long Episcopate*. New York: Macmillan, 1900.

White, Christine Schultz, and Benton R. White. *Now the Wolf Has Come: The Creek Nation in the Civil War*. College Station: Texas A&M University Press, 1996.

Wiley, Bell Irvin. *The Life of Billy Yank: The Common Soldier of the Union*. Baton Rouge: Louisiana State University Press, 1952.

———. *The Life of Johnny Reb: The Common Soldier of the Confederacy*. Baton Rouge: Louisiana State University Press, 1943.

Wilkins, David E., and Heidi Kiiwetinepinesiik Stark. *American Indian Politics and the American Political System*, 3rd edition. Lanham, MD: Rowman and Littlefield, 2011.

Wilkinson, Charles F. *American Indians, Time, and the Law: Native Societies in a Modern Constitutional Democracy*. New Haven, CT: Yale University Press. 1987.

Wimberly, Dan B. *Cherokees in Controversy: The Life of Jesse Bushyhead*. Macon, GA: Merce University Press, 2017.

Winston, Robert W. *Andrew Johnson: Plebian and Patriot*. New York: Henry Holton, 1928.

Woodward, Grace Steele. *The Cherokees*. Norman: University of Oklahoma Press, 1963.

Wooster, Robert. *The Military and United States Indian Policy, 1865–1903*. New Haven, CT: Yale University Press, 1988. Reprinted, Lincoln: University of Nebraska Press, 1995.

Articles

Ashcraft, Allan C., and William Steele. "A Civil War Letter of General William Steele, CSA." *Arkansas Historical Quarterly* 22, no. 3 (Autumn 1963): 278–81.

Baird, W. David. "Fort Smith and the Red Man." *Arkansas Historical Quarterly* 30, no. 4 (Winter 1971): 337–48.

Bearss, Edwin. "The Battle of Pea Ridge." *Arkansas Historical Quarterly* 20, no. 1 (Spring 1961): 74–94.

———. "The Civil War Comes to Indian Territory, 1861: The Flight of Opothleyoholo." *Journal of the West* 11, no. 1 (January 1972): 9–42.

Blunt, James G. "General Blunt's Account of His Civil War Experiences." *Kansas Historical Quarterly* 1, no. 3 (May 1932): 211–65.

Britton, Wiley. "Some Reminiscences of the Cherokee People: Returning to Their Homes the Exiles of a Nation." *Chronicles of Oklahoma* 6, no. 2 (June 1928): 163–77.

Brown, Walter L. "Albert Pike and the Pea Ridge Atrocities." *Arkansas Historical Quarterly* 38, no. 4 (Winter 1979): 345–59.

Carter, Jent. "Deciding Who Can Be Cherokee: Enrollment Records of the Dawes Commission." *Chronicles of Oklahoma*. 69, no. 2 (Summer 1991). 174–205.

Coffman, Edward M., ed. "Ben McCulloch Letters." *Southwestern Historical Quarterly* 60, no. 1 (July 1956): 118–22.

Collins, Richard B. "A Brief History of the U.S.-American Indian Nations Relationship." *Human Rights* 33, no. 2 (Spring 2006): 3–4, 24.

Dale, Edward Everett. "Some Letters of General Stand Watie." *Chronicles of Oklahoma* 1, no. 1 (January 1921): 30–59.

Daniel, Michelle. "From Blood Feud to Jury System: The Metamorphosis of Cherokee Law from 1750 to 1840." *American Indian Quarterly* 11, no. 2 (Spring 1987): 97–125.

DeLay, Brian. "Indian Polities, Empire, and the History of American Foreign Relations." *Diplomatic History* 39, no. 5 (2015), 927–42.

DeMotte, William H., "The Assassination of Abraham Lincoln." *Journal of the Illinois State Historical Society (1908–1984)* 20, no. 3 (October 1927): 422–28.

Edwards, John. "My Escape from the South in 1861." *Chronicles of Oklahoma* 53, no. 1 (Spring 1965): 58–89.

Fischer, LeRoy H., and Kenny A. Franks. "Victory at Chusto-Talasah." *Chronicles of Oklahoma* 49, no. 4 (Winter 1971–72): 452–76.

Fischer, LeRoy H., and William L. McMurry. "Confederate Refugees from Indian Territory." *Chronicles of Oklahoma* 57, no. 4 (Winter 1979–80): 451–62.

Fischer, LeRoy H., and Lary C. Rampp. "Quantrill's Civil War Operations." *Chronicles of Oklahoma* 46, no. 2 (Summer 1968): 155–82.

Ford, Harvey S. "Van Dorn and the Pea Ridge Campaign." *Journal of the American Military Institute* 3, no. 4 (Winter 1939): 222–36.

Foreman, Grant, ed. "The Murder of Elias Boudinot." *Chronicles of Oklahoma* 12, no. 1 (March 1934): 19–24.

Franks, Kenny A. "Operations Against Opothleyahola, 1861." *Military History of Texas and the Southwest* 10, no. 3 (1972): 187–96.

Genetin-Pilawa, C. Joseph. "Ely Parker and the Contentious Peace Policy." *Western Historical Quarterly* 41, no. 2 (Summer 2010): 196–217.

Green, Fletcher M. "Georgia's Forgotten Industry: Gold Mining. Part I." *The Georgia Historical Quarterly* 19, no. 2 (June 1935): 93–111.

Hale, Douglas. "Texas Units in the Civil War." *Chronicles of Oklahoma* 68, no. 3 (Fall 1990): 228–65.

Heath, Gary N. "The First Federal Invasion of the Indian Territory." *The Chronicles of Oklahoma* 46, no. 4 (Winter 1966–67): 409–19.

Hoffman, William S. "Andrew Jackson, State Rightist: The Case of the Georgia Indians." *Tennessee Historical Quarterly* 11, no. 4 (December 1952): 329–45.

Johnston, James J. "Reminiscence of James H. Campbell's Experiences during the Civil War." *Arkansas Historical Quarterly* 74, no. 2 (Summer 2015): 147–77.

Jones, Trevor. "In Defense of Sovereignty: Cherokee Soldiers, White Officers, and Discipline in the Third Indian Home Guard." *Chronicles of Oklahoma* 82, no. 4 (Winter 2004–2005): 412–27.

Kelman, Ari. "John Ross's Decision in 1861." *Chronicles of Oklahoma* 83, no. 1 (Spring 1995): 80–103.

Lale, Max. "The Boy-Bugler of the Third Texas Cavalry: The A. B. Blocker Narrative, Part I." *Military History of Texas and the Southwest* 14, no. 2 (1978): 71–92.

Lindberg, Kip, Matt Matthews, and Thomas Moonlight. "'The Eagle of the 11th Kansas': Wartime Reminiscences of Colonel Thomas Moonlight." *Arkansas Historical Quarterly* 62, no. 1 (Spring 2003): 1–41.

Littlefield, Daniel F. Jr., and Lonnie E. Underhill. "The Cherokee Agency Reserve, 1828–1886." *Arkansas Historical Quarterly* 31. no. 2 (Summer 1972): 166–80.

———. "Fort Wayne and Border Violence, 1840–1847." *Arkansas Historical Quarterly* 36, no. 1 (Spring 1977): 3–30.

McCluggage, Robert W. "The Senate and Indian Land Titles, 1800–1825." *Western Historical Quarterly* 1, no. 4 (October 1970): 415–25.

McLoughlin, William G. "Cherokee Slaveholders and Baptist Missionaries, 1845–1860." *The Historian* 45, no. 2 (February 1983): 147–66.

———. "Georgia's Role in Instigating Compulsory Indian Removal." *Georgia Historical Quarterly* 70, no. 4 (Winter 1986): 605–32.

McFadden, Marguerite. "Colonel John Thompson Drew: Cherokee Cavalier." *Chronicles of Oklahoma* 59, no. 1 (Spring 1981): 31–53.

McMurtrie, Douglas C. "Pioneer Printing in Georgia." *Georgia Historical Quarterly* 16, no. 2 (June 1932): 77–113.

Meserve, John Bartlett. "Chief John Ross." *Chronicles of Oklahoma* 13, no. 4 (December 1935): 421–37.

Michaelis, Patricia. "Quantrill's Raid in Kansas Memory." *Kansas History: A Journal of the Central Plains* 36, no. 3 (Autumn 2013): 198–209.

Miles, Edwin A. "After John Marshall's Decision: Georgia and the Nullification Crisis." *Journal of Southern History* 39, no. 4 (November 1973): 519–44.

Nelson, Megan Kate. "The Civil War from Apache Pass." *Journal of the Civil War Era* 6, no. 4 (December 2016): 510–35.

Oats, Stephen B. "Supply for Confederate Cavalry in the Trans-Mississippi." *Military Affairs* 25, no. 2, Civil War issue (Summer 1961): 94–99.

Oman, Kerry R. "The Beginning of the End: The Indian Peace Commission of 1867–1868." *Great Plains Quarterly* 22, no. 1 (Winter 2002): 35–51.

Perdue, Theda. "Traditionalism in the Cherokee Nation: Resistance to the Constitution of 1827." *Georgia Historical Quarterly* 66, no. 2 (Summer 1982): 159–70.

———. "The Conflict Within: The Cherokee Power Structure and Removal." *Georgia Historical Quarterly* 73, no. 3 (Fall 1989): 467–91.

———. "The Legacy of Indian Removal." *Journal of Southern History* 78, no. 1 (February 2012): 3–36.

Prucha, Francis Paul. "Distribution of Regular Army Troops Before the Civil War." *Military Affairs* 16, no. 4 (Winter 1952): 169–73.

———. "Protest by Petition: Jeremiah Evarts and the Cherokee Indians." *Proceedings of the Massachusetts Historical Society*, Third Series 97 (1985): 42–58.

Ramage, B. J. "Georgia and the Cherokees." *American Historical Magazine and Tennessee Historical Society Quarterly* 7, no. 3 (July 1902): 199–208.

Rampp, Lary C., and Arnold L. Rampp. "The Civil War in Indian Territory: The Union Counter, 1862–1863." *Military History of Texas and the Southwest* 10, no. 2 (1972): 93–114.

Rampp, Lary C., and Donald L. Rampp. "The Civil War in Indian Territory: Blunt's Pursuit." *Military History of Texas and the Southwest* 10, no. 4 (1972): 249–72.

———. "The Civil War in the Indian Territory: The Confederate Advantage, 1861–1862. *Military History of Texas and the Southwest* 10, no. 1 (1972): 29–42.

Rein, Chris. "The U.S. Army, Indian Agency, and the Path to Assimilation: The First Indian Home Guards in the American Civil War." *Kansas History: A Journal of the Central Plains* 36, no. 1 (Spring 2013): 2–21.

Schreier, Jesse T. "Indian or Freedman?: Enrollment, Race, and Identity in the Choctaw Nation, 1896–1907." *Western Historical Quarterly*. 42, no. 4 (Winter 2011): 458–79.

Strum, Circe. "Blood Politics, Racial Classification, and Cherokee National Identity: The Trials and Tribulations of the Cherokee Freedmen." *American Indian Quarterly*. 22, nos. 1–2 (Winter–Spring, 1998). 230–58.

Sundquist, Matthew L. "*Worcester v Georgia*: A Breakdown in the Separation of Powers." *American Indian Law Review* 35, no. 1 (2010–11): 239–55.

Trickett, Dean. "The Civil War in the Indian Territory, 1861." *Chronicles of Oklahoma* 17, no. 3 (September 1939): 315–27.

———. "The Civil War in the Indian Territory, 1861 (continued)." *Chronicles of Oklahoma* 17, no. 4 (December 1939): 401–12.

———. "The Civil War in the Indian Territory, 1861 (continued)." *Chronicles of Oklahoma* 18, no. 2 (June 1940): 142–53.

———. "The Civil War in the Indian Territory, 1861 (continued)." *Chronicles of Oklahoma* 18, no. 3 (September 1940): 266–80.

Vaught, Elsa. "Captain John Rogers: Founder of Fort Smith." *Arkansas Historical Quarterly* 17, no. 3 (Autumn 1958): 239–64.

Vipperman, Carl J. "The 'Particular Mission' of Wilson Lumpkin." *Georgia Historical Quarterly* 66, no. 3 (Fall 1982): 295–316.

———. "The Bungled Treaty of New Echota: The Failure of Cherokee Removal, 1836–1838." *Georgia Historical Quarterly* 73, no. 3 (Fall 1989): 540–58.

Warde, May Jane. "Civilian Civil War." *Chronicles of Oklahoma* 71, no. 1 (Spring 1993): 64–87.

Willey, William A. "The Second Federal Invasion of Indian Territory." *Chronicles of Oklahoma* 46, no. 4 (Winter 1966–67): 420–30.

Williams, H. David. "Gambling Away the Inheritance: The Cherokee Nation and Georgia's Gold and Land Lotteries of 1832–33." *Georgia Historical Quarterly* 73, no. 3 (Fall 1989): 519–39.

Young, Mary. "The Exercise of Sovereignty in Cherokee Georgia." *Journal of the Early Republic* 10, no. 1 (Spring 1990): 43–63.

Zellar, Gary. "First Indian Home Guard." *Chronicles of Oklahoma* 76, no. 1 (Spring 1998): 48–71.

INDEX

abandonment of Indian Territory, 18, 21, 27, 62–63, 71–73, 77–78, 100, 112, 142, 147, 175, 177, 189n12
abolition (abolitionist), 12, 57–59, 61, 64, 80–81, 106, 124
acculturation, 8–9, 18–20, 135–36, 155–57, 160–62, 164, 166
Adair, William P., 81–83, 85
Adair-Bell letter, 81–85
African Americans, 11–12, 85, 88, 108, 124, 126, 166, 168, 171–73, 175, 177, 203n35
African slave trade, 181n42
Alabama, 32, 34, 135
Allen, Lucy, 174
Allen v. The Cherokee Nation Tribal Council (2006), 174
allotment, 158, 165, 168, 172
American Revolution, 7
annuities, 41–42, 56, 70, 75, 133, 135, 140–41, 145–46, 152
Apache Pass, Ariz., 180n13
Apaches, 19, 54, 136, 155
Appomattox, Va., 129, 164
Arapahos, 18–20, 136, 153, 155
Arbuckle, Matthew, 15–16, 54–55
Arizona, 180n13
Arkansas, 13, 17, 21, 32, 46, 54, 58, 61, 64, 66–68, 88–89, 92, 97–98, 100, 107, 109, 125, 139, 153, 188n79, 198n9; population of, 16; secession, 13, 60–61, 64, 66, 187n43; statehood, 54
Arkansas River, 32, 61, 74, 87, 92, 95, 110, 115, 120, 124–27, 144, 155
Arkansas Territory, 32, 34
Arkansas troops, 27, 95, 110

Armstrong Academy, 140
Army of Northern Virginia, 119
Army of the Frontier, 120–21
Articles of Confederation, 7–8
assimilation, 21, 26–27, 80, 150, 155–56, 160, 164, 166, 169
Averell, William W., 63–64

Banner, Stuart, 25
Bateman, M. W., 45
Battle of Antietam, 20, 119
Battle of Bull Run, First, 74–75
Battle of Cabin Creek: First, 2, 114, 126; Second, 127
Battle of Gettysburg, 20
Battle of Greenleaf Prairie, 126
Battle of Honey Springs, 83, 127, 188n74
Battle of Pea Ridge, 101–6, 144, 147, 188n74, 194n31
Battle of Wilson's Creek, 66, 76, 78, 83, 105
Baxter Springs, Kans., 108–10, 114, 126
Bayou Maynard, Indian Territory, 116
Beauregard, Pierre G. T., 74–75
Beeson, John, 131
Bell, James M., 81–85
Benge, Pickens M., 94
Benton County, Ark., 100
Bentonville, Ark., 100
Bentonville Detour, 100, 102
Berrian, J. M., 35
Bird Creek, Indian Territory, 91–94, 99, 103, 144, 147
Bixby, Okla., 92
Black troops, 108, 124, 126

Bleeding Kansas, 57
Blunt, James G., 106–8, 110–18, 120, 124–27, 188n74; letter to Lincoln, 117
Board of Indian Commissioners, 20
Boudinot, Elias, 36, 38–39, 43, 47; execution of, 10, 46, 55, 65; support for Ross, 37
Bozeman Trail, 153, 155, 161
Brown, James, 74
Brown, John, 57
Buchanan, James, 63, 134; administration of, 58, 137
Bureau of Indian Affairs, 5–6, 14–16, 55–56, 58, 67, 110, 113, 122, 125, 127, 133–34, 136, 138, 151, 173, 181n44; incapacitated by secession, 17, 58
Butler Creek, Creek Nation, 125–26

Caddo-Confederate alliance, 74
Calhoun, John C., 5, 14
California, 16, 54, 153, 174
Canadian River, 89
Cane Hill, Ark., 67
capitalism, 9, 135, 161
Carruth, Edwin H., 115–16
Cary, Matthew, 36
Cass, Lewis, 15, 41, 45
Charleston, S.C., 63
Chatterton, Charles W., 17
Cherokee Citizenship Law of 1983, 171, 173–74
Cherokee-Confederate alliance, 13–14, 17–18, 21, 24, 47, 49, 77–79, 81, 86–87, 95, 98–99, 103–4, 108–9, 112, 117–18, 122, 129–30, 141–49, 152, 157, 175, 177; abrogated, 123
Cherokee constitution, 5, 9–10, 23, 33, 37, 39, 41, 43, 59, 136, 141, 172–74, 176; of 1975, 170, 173–74; of 2003, 173
Cherokee Council House, 127
Cherokee delegations to Washington, 7, 14–15, 18, 33, 37, 40, 43, 45–47, 57–59, 123, 131, 180n20
Cherokee Executive Council, 33–34, 64–65, 73–74, 84, 130, 139, 189n11, 192n92

Cherokee freedmen, 12, 148–49, 165, 168, 170–76; descendants of, 12, 165, 168, 170, 172, 175–76
Cherokee government, 10, 115, 150, 165; restoration of, 170; governmental model, 33
Cherokee landholdings, 7, 9, 14, 19, 28–37, 40, 43, 50, 53, 57–58, 68–70, 133, 135, 139–41, 143, 146, 148, 152, 159–60, 165, 171, 178
Cherokee Mounted Volunteers. *See* Watie's troops (Cherokee Mounted Volunteers)
Cherokee Nation: becomes centrally organized, 33; devastation of, 128; gold discovered, 35; mass meeting, 42, 75–76, 78–79, 81; population of, 9, 11–13, 168–69; restoration of, 21, 107, 121, 128–30, 139, 141–42, 163, 165
Cherokee National Committee, 12, 33, 123
Cherokee National Council, 5, 10–12, 29, 33, 36–42, 45–46, 50–51, 53, 56, 58, 60, 69–70, 73, 81, 84, 86, 122–23, 128–29, 131–32, 141, 144, 165; established, 33
Cherokee Neutral Lands, 133
Cherokee Phoenix, 39
Cherokee Question, The, 147
Cherokee regiment. *See* Drew's regiment (1st Cherokee Mounted Rifles)
Cherokees, factionalism within, 22, 37; voluntary emigration of, 15, 32, 36, 40, 43, 46
Cherokee Supreme Court, 12, 176; established in 1822, 33
Cherokee troops, 88, 90, 119–20, 132, 188n79; at Wilson's Creek, 76
Cheyennes, 18–20, 136, 153, 155
Chickasaw-Confederate alliance, 70, 74, 149, 175
Chickasaw Nation, 60, 63,189n12
Chickasaws, 60–61, 69, 127, 136, 148, 168, 175
Chickasaw troops, 100
Chippewas, 56
Chiricahuas (Apache), 180n13

Chivington, Colonel John, 18, 153
Choctaw and Chickasaw regiment, 64
Choctaw-Confederate alliance, 70, 74, 149, 175, 177
Choctaw freedmen, 148
Choctaw Nation, 115, 127–28, 140, 177, 204n53
Choctaws, 60–61, 69, 136, 148, 161, 168, 175
Choctaw troops, 64, 100
Christie, Smith, 132, 141
Cincinnati, Ohio, 81
citizenship: Cherokee, 165, 168, 170–75; Cherokee freedmen, 112, 148, 170–72, 174–76; Cherokee freedmen descendants, 12, 170; Chickasaw freedmen, 148; Choctaw freedmen, 148; Creek, 172; Creek freedmen, 148; Seminole freedmen, 148; U.S., 168
Civil Rights Movement, 169
Clark, George W., 81
Clarkson, James L., 111
Cloud, William, F., 117
Cochise, 180n13
Coffin, William G., 17, 64, 106, 113, 121, 124, 126, 128, 133
Colorado troops, 18
Colston, Daniel, 74
Comanche-Confederate alliance, 74
Comanches, 19, 54, 136, 155
commissioner of Indian affairs, 6–7, 14–15, 17, 26, 50, 56, 58, 105, 107, 122, 134–36, 138, 146, 155, 160, 163; Confederate, 59, 68–69
Committee on Indian Affairs, 152; House, 34; Senate, 41
Committee on Military Affairs (House, Senate), 152
Concharta, Indian Territory, 92
Confederate Army, 63, 66, 71, 76, 110, 124, 189n12; in Arkansas, 64; occupation of Indian Territory, 24, 47–48, 63–64, 71, 73; support of Watie, 49
Confederate Department of War, 64
Confederate government, 68, 70–71, 74, 95

Confer, Clarissa W., 2, 4
Congressional Black Caucus, 175
Conscription Act of April 1862, 68
Constitution of the United States, 3, 8, 22–23, 30–31, 33, 37, 44, 50, 52, 158–59, 170, 182n8
Coodey's Bluff, Indian Territory, 89–91, 93
Cook, H. Dale, 171
Cooley, Dennis N., 138–47, 149, 160–61
Cooper, Douglas H., 64, 88–89, 91–95, 99, 103, 115, 125, 127, 192n92; troops, 89–90
Council of the Cherokee Nation, 170–71, 174. *See also* Cherokee National Council
Cowart, Robert J., 17, 58
Cowskin Prairie, 110–11, 122–23, 129, 133, 145, 165
Crawford, John, 17
Crawford, Thomas Hartley, 50–51
Creek Agency, 61
Creek and Seminole Battalion, 90
Creek-Confederate alliance, 3, 70, 74, 76, 87, 89, 133, 141
Creek freedmen, 148
Creek General Council, 88
Creek landholdings, 133, 166
Creek Nation, 11–12, 27, 60, 81, 85–88, 90, 115, 141, 145
Creek Reservation, 158–59
Creeks, 1, 3, 30, 60–61, 64, 136–37, 148, 168, 182n8–9
Creek troops, 86, 90, 100
Cripps, John, 174, 176
Crows, 155
Currey, Benjamin F., 40
Curtis, Samuel R., 100–102, 120, 122, 125
Custer, George Armstrong, 164

Dallas County, Tex., 57
Davis, Jefferson, 100, 104
Davis, Porum, 91
Davis, William M., 43–45
Dawes Act of 1887. *See* Indian Allotment Act of 1887

Dawes Commission, 168, 170, 172
Dawes Rolls, 168, 170–72; and freedmen, 168, 171–73
Debo, Angie, 4
Delaware-Confederate alliance, 13
Delaware Indians, 56; as Cherokee citizens, 170
Deloria, Vine, Jr., 26
DeMallie, Raymond J., 26
Denton County, Tex., 57
Denver, James W., 134–35
Department of Kansas, 106
Department of the Interior, 6, 14, 20, 122, 127, 131, 133, 139–40, 146, 151, 170–71, 173, 176
Department of the Mississippi, 105
Department of War, 5–6, 14, 20, 35, 62–63, 71, 104, 106, 110–11, 113, 151; Confederate, 64
discovery doctrine, 51–52
District of Western Arkansas and Indian Territory, 122
Dole, William Palmer, 17–18, 63–64, 104–5, 109, 117–18, 120, 130–33, 136–40
Doublehead, 29, 32
Downing, Lewis, 123, 131–32, 139
Drew, John, 12, 64, 74, 80, 88, 90, 93, 95
Drew's regiment (1st Cherokee Mounted Rifles), 80, 90–91, 94–96, 99–103, 111, 122, 124, 131
Dunn, J. W., 146

Eaton, John, 14
11th Texas Cavalry, 96
Elk Creek, Indian Territory, 127
Elkhorn Tavern, Ark., 101
Ellithorpe, Albert C., 116
Elm Springs, Ark., 100–102
Emancipation Proclamation, 18, 119, 123, 165
Emory, William H., 62–64
Ewing, Thomas, 165

Fayetteville, Ark., 99–100
Federal Indian Brigade, 68, 98, 116, 120–22, 124–27, 129–30, 132, 188n79

Fetterman, William J., 153, 161
Fetterman Commission, 162
Fillmore, Millard, 136; administration of, 56
1st Arkansas Cavalry, 125
1st Choctaw and Chickasaw Mounted Rifles, 90. *See also* Pike's brigade (1st Choctaw and Chickasaw Mounted Rifles)
1st Division, Army of the Frontier, 121
1st Indian Home Guard, 106, 116, 125
1st Kansas Colored Infantry, 126
Fischer, LeRoy H., 2
Five Tribes, 64, 71, 138–39, 148–49, 159–60, 166, 168
Flandrau, Charles E., 118
Florida, 30, 90
Ford's Theater, 27, 157
Foreman, Grant, 39
Fort Arbuckle, Indian Territory, 54, 63–64, 100
Fort C. F. Smith, Mont., 153
Fort Cobb, Indian Territory, 74–75
Fort Davis, Indian Territory, 115–16
Fort Gibson, Indian Territory, 1–2, 12, 15, 54, 61, 67, 87–91, 93–95, 106–7, 114–16, 120, 122, 125–27, 132
Fort Laramie, Wyo., 153, 155
Fort Leavenworth, Kans., 62–64, 112, 120
Fort Moultrie, S.C., 63
Fort Phil Kearney, Wyo., 153
Fort Reno, Wyo., 153
Fort Scott, Kans., 54, 108, 111, 114, 116–17, 120, 122, 124
Fort Smith, Ark., 1, 15, 54, 64, 95, 100, 103, 120, 127, 139–40
Fort Smith Council, 19–21, 25, 139–52, 156–57, 159–60, 162–63, 175, 177–78, 201n90
Fort Sumter, S.C., 13, 59, 62–63
Fort Washita, Indian Territory, 54
4th Texas Cavalry, 89, 93, 191n66, 191n71
Frémont, John C., 92

full-blood Indians, 9, 80–81, 163, 169, 172; support for Ross, 33
Furnas, Robert W., 106, 116

Gaines, J. J., 187n45
Georgia, 9, 13, 17, 31–32, 34–38, 42–43, 47–48, 50, 52–56, 58, 135, 178; attack on Cherokee sovereignty, 14; gold discovered on Cherokee land, 35; government of, 10; role in removal, 16; sovereignty of, 9; starting point for Trail of Tears, 10
Georgia Compact of 1802, 31, 34–35
Georgia Guard, 36, 43
Ghost Dance, 164
Gilmer, George R., 35–36
gold: in Georgia, 35–36; in California, 16, 54, 153
Gorsuch, Neil, 158
Graham, George, 32
Grand River, 95, 109, 111, 116, 126
Grand Saline, Indian Territory, 114
Grant, Ulysses S., 19–20, 129, 136, 140, 149, 151–53, 155, 163–64; administration of, 21
Grayson, George Washington, 1–2
Great Britain, 182n9
Great Depression, 169
Great Plains, 20, 133, 136, 164, 166
Great Plains tribes. *See* Plains Indians
Greeno, Harris S., 115
Greenwood, Alfred B., 58, 104, 134–35
Greusel, Nicholas, 102
Gross, Ariela, 172

Hagan, Thomas F., 176
Halleck, Henry W., 105, 107–8
Harlan, James, 17, 139–40, 142, 146–47
Harlan, Justin, 17, 120, 145–46
Harlan, Mary, 139
Harney, William S., 140
Harper's Ferry, Va., 57
Harris, Cyrus, 60–61
Harrison, M. LaRue, 67
Harrison, William Henry, 50

Hebert, Louis, 100, 102, 193n15
Henbree, Todd, 176
Henderson, John B., 152–53
Hicks, C. R., 81
Hitchcock, C. M., 45
Honey Creek, 110
Honey Springs Depot, Indian Territory, 83, 127. *See also* Battle of Honey Springs
Hooper, Jonathan L., 45
Houston, Sam, 181n42
Hubbard, David, 59, 68–69
Humboldt, Kans., 114

Illinois, 120, 157
Illinois River, 126
Indian Allotment Act of 1887, 165, 175–76
Indian Appropriations Act of 1871, 26, 156
Indiana troops, 102
Indian Citizenship Act of 1924, 169
Indian Civil Rights Act of 1968, 170
Indian Expedition, 17–18, 24–25, 107–16, 120–22, 144, 147–48, 194n31, 195n68
Indian Removal Act of 1830, 5, 184n74
Indian Reorganization Act of 1934, 169
Indian Territory: devastation of, 127–28; establishment of, 34; population of, 166
Indian Wars, 27, 150, 152
intermarriage, 9, 11, 80, 135
Iowa, 17
Iowa troops, 101, 139
Iroquois Confederacy, 149

J. R. Williams (Federal steamboat), 1–3, 127
Jackson, Andrew, 5–7, 10, 15, 23, 31, 35–44, 48–49, 52, 54–55, 128, 143, 178, 184n74; administration of, 45; commander of Tennessee militia, 32, 36; election of, 37, 40
Jacksonian Democrats, 14, 55, 184n74
Jayhawkers, 57, 126
Johnson, Andrew, 19, 25, 130, 133, 139–40, 142–43, 146, 149, 151–53, 159, 163–64, 178; administration of, 21, 25, 133–34, 138–40, 142–43, 149, 152, 177

Johnson v. McIntosh (1823), 51
Jones, Evan, 80, 105, 108, 118, 131
Judicial Appeals Tribunal, 170, 173–74, 176
Judson, William R., 109
Jumper, John, 90
Jumper's troops, 90

Kannady, J. R. 64–66, 69
Kansas, 17, 27, 54, 57–59, 61, 64, 76, 81, 89–91, 96, 106, 111, 113–15, 117, 122, 124–27, 133, 141, 153; population of, 16, 181n51; refugee camps in, 4, 99; refugees, 105–6, 110, 121, 124
Kansas-Nebraska Act of 1854, 16, 56–58
Kansas Territory, 56–57
Keetoowah Society, 80–81, 94, 108
Kempthorne, Dirk, 173
Kennard, Motey, 85–89
Kennedy, Henry H., Jr., 173
Kentucky, 29
Kiowas, 19, 54, 136, 155
Knight, Wilfred, 2
Knights of the Golden Circle, 81–83, 85
Knox, Henry, 29

Lakotas (Sioux), 164
Lane, James, 64, 66
Lasley, Hanna, 171
Law of Blood Revenge, 29, 32, 39, 46
Law of July 5, 1862, 131, 142, 144, 159, 162–63
Lawrence, Kans., 57
Lea, Luke, 56, 136–38
Lee, Robert E., 119, 129, 149
Leeds, Stacy L., 174
Leetown, Ark., 101–2
Lincoln, Abraham, 3, 7, 16–19, 21–22, 24–25, 28, 48, 63, 87, 104–7, 109, 117–20, 124, 128–31, 138–39, 142–43, 145–46, 152, 157, 159–60, 163; administration of, 7, 12, 99, 107, 109, 120, 122–23, 129–33, 136, 138–40, 142–43, 147–48, 157; assassination of, 7, 19, 21, 25, 48, 128, 130, 133, 139–40, 148–49, 152, 157, 160, 164; call for volunteers, 13, 62; election of, 7, 12, 16, 59, 63; meeting with Ross, 18, 48, 118–19, 130; restoration of Cherokees, 21, 107, 121, 129–30, 139, 141–42, 163, 165; return of troops to Indian Territory, 17, 24–25, 105, 107, 109, 117, 130
Lincoln, Robert Todd, 139
Little Bighorn, 20, 27, 164
Little Crow, 118
Little Sugar Creek, 101
Lone Wolf v. Hitchcock (1903), 52–53, 158
Louisiana, 22, 129
Louisiana Purchase, 27
Lumpkin, Wilson, 43
Lyon, Nathaniel, 105

Maine, 106
Manassas, Va., 74. *See also* Battle of Bull Run, First
Mangas Coloradas, 180n13
Manifest Destiny, 162, 166. *See also* westward expansion
Manypenny, George W., 134–35
Marshall, John, 51–52
Maryland, secession of, 13
Massachusetts, 152
Matlock, Darell R., Jr., 170, 173
Mayes County, Okla., 2
Maysville, Ark., 92
McCluggage, Robert W., 35
McCulloch, Benjamin, 64, 66, 68–69, 71, 81, 85, 92, 95, 100–103, 113; killed, 102
McDaniel, James, 90
McDowell, Irvin, 74
McGirt, Jimcy, 158
McGirt v. Oklahoma (2020), 159
McIntosh, Chilly, 90
McIntosh, D. N., 90
McIntosh, James, 95, 99–101; killed, 102
McIntosh's troops, 90
McLean, John, 39
McMinn, Joseph, 32
Medicine Lodge Creek, 155
Meeker County, Minn., 118
Meiggs, Return Jonathan, Sr., 8

Meriwether, David, 32
Mexico, 40, 54; destination for escaped slaves, 11; war with United States, 16, 105
Michigan Territory, 34
Minnesota, 21, 118119, 131; Sioux uprising, 18
missionaries: among Cherokees, 36; among Creeks, 79; imprisoned by Georgia, 38
Mississippi, 58
Mississippi River, 5, 10, 32, 34, 40, 44, 52, 54, 91, 100, 122, 136, 138, 159, 161
Mississippi Territory, 9, 31
Missouri, 21, 34, 87, 93, 97–101, 105, 107, 111, 114, 120, 125, 152; Confederate troops from, 27; refugee camps, 99; secession of, considered, 13
Missouri troops, 101–2
Mix, Charles E., 134, 162
mixed-blood Indians, 5, 9–11, 33, 66, 70, 81, 99, 150, 163, 168, 172; support for Ross, 34
Monroe, James, 34
Montana, 161
Montgomery, Hugh Lawson, 14

Nash, Raymond, 174–75
Navajo Indians, 169
Nebraska, 153
Nebraska Territory, 56
Nero, Abe L., 172
Nero, Jesse, 171
Nero, Roger Henry, 171–72
Nero, Sarah, 171–72
Nero v. Cherokee Nation of Oklahoma (1989), 171, 173
neutral Indians, 89–91, 93–95, 113, 118, 147, 149
neutrality, 24, 59, 61, 65–66, 68, 70–71, 73–79, 82, 84–86, 89
New Echota, Ga., 42, 55. *See also* Treaty of New Echota (1835)
New Mexico, 180n13
Newtonia, Mo., 119–20

New Ulm, Minn., 118, 139
New York City, 30, 109
9th Texas Cavalry, 191n66, 191n71
non-Confederate Cherokees, 97, 99, 127, 147
non-Confederate Creeks, 133
non-Confederate Indians, 140
North Carolina, 45, 55, 59, 182n8; and secession, 13
North Platte River, 153

Obama, Barak, 175
Ohio, 8
Oklahoma, 91, 158–59, 203n34; population of, 168–69, 203n35; statehood, 165–66, 168
Oklahoma land run, 166
Oklahoma Territory, 166, 203n34; population of, 166
Old Settlers, 15
Old Tassel, 29
Opothle Yahola, 3–4, 24, 76, 81, 84–96, 106, 133, 144, 147–48, 191n78, 192n92
Osage-Confederate alliance, 86
Osages, 56, 83–84, 144, 147

Pacific Ocean, 16, 153
Parker, Ely Samuel, 19–20, 26, 140, 143, 149–53, 155–56, 159–60, 162, 164, 178, 201n90
Park Hill, 64, 66, 73, 83, 98, 108, 112, 115, 117, 125, 127
Pea Ridge, Ark,, 100, 102–3, 105. *See also* Battle of Pea Ridge
Peace Commission of 1867, 20, 153, 155, 162
Pegg, Thomas, 93, 122, 132, 192n92
Perdue, Theda, 135
Perryville, Indian Territory, 127
Philadelphia, Pa., 18, 36
Phillips, James A., 108–9
Phillips, William A., 98, 114, 116–17, 119, 121–22, 124–27
Pierce, Franklin, 57; administration of, 134

Pike, Albert, 17, 67–71, 74–76, 81–83, 85, 87, 99–100, 103, 109, 113, 117, 147; letter of August 1, 70–71, 73–74, 76–78, 83, 86, 145
Pike's brigade (1st Choctaw and Chickasaw Mounted Rifles), 88, 90, 100–102
Pine Ridge Agency, 164
Plains Indians, 18–21, 54, 70, 75, 133–34, 136, 138, 143, 152–53, 155, 157, 159–60, 162
Platte Road, 153, 155
Pleasant Bluff, Indian Territory, 1–2, 28
Polk, James K., 15; administration of, 65
Pope, John, 156
Pottawatomie Creek, 57
Powder River, 153, 155
Price, James C., 45
Price, Sterling, 100–101
Princeton University, 74
Principal Chiefs Act of 1970, 170, 173
Proclamation of Amnesty and Reconstruction, 129
Proclamation of Neutrality, 65, 69, 74
pro-Confederate Cherokees, 1–2, 4, 19, 67, 75, 85, 89, 107, 109, 111, 114, 140, 142, 147, 152, 165
protection, 6, 17, 29–31, 33, 35, 47, 53–55, 58–59, 61, 64, 69–78, 85, 88, 96, 104–9, 112, 117, 119, 122, 124, 137, 151, 158, 173, 178
Prucha, Francis Paul, 14, 19, 26, 31, 53, 160
Pryor Creek, Indian Territory, 116
Pueblo Indians, 161

Quantrill, William Clarke, 114
Quapaw-Confederate alliance, 86
Quapaws, 56, 83–84, 147
Quayle, William, 89–90, 191n71

Read, Rhesa Walker, 2, 28
Reconstruction, 129, 139, 149
Rector, Elias, 17, 58, 61, 137, 187n45
Rector, Henry, 17, 61, 64, 113, 187n45
Red Cloud, 153, 155

Red River, 12, 27, 57, 87, 125, 127
Red River Campaign, 198n9
Reeder, Andrew H., 57
Reese, H. D., 103, 142, 144, 146
refugees, 12, 17, 27, 98–99, 105–7, 110–11, 121, 124–27
Removal Era, 22, 32, 48, 178
Resolutions of 1838, 50, 53, 170–71
Revolutionary War, 29
Richmond, Va., 88
Ridge, John, 10, 22–23, 36, 38–43, 48, 52, 80, 82; execution of, 10, 46, 55, 65; support for Ross, 36–37
Ridge, Major ("the Ridge"), 10, 29, 80; execution of, 10, 46, 55, 65; support for Ross, 36–37
Rifle and Peace Pipe Policy, 164
Riggs, Bernice, 173–74
Riggs v. Ummerteskee (2001), 173–74
Ritchey, John, 106, 111
Robertson, W. S., 79
Rocky Mountains, 138
Rose Cottage (Ross's home), 127
Ross, Allen, 46
Ross, Andrew, 52
Ross, Daniel, 121
Ross, John: arrest of, 10, 18, 55, 76, 89, 115, 117, 127; correspondence of, 5, 14–17, 69, 89, 132, 147, 181n46, 191n78; death of, 149, 178; deposed at Fort Smith, 25, 146–47, 150, 152, 160; meeting with Lincoln, 18, 118–19, 130–31; as slaveholder, 9–10, 80
Ross, Joshua, 81
Ross, Lewis, 91
Ross, William Potter, 60, 74, 89, 94
Round Mountain, 91, 94
Runnels, Hardin Richard, 181n42

Saline District, 12
Salomon, Frederick, 109–10, 115, 117, 120
Sand Creek, Colo., 18, 153
Santee (Dakota) Sioux, 118, 131
Schermerhorn, John F., 40–42, 44–45, 47
Schofield, John M., 120–22, 126

Scott, Winfield, 44, 50, 62–63, 71
Scraper, George W., 132
secession, 24, 58, 60–61, 63–64; in Arkansas, 60–61, 64, 66, 187n43; in Kentucky, 13; in Maryland, 13; in Missouri, 13, 60–61, 77, 187n43; in North Carolina, 13; in South Carolina, 12; in Tennessee, 13; in Texas, 60–61, 187n43; in U.S. South, 12, 17; in Virginia, 13, 62
2nd Indian Home Guard, 106, 111, 116, 198n9
secretary of the interior, 6, 14, 17, 58, 63, 105, 107, 120, 139
secretary of war, 6, 14–15, 38–39, 44, 107
Sells, Elijah, 127, 140
Seminole-Confederate alliance, 70, 74
Seminole Nation, 158
Seminoles, 61, 90, 95, 136, 148, 168; freedmen, 148; landholdings, 166
Senate Bill 459, 144
Seneca and Shawnee-Confederate alliance, 86
Senecas, 19, 83–84, 147, 149–50, 163
7th U.S. Infantry, 54
Shawnees, 56, 83–84, 147; as Cherokee citizens, 170
Sherman, William Tecumseh, 155
Shoal Creek (Chustenahlah), Indian Territory, 95
Shreveport, La., 198n9
Sibley, Henry H., 118
Sims, William B., 93, 101, 191n66, 191n71
Sioux, 18–20, 56, 118, 131, 136, 153, 155, 161
6th Kansas Cavalry, 125–26
6th Texas Cavalry, 96, 101
slavery, 9–14, 16–17, 32, 57–61, 65–68, 80–83, 85–86, 88, 109, 114, 123–24, 135, 143, 150, 165, 168, 171–72, 175, 177; abolished by Cherokees, 12, 123–24, 165; in Texas, 181n42
slaves, population of, 13
Smith, Caleb Blood, 17, 63, 104–5, 109, 117–18, 120, 130, 140
Smith, Chadwick, 174–75

Smith, Crab Grass (Cabbin), 91
Society of Friends, 140
South Carolina, 60, 135; secession, 12
South Dakota, 164
sovereign immunity, 171, 173
Spring River, 109
Stanton, Edwin M. 105–6, 112, 132, 152
Stapler, John W., 84–85
Steele, Frederick, 67, 198n9
Steele, William, 2
Stimson, Track, 86
Stokes, Montfort, 55
Sturgis, Samuel D., 105
superintendent of Indian affairs, 14–15, 58, 106, 113, 137

Tahlequah, Indian Territory, 3, 15, 27, 64, 74, 78–79, 84–85, 87, 93, 100, 115–16, 120, 127
Tamaha, Okla., 2
Taylor, Nathaniel G., 134–36, 161–62, 199n31
Tennessee, 7, 14, 29, 32, 41, 135; secession, 13
Ten-Percent Plan, 22, 129, 157
Texas, 2, 12–13, 21, 24, 57, 88–89, 125, 127, 178, 180n42; annexation of, 16; as possible destination for removal, 40; independence, 54; occupation of Indian Territory, 17; population of, 16, 181n51; troops, 27–28, 71, 87, 95, 102, 126–27; secession, 60–61, 187n43
3rd Indian Home Guard, 114, 119, 121, 198n9
3rd Iowa Cavalry, 102
3rd Kansas Battery, 125
Thirteenth Amendment, 173
36th Illinois Infantry, 102
Thompson, Jacob, 58–59, 104
Toombs, Robert, 69–70
Trail of Tears, 5, 10, 15, 23, 32, 44–46, 50, 53–54, 128, 171, 175
Trans-Mississippi theater, 100, 128
Treaty of 1833, Creek, 159
Treaty of 1865, 145–46, 157

Treaty of 1866, 12, 148–49, 153, 159–60, 165, 168, 171–73, 175–78
Treaty of Fort Laramie (1851), 153
Treaty of Holston (1791), 8, 14, 30–32, 52, 60, 177–78
Treaty of Hopewell (1785), 7–8, 29–30, 37, 40, 48, 177
Treaty of New Echota (1835), 22–23, 42–48, 50–54, 57, 62; ratified by Senate, 45
Trott, James J., 45
Tulsa, Okla., 89, 181n46
Tulsey Town, Indian Territory, 93
Turkey Town, Cherokee Nation (East), 34
Turner, Frederick Jackson, 4
29th Texas Cavalry, 2, 126
Tyler, John, 15, 50, 54

U.S. Army, 15, 20, 22, 25, 53–54, 62, 71, 106, 118, 160, 164; enforced removal, 10, 50; return to Indian Territory, 18, 25, 27, 77, 87, 89, 103, 105, 109, 124, 165; withdrawal from Indian Territory, 17–18, 21, 24–25, 27, 62, 104–5, 178
U.S. Census Bureau, 166, 181n50, 203n35
U.S. Constitution. *See* Constitution of the United States
U.S. constitutional law, 7, 14, 22, 24, 32, 37–38, 44, 47–48, 131, 143, 146, 163, 177–78
U.S. District Court for the District of Columbia, 176
U.S. District Court for the Northern District of Oklahoma, 171
U.S. House of Representatives, 14, 26, 34, 45, 174
U.S.-Mexican War, 16, 105
U.S. Postal Service, 67
U.S. Senate, 26, 38, 40–41, 44–45, 47, 50, 133, 178, 184n74
U.S. Supreme Court, 14, 22, 36, 38–39, 41, 44, 48, 50, 52–53, 158–59
U.S. Tenth Circuit Court of Appeals, 171

U.S. War Department. *See* Department of War
unassigned lands, 165–66
Utley, Robert, 164

Van Buren, Martin, 15, 44, 50, 54
Van Dorn, Earl, 100, 102
Vann, James, 192n92
Vann, Joseph, 11–12, 74, 86–88
Vann, Marilyn, 173, 175
Verdigris River, 89, 95
Vipperman, Carl J., 31, 46
Virginia, 58, 63, 75, 119; secession, 13
Voorhees, Daniel W., 165

Wagoner County, Okla., 158
Walker, L. P., 64
Warde, Mary Jane, 2, 4
War of 1812, 182n9
Washington, George, 29, 34; administration of, 182n8
Washington County, Ark., 64–66
Watie, Stand, 2, 10, 22–24, 28, 38, 43, 46–49, 66, 75–77, 81–85, 107–10, 112–15, 117, 120, 123, 125–28, 130, 132, 147, 165, 188n74; absent from battle, 66; attack on Opothle Yahola, 96; commission of, 66, 81; declared chief by troops, 10, 127; early support for Ross, 37; last to surrender, 128; as slaveholder, 10; on slavery, 67; reluctance to enter war, 24, 66
Watie's troops (Cherokee Mounted Volunteers), 2–3, 67–68, 82, 95–96, 99–102, 110–11, 116–17, 120–21, 126, 132, 188n74, 188n79
Watson, Diane, 174–75
Webber's Falls, Indian Territory, 83, 126
Weer, William, 106, 108–15, 147; arrest of, 115–17; letter to Ross, 111–13
Welch, Otis G., 100–102
westward expansion, 4, 8, 16, 27, 29, 134, 138, 151, 157, 159, 161–62, 166. *See also* Manifest Destiny

Wheeler v. United States Department of the Interior (1987), 171
White, Hugh Lawson, 41
White River, 32
Wichita Agency, 74–75, 189n12
Wichita-Confederate alliance, 74
Wichita Nation, 144
Wilkinson, Charles F., 160
Williams, James M., 126
Wilson, Henry, 152
Wisconsin, 109
Wistar, Thomas, 140
Wolf Creek, Indian Territory, 112, 115, 117
Wooster, Robert, 20
Worcester v. Georgia (1832), 14, 22, 38, 41, 48, 51–52, 158
Wounded Knee, 20, 27, 164, 166

www.ingramcontent.com/pod-product-compliance
Lightning Source LLC
Chambersburg PA
CBHW032249150426
43195CB00008BA/376